CW00839994

DANGEROUS SEAS

Ian M. Malcolm

4 BOOKS

Dangerous Voyaging
Dangerous Voyaging 2
Fortunes of War
Mined Coasts

Dangerous Seas
First published in 2017 by
Moira Brown
Broughty Ferry
Dundee. DD5 2HZ
www.publishkindlebooks4u.co.uk

ISBN 978-1-5207-5377-5

Copyright © Ian M. Malcolm 2017
Layout and cover design: Moira Brown

The right of Ian M. Malcolm to be identified as the Author
of this work has been asserted in accordance with the
Copyrights, Designs and Patents Act 1988.

DANGEROUS
VOYAGING
- in the Merchant Navy

1939 † 1945

Ian M.Malcolm

DANGEROUS
VOYAGING 2
- in the Merchant Navy

1939 † 1945

Ian M.Malcolm

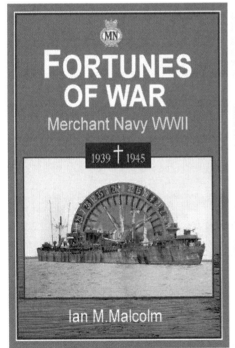

FORTUNES
OF WAR
Merchant Navy WWII

1939 † 1945

Ian M.Malcolm

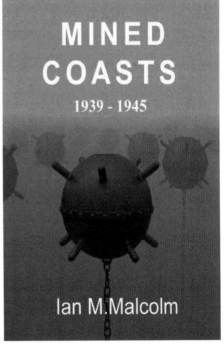

MINED
COASTS
1939 - 1945

Ian M.Malcolm

DANGEROUS VOYAGING

- in the Merchant Navy

Ian M. Malcolm

INTRODUCTION

Although the Second World War could not have been fought and won without the British and Allied Merchant Navies, this fact is generally ignored by historians so that few people today have even heard of the Merchant Navy. It is my opinion that the reason for this is that successive British Governments and the British Legion wish to promote the Armed Forces of the Crown, and the Merchant Navy was (for there is very little of it left) a civilian service.

The War began on 3 September 1939 and the Donaldson liner, Athenia, was torpedoed and sunk in the North Atlantic on the evening of that same day. The German forces surrendered on 7 May 1945, the same day that the *Avondale Park* was torpedoed and sunk in the Firth of Forth. Four thousand seven hundred ships flying the Red Ensign were sunk during the conflict and 33000 men, of various nationalities and aged between 14 and 70, died. And death didn't always come quickly, as when, for example, a man was trapped in the engine room, or his cabin, or was floating in a sea of burning oil.

As MN ratings wore no uniform, they were sometimes thought to be draft dodgers and, when a survivor of a Russian convoy disembarked at Scrabster, in Caithness, in 1942, the Salvation Army refused him a cup of tea because he was not in one of the Armed Forces.

While I anticipate that these two small books will be read mainly by post-war seafarers, I hope that they, the readers, will make younger people aware of the sacrifices made by the men, and also a few women, of the wartime Merchant Navy.

1. THE SOUTHERN EMPRESS

This investigation was sparked off by seeing the name Donald Bremner Ryrie, Senior Radio Officer MN, on the war memorial beside the road to John o' Groats, on the northern outskirts of the wind-swept village of Keiss in Caithness where he was brought up. Because I had followed the same profession, I was particularly interested, and, when I looked up his name in the Merchant Navy Roll of Honour in the Scottish War Memorial at Edinburgh Castle, I learned of the *Southern Empress*. At the time of his death, Danny, as he was known, was married with a six-year-old daughter and a son of four, and his home was in Monymusk, Aberdeenshire. Danny's granddaughter has told me that her grandmother would not accept that her husband had died and would send her mother out to watch for his arrival.

The 12398 grt *Southern Empress* (Captain Olaf Hansen) registered in the Falkland Islands and owned by Christian Salvesen of Leith, sailed from Liverpool on 25 February, 1942. A whaling factory ship converted to carry oil, she sailed in ballast, but carried a number of merchant seamen as supernumeries/passengers who were to join ships in the United States and who disembarked when the vessel arrived in Brooklyn, New York on 17 March. (*Her registry was changed to Leith during the voyage.*)

The ship then proceeded to Houston, Texas where she remained for three weeks; under-going repairs before loading 11700 tons of fuel oil. From Houston, she sailed to New Orleans to load 21 invasion barges as deck cargo.

Her next port-of-call was again New York where she embarked 50 DBS (Distressed British Seamen), most of whom were survivors of torpedoed ships. This made a total of 51 DBS as it is recorded that one had already joined in Charleston, South Carolina on 29 August although I have no evidence of the ship having called there. Together with her 69 crew and 6 DEMS (Defensively Equipped Merchant Ships) gunners (4 RN and 2 Maritime Regiment of the Royal Artillery), her total complement was 126.

On 3 October, she sailed north in the New York section of Convoy SC.104 to rendezvous with the Halifax, NS and Sydney, NS sections which departed these ports on 6 and 7 October respectively. When the sections combined, 51 ships proceeded eastwards in 11 columns which consisted mainly of 5 ships. In position 94, the *Southern Empress* was 4th in column 9. The [1]*Merchant*

---

[1] This turned out to be an unhappy ship and the Commodore, Captain Taylor, DSC RN retired, reported that the ship was unsuitable for commodore duty.

Royal, the Commodore's ship, was No.61 and the *Mariposa*, the Vice-Commodore's, No.31. The escort consisted of the Royal Navy F Class destroyer *Fame*, the Thornycroft V Class destroyer *Viscount*, the Royal Navy flower class corvettes *Acanthus* and *Eglantine* and the flower class corvettes *Montbretia* and *Potentilla* of the Royal Norwegian Navy. The rescue ship was the *Gothland*; a vessel of less than 2000 tons which kept station astern of the convoy and whose job was to pick up survivors.

Two U-boat wolf packs were operating in the North Atlantic and, on 8 October, the Wotan group, consisting of 10 boats, was 300 miles northeast of Newfoundland while the larger Panter group, was spread over an area 700 to 800 miles west of the North Channel. On 11 October, 8 boats were detached from the Panter group to form the Leopard group and, having failed due to bad weather in an attack on a section of the westbound ONS 136 convoy, the Leopard boats were ordered west to join in the search for SC.104. (ON = United Kingdom to North America (Outward North-bound), Speed 9 knots. SC = Sydney, Cape Breton or Halifax, Nova Scotia or New York to United Kingdom, slow.)

Although the position of SC.104 was still unknown to German intelligence, they were aware of its existence and the Wotan group expected to sight it on 11 October. But, although U-258 reported briefly seeing a corvette heading north-east that afternoon, it was 12 hours later before the other boats were ordered to proceed in that direction at full speed due to the report being delayed for 12 hours. The convoy was sighted on the evening of the 12th, the Wotan group began the attack the following evening and were joined by the Leopard group on the 14th. By the time the attack commenced, SC.104 had been reduced to 48 ships: on 7 October, the [2]*Millcrest* had sunk after being in collision with the *Empire Lighting* and the latter had returned to Halifax. Also, the Swedish *Porjus* had returned to Halifax and the Norwegian *Bonde* to Sydney for other reasons.

At 2000 hours on the evening of 13 October, the *Southern Empress* was proceeding at full speed to regain her position in the convoy due to having fallen behind because of a fault in her steering telemotor. And, when flares were fired by other ships in the convoy and a ship was seen sinking on her starboard bow, Captain Hansen sounded the alarm bells and ordered crew and DBS passengers to their boat stations. Twenty minutes later, a torpedo struck

---

[2] This vessel is not shown on convoy plan and not included in figures.

4

the ship and, although she was still underweigh and a heavy sea and swell running, 9 DBS attempted to launch a lifeboat against orders and were lost.

Although an inspection by Mr Froggatt, her 1st Mate, and Mr Skinner, her Chief Engineer, revealed a large hole on the starboard side, from the top of No.5 tank to the flensing deck, and that water had entered the 'tween deck, it was decided that there was no immediate danger of the vessel sinking. But, considering the extensive damage, Captain Hansen set a course for the nearest port in Newfoundland and, as all steering had gone, together with all communication between bridge and engine room, the ship had to be hand steered.

The ship had developed a heavy list to starboard and, when an attempt was made to correct this, it was found that the main steam line from the boilers to the pumps had been smashed so that the cargo pumps could not be used. And, when the fuel pump in the engine room was resorted to, it was discovered that the whale oil bunkering line had also been broken. Nevertheless, a small correction had been made by filling the port side tanks by gravity feed.

At 2300 hours, Mr Froggatt informed Captain Hansen that the water was gaining in the 'tween deck and that he believed that the ship was sinking. Acting on this information, Captain Hansen stopped the ship and, as the lifeboats on the starboard side had been carried away by the list and her rolling in the swell, laid her starboard side to the weather and ordered all boats except No.6 to be launched. When No.8 boat was being launched, it carried away the pudding spar and swung inboard, but Nos. 2, 4 and 10 boats were successfully launched. Some twenty minutes later, No.6 boat was being swung out, with great difficulty due to the heavy list, when a second torpedo struck the starboard side of the ship directly under it; smashing it and laying the ship on her side. The order was given 'every man for himself' and the ship sank within 5 minutes in position 53°50′N 40°40′W.

Subsequently, 48 homes in the UK were informed that their husbands or sons were 'missing/presumed dead' or 'believed drowned/missing' as 24 crew, the 4 RN DEMS gunners and 20 DBS of the *Southern Empress* perished that night. The majority of the survivors were picked up by the Norwegian corvette *Potentilla*, but were transferred to the Norwegian tanker *Suderoy* which had 71 survivors on board when she arrived in Gourock on 21 October. And another 5 were landed in Liverpool the same day.

Other ships in the convoy which fell to the U-boats were the *Susana* (US), *Senta* (Nor), *Asworth*, *Nikolina Matkovicu* (Yug), *Fagersten* (Nor), *Empire Mersey* and *Nellie* (Gr). With the exception of the *Nellie*, the last ship in column 2, all were on the starboard wing of the convoy; in columns 9, 10 and 11. The *Southern Empress* and 4 of the others were sunk by U.221 commanded by 26-year-old Hans Trojer.

The enemy, however, also suffered losses. On 15 October, U.661 was rammed and sunk by HMS *Viscount* and, the following day, HMS *Fame* rammed and sank U.353; both were on their first patrol. U.661 went down with all hands, but 20 survivors of U.353 were picked up by HMS *Acanthus*. Owing to the damage they incurred, *Viscount* and *Fame* detached from the convoy. And retribution came to U.221 on 27 September, 1943 when, still commanded by Trojer, she was sunk with all hands by Halifax 'B' of 58 Squadron of the RAF. The 'plane was shot down by AA fire, but 6 of her crew were rescued by the destroyer *Mahratta*.

The *Southern Empress* was 527 feet long and travelling at such a slow speed that she presented an easy target for the enemy. And there was the additional danger of being a laden tanker. Yet, because she had surplus accommodation, necessary in her whaling days, 51 DBS were being conveyed home on her as passengers. This was reasonable if you were directing operations from the safety of an office in the UK, but the 'passengers', most of whom were already survivors of torpedoed ships, must have experienced trepidation at having to cross the U-boat infested North Atlantic on such a vessel. Indeed, all Salvesen's whaling factory ships were lost during the War.

I do not believe that mere tradition dictates that the Master is the last man to leave a sinking ship, but that it is his awareness of his responsibility for those under his command and must see to their safety before considering his own. Captain Olaf Hansen was obviously of this breed as was his 21-year-old 3rd Mate, John (known as Ian) Barbour Wylie, who must have held Captain Hansen in such high regard that, no doubt in spite of Captain Hansen's pleas to the young man to see to his own safety, chose to remain with him on the bridge until both went down with the ship. (Captain Hansen, OBE, was master of the *New Sevilla* when she was torpedoed and sunk off Malin Head in September, 1940. And, as a 1st-year apprentice, Ian Wylie had spent 19 days in a lifeboat after the *Baron Nairn* was torpedoed off the Azores. He and William Skinner, OBE, the Chief Engineer, who also died, were 'Commended for brave conduct' in the Third Supplement to the London Gazette of Tuesday, 2 March, 1943.)

It had also become traditional in the Merchant Service that the 1st Radio Officer marginally preceded the Master in leaving a sinking vessel. The fact that the other two radio officers survived when Danny Ryrie did not, suggests

6

that he told them to get into the lifeboats while he remained at his station on the stricken vessel. In peacetime, ships of this size generally carried only one radio officer who kept an 8-hour watch, but, in order to keep a continuous 24-hour human watch during the War, the entrance qualification was lowered and three R/Os were carried. But Danny and his No.2, David W. Miller, both held 1st Class PMG Certificates.

The oldest of the casualties were D. Dalgleish, a greaser aged 64, Captain Olaf Hansen, aged 42, Chief Engineer William Skinner, aged 42, and 1st R/O Donald Bremner Ryrie, aged 41. But almost all were young and, although all the loss of life is heart-breaking, it is particularly so in the case of boys in their teens and Mess Boys Ernest Boots and John McNally were only 15.

The Merchant Navy suffered a higher percentage of casualties during the Second World War than any of the Armed Forces of the Crown, but, because it was a civilian Service, bravery was not generally recognized by the award of decorations.

Acknowledgments
P.J. Chapman of Fishguard, former Surgeon on Salvesen's Whaling Expeditions.
W.M.B. Greenfield, Secretary/Treasurer, Salvesen Ex-Whalers' Club.
A Hague, World Ship Society.
Naval Historical Branch, Ministry of Defence.
D.G.M. Cameron, former Midshipman, Alfred Holt & Co. and 3rd Mate, Cunard Line.

Bibliography
Ministry of Defence (Navy). German Naval History - "THE U-BOAT WAR IN THE ATLANTIC" 1939 -1945. Facsimile Edition First published 1989 by HMSO. Volume II January 1942 - May 1943 Chapter V July - December, 1942.
Mr Froggatt's report dated 20 October, 1942.
The Fourth Service by John Slader.
The Empire Ships by Mitchell and Sawyer.
The Whalers of Anglesey by Alun Owen.
From 70 North to 70 South (A History of the Salvesen Fleet) by Graeme Somner.
British Vessels Lost or Damaged by Enemy Action During The Second World War. HMSO.

Those interested in a more detailed account of the loss of the *Southern Empress*, giving names, wages, certificates held, etc., should consult copies of the project I have given to Amlwch Library, Amlwch Heritage Centre (Anglesey), Edinburgh University Library, Merseyside Maritime Museum, Shetland Library, Wick Library and Wick Heritage Centre.

2. CONVOY SC.121

In his book, *The Critical Convoy Battles of March 1943*, Professor Dr. Jürgen Rohwer wrote "In the first 20 days of March 1943 the U-boats came nearest to their aim of interrupting the lines of communication between the Old World and the New when they sank 39 merchant ships out of four successive convoys." SC.121 was one of those convoys and it may be the case that more merchant seamen were lost during its west to east crossing than in any other convoy of the Second World War. The letters SC stood for 'Sydney (Cape Breton) or Halifax or New York to UK (Slow)' and, as the convoy's average speed was 7¼ knots, this was slow indeed; particularly on the North Atlantic in winter when heavy seas, snow blizzards and U-boat packs lay in its path. Indeed, the severity of the weather cannot be overemphasized. Reputed to be the worst in 50 years, it resulted in ships not being able to see their neighbours, even in daylight, and several ships straggling with disastrous results. Likewise, it made it impossible, at times, for the Commodore and Escort to know exactly what was happening.

The New York Section, sailing from New York at 0800 on 23 February, 1943, included the *Trontolite*, *Vancolite* and *Baldbutte*, but these three detached for Halifax at 1800 on the 28th, together with the *Zouave* which had developed engine trouble. That same day, the *Parkhaven* fell behind and returned to port while the *Badjestan*, *Porjus*, *Brant County* and *Reavely* also returned for various reasons. The Halifax Section, sailing at 1645 on the 26th, consisted of the *Leadgate*, *Stavadin*, *Etrac*, *British Progress*, *Melrose Abbey* (Rescue Ship), *Empire Opossum*, *Empire Grebe*, *Manchester Progress*, *Lorient*, *Halfried*, *Fort Remy* and *Gatineau Park*. The St. John's (Newfoundland) Section, sailing at 0900 on 3rd March, consisted on the *Empire Planet*, *Empire Bunting* and *Standford*. The New York Section was the largest and, according to Convoy Form D, 51 ships actually sailed in the Convoy. The Commodore, RC Birnie, RNR, was on board the Norwegian ship, *Bonneville*, in position 81, and the Vice Commodore, Arthur Cocks, RNR, was on the *Empire Keats*, in position 51. At the outset, the Convoy advanced in 14 columns. No.81 headed the 8th column and No.51, the 5th.

The Ocean Escort, US Escort Group A3, consisted of the US destroyers *Babbitt* and *Greer*, the US Coast Guard Cutter *Spencer*, and the Canadian corvettes *Dianthus*, *Rosthern* and *Trillium*. The *Spencer*'s commander was Senior Officer Escort (SOE).

By 4 March, U-boats of the Wildfang and Burggraf Groups waited south of Greenland in a line running northwest to southeast, but the Convoy eluded them and continued undetected until sighted, some 90 miles to the north, by a boat of the Neptun Group. Seventeen boats, from the three Groups were then ordered in pursuit while 11 boats of a new Group, the Neuland, formed a patrol line off the west coast of Ireland - ahead of the expected course of the Convoy.

According to Convoy Form D, completed by the Vice Commodore, it was noon on Saturday, 6 March, when they became aware that there were U-boats in the vicinity and, that 'at 2040 ship on port wing fired two white rockets and reported by W/T that a submarine was passing ahead on outside of columns. At 2315, No.61 (it was 62) *Egyptian* was torpedoed, visibility 2 miles. No further enemy reports that night.'

The U-boat website, however, gives a somewhat different version which is that U.566 and U.230 contacted the Convoy on the 6th and, during the night, the latter sank a ship. Due to the severe weather, the sinking was noticed by only another merchantman which, due to stopping to pick up survivors, became a straggler and was herself torpedoed, towards morning, by U.591.

The preceding paragraph seems to be the more accurate, as, although not recorded by the Vice Commodore, the *Empire Impala* was also sunk that night - by U.591 whose commander did not record the date and time. But, as U.230 noted that she sank the *Egyptian* at 2349 on the 6th and a second ship was torpedoed 'towards morning', we can deduce that it was the *Empire Impala*, No.25, which went to the aid of the *Egyptian*.

Yet another version, and in view of the time lapse between the sinkings would appear to be even more accurate, is given in The Empire Ships by Mitchell & Sawyer: 'The straggling *Empire Impala* came upon survivors (of the *Egyptian*), stopped at about 0900 hours and herself was sunk…….'

On 8 March, the *Guido* was torpedoed when she had romped ahead of the Convoy. In his report, her Master stated that owing to heavy seas and wind, he had found it difficult to maintain the Convoy course and that, early on the 8th (he must have meant the 7th), he had been forced to increase to full speed to prevent the ship 'broaching to'. Full speed was maintained until 1630 when he was again able to reduce to the Convoy speed of 7 knots. But, at 0650 on the 8th, he was still 6 miles ahead of the Convoy when the torpedo struck.

8 March was a successful day for the U-boats as they also sank the *Fort Lamy*, carrying LCT 2480 (Tank Landing Craft) on deck, and the *Vojvoda*

Putnik, which, again due to the weather, had both become stragglers. The Escort strength was added to that day by the arrival of the corvette HMS *Mallow* and it would appear that the Convoy had air cover of a sort as the Vice Commodore noted 'At 1402 aircraft made by R/T "Am attacking submarine 247 degrees 11 miles from convoy."'

On 9 March, the Escort was further reinforced by the arrival of the US destroyer *Babbitt*, the US Coastguard Cutters *George M Bibb* and *Ingham*, and the British corvette *Campion*. This did not, however, prevent the sinking that night of the *Malantic*, the Escort Oiler *Rosewood*, the Commodore's ship *Bonneville*, carrying LCT 2341 on deck, and the *Nailsea Court*. The *Coulmore* was also torpedoed, but did not sink.

At 0829 on the 10th, the merchant ship *Scorton* reported a submarine 'right ahead' and, almost immediately after, that she had definitely rammed it. This has been confirmed by reference to the U-boat website and all 43 of U.633's crew perished. A similar report of ramming a U-boat had been made by the merchant ship *Kingswood* at 1922 on the 8th, but this is not substantiated.

The final losses, occurring on the 11th, were the *Empire Lakeland*, *Leadgate* and *Milos* - all of which had straggled.
The casualties suffered as follows:

Bonneville (Nor.) (Gen. & Expl.)	Few survivors (36)
Coulmore (Br.)	7 survivors (40)
Egyptian (Br.)	4 survivors (44)
Empire Impala (Br.)	No survivors (48)
Empire Lakeland (Br.)	No survivors
Fort Lamy (Br.)	3 survivors (47)
Guido (Br.)	10 survivors (35)
Leadgate (Br.)	No survivors
Nailsea Court (Br.)	3 survivors (48)
Malantic (US) (Ammo.)	Few survivors (25)
Milos (Swedish)	No survivors (30)
Rosewood (Br.)	No survivors (42)
Vojvoda Putnik (Yugo.)	No survivors

The number of dead, shown in brackets, may, in some cases, be slightly inaccurate and if we take it that, on average, the ships where the number is not shown had crews of about 45, the death total was in the region of 500 men.

Figures alone, however, do not reflect the horror and hardship experienced, but survivors' reports rectify this to some extent.

Extracts from the Report of Captain Mussared, Master of the ss *Guido*

'....... The crew, including 6 naval and 2 army gunners, numbered 45, ten of whom are missing, amongst them the 2nd Engineer and 2 naval gunners ....The vessel did not list, but at once started to settle, sagging amidships, with the bow and stern rising out of the water. The remaining lifeboat was lowered without difficulty, the men carrying out their duties as if at boat drill, and 28 of the crew abandoned ship in this boat. Four men, including myself, jumped overboard as we could hear the vessel breaking in two. The two rafts in the after rigging were also released. The 3rd Engineer sat on a spare raft kept amidships on deck, which floated off as the ship sank, 8 minutes after being torpedoed. The majority of the crew were clear of the ship within 3 minutes of her being struck. ....With regard to the two missing gunners, Perry and Dryden, I think they jumped overboard soon after the explosion, together with the Steward and a donkeyman. Perry was seen in the water by the Steward, swimming away from the ship with his lifejacket on, but neither he nor Dryden was seen again.

We had been unable to send out a distress message as the main and emergency wireless sets were smashed by the explosion, although the 1st Wireless Operator returned to the wireless room to try and effect repairs. He was forced to jump overboard before anything could be done with the set. The boat's wireless set was left behind in the wireless room. We had had a box specially made for this set in order to keep it near the lifeboat, but a Government Inspector had ordered the set to be kept in the wireless room with instructions for the Operator on duty to take it to a lifeboat in the event of a casualty, but it was forgotten.

I was picked up by the port lifeboat almost immediately, and after about an hour we were rescued by the USS *Spenser*, which brought us to Londonderry, where we landed on the 13th March. The Steward and a donkeyman, who were in the water for about an hour, were in a very bad state when rescued, as the water was very cold, about 28°, and both men were taken to hospital. They have since recovered. All the crew behaved extremely well and there was no sign of panic at any time.'

Extracts from the Report of Mr F.H. Millbank, 4th Engineer of the ss *Fort Lamy*

'We sailed from New York bound for Loch Ewe loaded with 4,000 tons of general cargo and explosives.......The crew numbered about 50; there were only three survivors, one gunner, the Galley Boy and myself....... 'The torpedo struck in the after end of the engine room on the starboard side. I was awakened by a terrific explosion. I dressed in about 2 minutes and rushed up on deck.......The three Wireless Operators, Chief Steward and 3rd Engineer were all on deck. The 3rd Engineer had been badly injured, blood was pouring from his face and his ears had been blown off. He was shouting for his lifejacket. I rushed down to the engine room, grabbed his lifejacket and hurried back. I managed to get him into his jacket then he collapsed on deck. The ship was settling fast.......a big wave swept the deck and I had to cling to the bulwarks to avoid being swept over the side.......the 3rd Engineer had disappeared. I think he must have been washed overboard.

(The *Fort Lamy* carried LCT 2480 as cargo and, as no lifeboat was available, Mr Millbank, who calls it a TLC, took refuge on it, together with a DEMS gunner and the Galley Boy. As the ship was sinking, the LCT broke its lashings and floated off the deck.)

'.......When we became unbearably thirsty we went up on deck and ate handfuls of snow which, although very cold, helped to moisten our mouths.......We drifted about for 10 days, by this time we were very weak. The Galley Boy could not walk on account of frostbite, his feet were absolutely black. My feet were frost bitten too.......At midday I heard the sound of an engine. As it became louder my excitement grew and I rushed up on deck.....suddenly the engines roared as the 'plane dived low over the water. I thought we must have been sighted.......to my bitter disappointment, however, the engines suddenly grew fainter and fainter.......On 20th March.......I heard an explosion.......The gunner came up on deck supporting the Galley Boy.......I realized we were being fired on. A shot landed in the water, just short of the TLC. We had no means of signalling.......Actually, quite unknown to us, we had drifted right through the middle of a convoy. One of the trawlers, sighting a large dark object in the water had decided to hold a practice for his 4" gun. He fired four shells at us.......luckily, a Corvette steamed over.......We waved wildly, shouted and jumped about on the deck.......but the Corvette did not see us and another shell landed in the water.......I then remembered my whistle and blew it as hard as I could. I think the Corvette must have heard because she steamed closer.......then shouted to know our nationality. ....We boarded HMS

Vervain sometime during the afternoon of the 20th March and were very thankful for a bowl of hot soup and then to crawl into bed and to sleep. ......After we had evacuated the TLC the trawler resumed her practice and after a few more shots succeeded in sinking the TLC which had been our home for 12 days. Had we known this would happen, we would have chopped up the wood from the decks and kept the fire burning, thus saving ourselves from becoming frost bitten.   ......we had drifted northwards......we were not far off the coast of Greenland.'   (They were taken to St John's, NF.)

Extracts from the Report of Mr H.C.C. Bette, 2nd Engineer of the *Nailsea Court*

'.......The crew, including 4 Army and 5 Naval Gunners, numbered 49; there were in addition 2 passengers, one a Mining Engineer, the other an Electrical Engineer, who came on board at Freetown. Of this number 48 are missing, including all officers (with the exception of myself), the gunners and the two passengers.......The 1st torpedo struck in No.1 hold on the port side.......The 2nd torpedo struck in the port side of No.2 hold.......I continued on my way to the engine room.......The 4th Engineer, Mr E.R. Dryden and the Fireman Barnes were still at their posts.......so we stopped the engines, also the circulating pump, as one lifeboat was directly over the discharge outlet and I did not wish to fill the boat up. The order was given on the telegraph to "abandon ship" three minutes after the second explosion.

.......During the previous day the port boat had been struck by a heavy sea and washed inboard where it had been secured, thus leaving only the starboard boat intact and this was ultimately very much overloaded. There was some delay in lowering this boat, as the forward fall became jammed, and one of the sailors who was trying to clear it got his hand in the block.......This starboard boat eventually had about 25 men in it and the remainder had to get away on rafts. Captain Lee, 2nd Officer Mr. Johansen, an apprentice and myself were left on board, so all four of us jumped from the boat deck.....

About the same time as we were torpedoed, the Commodore's ship *Bonneville* and the ss *Coulmore* were also torpedoed and I should think that the attacks occurred at intervals of between 3 to 4 minutes.

.......after picking up several men from the water, some of whom I think were from the *Coulmore*, there were 37 in the boat. She became water-logged.......The Canadian Corvette *Dauphin* which came over to rescue us suddenly stopped when she was about 250 yards from us. The Captain shouted through his loud hailer telling us that his steering gear had broken down and that he was unable to reach us. We signalled telling him that our boat was sinking rapidly. Again the Captain told us that he could not possibly reach us and that we were to try to reach him. This, of course, was quite impossible owing to the crowded condition of our boat and about half-an-hour later it capsized.......Many of the men were exhausted and washed away by the heavy seas until eventually there were only 17 left, clinging to the keel of the upturned boat. Gradually many of these men were washed away until finally there were only 7 of us left.......At approximately 0200 on the 10 March, the Corvette came along for the second time. We had now been hanging on to the bottom of the boat for about 3½ hours. Only another man and myself were strong enough to lift our hands in order to be dragged aboard.......

There were also two men on the port raft, but only one was rescued, the other being already dead.......The 3 survivors rescued by the corvette were the Mess Room Steward, a greaser named Perks and myself......We were eventually landed at Londonderry at 0800 on the 13th March, 1943.

Owing to the frequency of the attacks prior to the disaster, the boat's wireless set was placed into the port boat in readiness, but this boat did not get away.

I would suggest that as the lifeboats frequently capsize, a rail fitted along each side of the keel would greatly assist men to hang on to the bottom of the upturned boats. In cold weather it is impossible to grip it tightly.

I would like to mention that all the crew behaved extremely well and that there was definitely no sign of panic.......'

Mr Bette made special mention of the bravery of Captain Lee, 2nd Officer Johansen, 4th Engineer Dryden and Greaser Perks. But, as he had previously named the man who remained in the engine room as Fireman Barnes, it appears that he got the names mixed up.

The steering gear failure experienced by the *Dauphin*, cost many lives, but she was not the only escort ship to suffer equipment failure as, due to having no respite from arduous duty, most were in bad shape.

<u>Extracts from the Report of Mr David R.H. Nichols, 2nd Radio Officer of the ss *Coulmore*</u>

.......Our crew numbered 47, including 5 Naval and 2 Military gunners. Of this number, 40 are missing.......At 1930 on March 7th, another submarine warning was intercepted.......After an hour, we received the "all clear", so I went below to lie down. Shortly afterwards, at 2210 on 9th March ....we were struck by a torpedo........The torpedo struck on the port side, forward, close to the stem.......

I made my way to the boat deck and placed the wireless transmitter in the starboard after lifeboat.......I climbed into the boat and we were pushed clear of the ship within about a quarter of an hour of the torpedo striking. This lifeboat had fourteen men in it. The ship carried two jolly boats and two lifeboats, but the starboard jolly boat was damaged and I believe the starboard after lifeboat was the only boat to be lowered successfully. I understand the port lifeboat was also lowered, but the after painter carried away and the boat drifted away with no-one in it.

The Chief Officer, who was still on deck, ordered us to bring our lifeboat alongside the ship, but in attempting to do so we drifted under the counter and the boat was damaged. We eventually managed to push it clear, but the boat rapidly filled and soon became waterlogged. This boat had previously been damaged during the bad weather on the outward voyage, but although it was repaired in New York, the seams were not properly caulked, and consequently she leaked very badly.......an Able Seaman instructed the others to make the sea anchor fast to the painter and put it out, but it was thrown over without being made fast and was lost. The boat gradually filled up and turned over, everyone being thrown into the water. Several of us managed to cling to the bottom of the boat, the remainder being washed away and lost. After clinging to the boat for about an hour, a raft, which had drifted off the ship, came close to us and the seven remaining survivors swam to it and climbed on board. This raft capsized twice, throwing everybody off each time, until eventually only three were left on the raft. By this time, I could not see the ship; the last I saw of her was about two hours after abandoning her, when she appeared to be well afloat.

We tried to get at the bottle of brandy, but the stores, which were kept in a tank in the centre of the raft, were battened down with a cross piece of wood. As we did not have a knife, and our hands were much too numb to break those wooden fastenings, we had to give up the attempt and stretched ourselves on the raft to wait until picked up.

We had previously seen a destroyer, a little before the raft capsized, when there were still seven survivors. We whistled and shouted and flashed our torches to attract attention, and whilst we were trying to attract attention a corvette came along and exchanged signals with the destroyer. The AB said that we must have been seen and we therefore imagined that we would be picked up at daybreak.

When daylight came, the AB saw the mast of a vessel which sighted us and came alongside and we drifted down to her. This vessel turned out to be the US Cutter *Bibb* which picked us up by 0910 on the 10th March. (It is evident that Mr Nichols got his dates wrong.) We were taken below, stripped of our wet clothing and given whisky. I cannot remember much; the last thing I remember clearly was being pulled on board and waking up in a bunk.......
I did not see the ship again, but on March 12th the Captain of the destroyer (it was a cutter) called our carpenter to the bridge and pointed out our ship which was still well afloat, but down by the head. He asked if we wished to reboard her, but Carpenter Smith said that he did not wish to do so.

The destroyer (cutter) was then [3] escorting a damaged ship and eventually continued until within 30 miles of Londonderry. As the destroyer (cutter) did not enter the port, we were taken back to Iceland, arriving at 0100 on Monday morning, 15th March.

I would like to place on record the fine behaviour of Deck Boy Triggs. This boy was only sixteen years old and making his first trip to sea. When the lifeboat capsized, Triggs, who could not swim, clutched AB Chalcroft for support. When he found he was pulling this man beneath the water, he deliberately released his hold and was drowned. His unselfish action undoubtedly saved Chalcroft's life, but at the sacrifice of his own.......'

Convoy Form D lists the ships in the first two columns as having been 'in company a.m. 10th March' while those in the third column, although on the Convoy Plan, are not mentioned. Conversely, the torpedoed *Leadgate* is not shown on the Plan.

---

[3] Somewhat confusing as the *Coulmore* was apparently the only ship damaged and it is reported that she was escorted by the British Corvettes *Aubrietia* and *Clover* and the RN Tug *Samsonis* when under tow by the RN Tug *Eminent*.

Egton	*Kingswood*	*Garnes* (Nor.)
British Freedom (Oil)	*El Grillo*	*USS Laramie*
Morska Wola	*Miguel de Larrinaga*	*Dilworth*
Thraki	*Harpefjell* (Nor.) (Ammo.)	*Manchester* *Progress*
Nadin	*Empire Grebe* (Explosives)	*Empire Advocate*
Sutlej	*Empire Forest*	*Alcoa Leader*
San Tirso	*Lobos*	*Katendrecht*
Astrid	*Ravnefjell* (Nor.) (TNT & Ammo.)	*Camerata*
Scorton	*Hollywood*	*Stavadin*
Bengkalis (Dutch)	*Raranga*	*Etrac*
Sinnington Court	*Clune Park*	*Gatineau Park*
Standford	*Empire Caxton*	*Empire Planet*
Eskdalegate	*Gascony*	*Empire Bunting*
British Progress (Oil)	*Lorient*	*Melrose Abbey*
Harperley (Nor.)	*Lombardy*	*Halfried*
Empire Keats	*Empire Opossum*	*Fort Remy* *Suderoy* (Nor.) (Oil)

It can be taken as a certainty that other ships carried dangerous cargoes such as those shown in brackets above, but my sources have not revealed this.

Although so many ships fell to the U-boats, the convoy system was, nevertheless, proved effective as, due to the severity of the weather, most of the victims were detached from the convoy's relative security by either straggling or romping.

A significant factor in the heavy losses suffered by convoys during this period, is that, due to the Germans making a change in Enigma machine settings, Bletchley Park was unable to decipher signals transmitted to the U-boats. Had they been able to do so, convoys would have been rerouted to avoid the danger area. Regrettably, the *Zouave*, which returned to port with engine trouble, was torpedoed and sunk on 17 March when in Convoy SC.122.

Acknowledgments: Mr Arthur Owen, who was 1st Radio Officer of the *Empire Grebe* and who supplied most of the information contained in this narrative. LtCdr. Arnold Hague, RN

Bibliography

Ministry of Defence (Navy). German Naval History - "THE U-BOAT WAR IN THE ATLANTIC" 1939-1945. Facsimile Edition First published 1989 by HMSO. Vol II Jan 1942 - May 1943
The Critical Convoy Battles of March 1943 and Axis Submarine Successes 1939-1945 by Professor Dr. Jürgen Rohwer
The Empire Ships by W.H. Mitchell and L.A. Sawyer
Convoy Plan and Convoy Form D
A Dictionary of Ships of the Royal Navy of the Second World War by John Young.
Enigma by Hugh Sebag-Montefiore
Survivors' Reports, www.uboat.net

3. THE SINKING OF THE DORYSSA

Names on war memorials have always intrigued me; those of merchant seamen in particular. And when I saw the name of Radio Officer William Stark Thomson on the war memorial in St. Andrews, Scotland, I researched his death with the following result.

Bill Thomson was 1st R/O of the *Doryssa*; an 8078 grt ton, 12½ knot motor tanker, owned by the Anglo-Saxon Petroleum Co. and built in 1938 by R.W. Hawthorn, Leslie & Co., Newcastle upon Tyne. Under the command of Captain W. Fraser, she sailed from Cape Town on 24 April, 1943. Her crew numbered 60 (22 British, including 5 Royal Navy DEMS gunners signed on as Deck Hands, and 38 Chinese) and she carried 2 passengers, employees of the Anglo-Iranian Oil Company. Her armament consisted of one 4.7" gun (situated aft), one 12-pounder, two Oerlikons, two Lewis guns, two rifles and four PAC rockets; and, in ballast and sailing independently, she was bound for Abadan in the Persian Gulf to load a cargo of oil.

As enemy submarines were known to be active in the area, those on board the *Doryssa* felt apprehensive as the ship proceeded east from Cape Town on the ordered zigzag course. And their apprehension was fully justified when at 1920 hours on 25 April a violent explosion occurred and a huge column of water enveloped her as she was suddenly struck by a torpedo; on the port side, by way of No.7 tank. She was doing 11 knots on a mean course of 120° and her position was 37° 03' South 24° 04' East.

Although she had taken on a 25° list to port, the *Doryssa* headed at full speed in the direction of the attack while Mr. Thomson transmitted the 'Being attacked by submarine' signal 'SSSS' followed by the distress message. And his transmission, on the calling and distress frequency of 500 kcs, must have been acknowledged, by perhaps Cape Town radio station (ZSC), as subsequent events show that the authorities were alerted.

The ship carried four lifeboats – Nos. 1 and 3 on the starboard side and Nos. 2 and 4 on the port. All the boats were swung inboard so that they had to be swung out ready for lowering. After clearing No. 4 boat, Mr Quick, the 3rd Mate, helped the 2nd Mate to clear No.3. The boats were not fitted with skates and the clearing of No.3 proved difficult. Meanwhile, the 1st Mate was opening valves to bring the ship back on an even keel.

On reporting back to the bridge that the two after lifeboats were ready for lowering, Mr Quick was ordered to check the bearing and distance from Cape

Agulhas and Cape Recife which he calculated as 305° 240 miles and 024° 196 miles respectively. It then became known that the Chinese had started to lower No.1 lifeboat and had left it hanging in the falls half way to the water. He was told to hoist it back into position and was engaged in this task when Captain Fraser shouted, "Submarine on the port beam", swung the ship hard to port towards it, and then, "Open fire". But as the 4.7" gun opened up, the submarine fired a second torpedo, from her stern tube, which struck the engine room on the starboard side. Once again there was another terrific explosion and as the 2nd Engineer and others in the engine room were never seen again, it was deduced that they were killed by it.

When, at 2030, the Chief Engineer reported that, with the engine room flooded, the engines were now out of commission, Captain Fraser gave the order "Abandon ship" and the code books, in their perforated lead box, were heaved overboard. The ship now had no list, but was rapidly settling by the stern. Mr Quick collected the lifeboat wireless set from the chart room and placed it beside No.2 boat which had an apprentice in charge. He then proceeded to his own boat, No.4, but finding it swamped and hanging in its falls, he went to No.3 boat which he found already in the water alongside with some of the crew climbing into it. He descended into the boat by the falls and when he was informed that the 2nd Mate was missing, he took charge of the boat.

While the lifeboat was lying alongside the ship, the bridge was turned into a blazing inferno by shellfire from the submarine. Mr Quick cast off and, seeing a man in the water, allowed the boat to drop astern to pick him up. This proved to be DEMS Gunner Crossman, who had jumped from the ship, and while he was being rescued, bullets were flying over their heads. Mr Quick ordered the boat's crew to row away from the ship and then to stop about ¾ of a mile away.

The amidships section of the *Doryssa* was now engulfed in flames and the submarine had ceased shelling. Nos. 1 and 2 lifeboats had succeeded in getting away and the submarine, on the port beam, was now using her searchlight in an effort to locate them. Sometimes the beam swung in the direction of No.3 boat, but somehow failed to spot it. Then, at 2145 and in the distance, those in the lifeboat heard machine gun fire followed by a brilliant red flash and, as Captain Fraser's motorized boat had 16 gallons of petrol on board, Mr Quick deduced it was this boat exploding.

The submarine was seen silhouetted against the burning *Doryssa*, shortly before she sank at 2245. She was heard again at 0200, but, when the new day dawned and there was nothing to be seen of her, Mr Quick searched for the other two lifeboats, without success.

Using the lifeboat compass, Mr Quick set a course for Cape Recife. The sea was choppy with a fresh south-easterly breeze and the boat made a steady 3 knots under sail. But, by 0230 on the 27th, the wind rose so that the main sail was lowered and, using only the jib, little progress was made. And when the weather became worse, Mr Quick hove to.

At 1240, hopes rose when a Hudson was seen flying south at a height of about 1000 feet. But, in spite of a red flare being burned, the plane failed to see the boat. With the weather continuing to deteriorate, the jib was taken in and the sea anchor streamed. By 1800, a full gale was blowing. The boat's occupants were wet and cold, but they had ample food and plenty of water and Mr Quick issued a welcome tot of brandy.

At 0130 on Wednesday, 28 April, a heavy sea swamped the boat and carried away the sea anchor. The crew commenced bailing out and the boat was allowed to drift towards the southeast which made them more comfortable. Tots of brandy were issued during the wet periods and, during the daylight hours, another two planes were sighted, but again they failed to see the lifeboat.

The weather was gradually moderating and at dawn on the 29th, the sails were again hoisted and a northerly course set. Sailing at an estimated speed on 2 knots, they saw yet another plane which did not see them.

A light westerly wind was blowing and it was fine and clear on Friday, 30th April, when, at 1130, an Avro Anson sighted and circled the lifeboat and dropped a questionnaire in an inflated Mae West lifejacket. The questionnaire read:

Are you from Doryssa? Raise one oar.
Raise number of oars for number of lifeboats which left ship.
Wave oars if you are in need of food and water.

On receiving the answers, the plane flew away, but returned shortly with the message, 'Help coming'.

HMSA Patrol boat [4]*Southern Barrier*, which had made smoke to attract their attention, was sighted at 1230. She came alongside and took the tired, but cheerful, survivors on board. All were fit and well apart from a young engineer who had been in poor health and had developed saltwater sores.

It was Tuesday, 4th May before the *Southern Barrier* returned the survivors to Cape Town as, throughout Saturday, Sunday and Monday, she continued searching for the missing lifeboats. But, regretfully, her search proved fruitless. And, as they were never heard of again and assuming that the submarine had indeed sunk Captain Fraser's boat, it is likely that she machine-gunned the two lifeboats she was able to locate. Of the 62 who been on board the *Doryssa*, 53 perished and only the 9 in No.3 lifeboat survived.

The survivors had, of course, no clue as to the identity of the submarine which had sunk their ship and in his report to the Interviewing Officer, Lieut. A.P. Cartwright, S.A.N.F. (V), Mr Quick refers to it as a u-boat. The sub was, in fact, not German, but the Italian Marconi Class *Leonardo da Vinci*, launched in Monfalcone (Trieste) in 1940 and commanded by Tenente di Vascello (Lieut.) Gianfranco Gazzana-Priaroggia. It had a surface speed of 18 knots and carried a crew of 57.

With 17 allied ships to her credit, the *Leonardo da Vinci* was the most successful Italian ship in the Battle of the Atlantic and, prior to entering the Indian Ocean, had sunk, on the night of 13/14 March, the 21517 ton *Empress of Canada* in position 1° 13' South 9° 57' West. And, ironically, many of those who died were Italian prisoners of war.

During this period, the *da Vinci* was working in collaboration with the submarine *Linzi*, commanded by Tenente di Vascello Mario Rossetto. The latter sank the 7,628 ton *Lulworth Hill* on the 18th, and the following day, transferred to the *da Vinci* diesel fuel, lubricants, water, three torpedoes, and provisions to allow her to continue into the Indian Ocean. In return, the *da Vinci* transferred to the *Linzi* the Italian surgeon lieutenant, Vittorio Del Vecchio, whom she had rescued from the *Empress of Canada*, and James Leslie Hull, described as a seaman/gunner. The *Linzi* docked in Bordeaux on 20th April.

After entering the Indian Ocean on 5 April, the *da Vinci* prowled off Durban and her first victim was the 6566 ton Dutch vessel *Sembilan* which she sank

---

[4] Formerly a whale catcher owned by the Southern Whaling & Sealing Co., Ltd., London, she was renamed "KOS 29" in 1946 and broken up in Stavanger in 1964.

in position 31°30' South 33°30' West on the 17th. The next day it was the turn of the 8007 ton British ship *Manaar*, in position 30°59' South 33°00' East, and, on the 21st, the 7177 ton US Liberty Ship *John Drayton* was disposed of in position 32°03' South 34°04' East.

The story of his experiences concerning the *John Drayton* is told by survivor Herman E. (Hank) Rosen in his book, 'Gallant Ship, Brave Men' – the proceeds of which go to the US Merchant Marine Academy. The ship was bound for Cape Town from Khorramshahr in the Persian Gulf where she had discharged her cargo of ammunition, tanks, jeeps, trucks, clothing and other supplies from New York. And, after being torpedoed, she was shelled by the submarine. Together with 23 other men, Mr Rosen, on his first trip to sea, entered a lifeboat which was to be their refuge for the next 30 days; until spotted by an aircraft and rescued by a Greek merchant ship. Throughout their ordeal, it was fiercely hot during the day, perishing cold at night and they lost all their supplies when the boat capsized. It took them eight hours to right it and clamber back in and, after that, their only sustenance was water absorbed in clothes spread out on the bottom of the boat when it rained. Nineteen of the occupants died from malnutrition and exposure so that only 5 survived. Mr Rosen's weight dropped from 140 to 90 pounds. In all, 21 crew and 2 of her Armed Guard, lost their lives.

The *Leonard da Vinci*'s last victim was the *Doryssa* and, on 28th April, flushed with success and with her fuel running low, she headed for her home base of Bordeaux.

During the return passage, a message was received from Bordeaux informing Gianfranco Gazzana-Priaroggia that he had been promoted Capitano di Corvette (Lieut. Cdr.). His delight, however, was to be short lived as when proceeding under water off Cape Finisterre, just before noon G.M.T. on 23 May, the sound of his engines was picked up by asdic and the *da Vinci* was depth charged and sunk by the destroyer HMS *Active* and the frigate HMS *Ness*. All hands were lost; including, Robert Gray, the 2nd Mate of the *Manaar* who had been taken prisoner.

Bibliography

The National Archives, Kew, Surrey.

4. CONVOY OB.288

My investigations often begin by seeing names on a war memorial and this one is no exception. On the Dundee Roll of Honour are the names Duncan Fox, Cabin Boy, aged 15 and David Gow, Galley Boy, aged 16. Both boys lost their lives on the *Temple Moat* and this led me to Convoy OB.288.

Containing ships bound mainly for North America, the main section of Convoy OB.288 sailed from Liverpool on 18 February, 1941. After being joined by ships which sailed from Loch Ewe on the 19th, it contained in the region of 46 vessels. The Commodore, Rear Admiral R.A.A. Plowden, was on board the *Sirikishna* and the Vice-Commodore on the *Harberton*.

In his book, The Allied Convoy System 1939-1945, Arnold Hague lists only two ships damaged and no ships sunk in the convoy. This, however, is because he never lists losses which occurred when ships were not actually in a convoy and even stragglers are omitted.

Three ships returned to port – the [5]*Empire Fusilier* (Br.), to Oban, because of trouble with her steering, the *Empire Steelhead* (Br.) because of engine trouble, and the [6]*Kasongo* (Belg.), to Belfast, to adjust her compass.

The first attack on OB.288 was made by a Focke Wolf 200 at 0700 on the 22nd. The Convoy advanced in nine columns of approximately six ships and, the plane flew down Column 5 firing machine guns and dropping bombs. The *Kitheron* (Gr.), [7]*Kingston Hill* (Br) and the *Keila* (Estonian) were damaged by bombs. The former continued in the Convoy, but the latter two were escorted back to the UK by [8]HMS *Picotee*, a Flower Class corvette, and the Smit Tug *Thames*. Captain Niven was the only casualty of the *Kingston Hill*.

The remaining Escort consisted of the 'A' Class destroyers [9]*Achates* and *Antelope*, the Town Class destroyer *Georgetown,* ex-USN *Maddox* (on board of which was the Senior Officer Escort (SOE), the Flower Class corvette *Heather*, and the armed trawler *Ayrshire*. At this stage of the War, escort vessels were thin on the ground and they were to be with the Convoy only as far as 18°W which was about the norm.

---

[5] Sunk later in the War
[6] Sunk later in the War
[7] Sunk by U.38 on 8 June
[8] HMS *Picotee* was sunk off Iceland by U-568 on 12 August.
[9] Sunk in the Barents Sea by the cruiser *Admiral Hipper* on 31 December, 1942.

Although C. in C. Western Approaches had been notified of the air attack and knew that the Convoy was being shadowed by the enemy, the escort left in the forenoon of the 23rd. Oddly enough, the Commodore kept the ships in formation until 2100 before ordering them to disperse, but to maintain Convoy Speed for half-an-hour after dispersal. This is why Hague does not record the losses, as the u-boats began to strike shortly *after* 2100 when the ships were still close together, but no longer in convoy.

Ships torpedoed and sunk between 2100 hours and midnight on the 23rd:

Anglo Peruvian (Br.) and *Svein Jarl* (Nor.)

Ships torpedoed and sunk on the 24th:

Cape Nelson (Br.), *Huntingdon* (Br.), *Linaria* (Br.), *Manistee* (Br.), *Marslew* (Br), *Sirikishna* (Br), *Temple Moat* (Br) and *Wayngate* (Br). HMS *Manistee* was a merchant ship requisitioned by the Admiralty and employed as an Ocean Boarding Vessel i.e. a vessel used for intercepting suspected enemy merchant ships and examining their cargoes. She had managed to continue after being torpedoed the previous evening, but was sunk by a second torpedo on the morning of the 24th.

Details of the ships

Anglo Peruvian – 5457 tons. (Captain C.M. Quick). Built 1926. Nitrate Producers Steamship Co. Ltd. Tyne for Boston. 3015 tons of coal. Crew 46. 29 lost, including the Master. The ship, the first to be sunk, suffered two hits and sank within minutes. At 2300 the *Harberton* (Captain A. Patterson) sighted the survivors on a raft and rescued them by using two of their own lifeboats. But one man of the *Anglo Peruvian* was lost when one of the boats capsized.

Svein Jarl – 1908 tons. (Captain M. Marsteen). Built 1919. Nordenfjeldske D/S. In ballast. Crew 22. No survivors.

Cape Nelson – 3807 tons. (Captain K.M. Mackenzie). Built 1929. Lyle Shipping Co. Ltd. Hull for New York. Crew 41. 4 lost – Captain McKenzie, 1st Radio Officer W. A. Bassom, 3rd Engineer C. Drysdale and Donkeyman Ali Abdulla. The vessel sank in about six minutes, but two lifeboats got away and, when the survivors were boarding the *Harberton*, one man fell between the boat and the ship and was lost. As, including her own crew of 41, the

Harberton now had 91 men on board and food for only ten days, Captain Patterson decided to make for Halifax. They arrived at noon on 4 March and in his report, he wrote: *"I suggest, for consideration, that as this attack occurred only twelve hours after the local escort left the convoy, in Longitude 18° West, it would be in the interest of British Shipping, that the Local Escort should not disperse from the convoy before Longitude 28°W."*

Huntingdon – 10,946 tons. (Ex-*Munsterland*) (Captain Styrin). Built 1920. Federal Steam Navigation Co. Ltd. Cargo general. Crew 66. All rescued by the *Papalemos* (Gr) which landed them in Horta, in the Azores, from where they were taken to Lisbon for repatriation to the UK.

Linaria – 3385 tons. (Captain H.T. Speed). Built 1924. Stag Line Ltd. Tyne for Halifax, N.S. Cargo coal. Crew 35. No survivors.

HMS *Manistee* – 5360 tons. (LtCdr. E.H. Smith). Built 1920. Elders & Fyffes Ltd. Crew 141. No survivors.

Marslew – 4542 tons. (Captain H.R. Watkins). Built 1926. Walmar Steamship Co. Ltd. Glasgow and Liverpool for Montevideo and Villa Constitution. Cargo general. Crew 36. 13 lost, including the Master. A torpedo struck the stern at 0028 and she sank shortly after that time. The survivors were rescued by the *Empire Cheetah*.

Sirikishna – 5458 tons. (Captain Robert. Paterson). Built 1936. Chr. Salvesen & Co. Avonmouth to Halifax, N.S. In ballast. Crew 43. A first torpedo struck the ship at about midnight on the 23rd. The Master ordered 'abandon ship', but she remained afloat for approximately another 6½ hours when another torpedo cut her in two and she went down. Although it appears that lifeboats were launched, there were no survivors.

Temple Moat – 4427 tons. (Captain T. Ludlow). Built 1928. Temple Steamship Co. Ltd. Crew. Cargo coal. Crew 42. No survivors.

Wayngate – 4260 tons. (Captain S.G. Larard). Built 1931. Turnbull Scott Shipping Co. Ltd. Newport, Mon. to Freetown. Cargo coal. Crew 44. All saved. *Wayngate* was torpedoed at 0220 and it was snowing heavily when the crew were in the lifeboats, prior to being rescued at 0830 by the Free French Chacal Class destroyer *Leopard*.

The U-boats and their victims

U.69 – Kapitänleutnant (Kptlt. Jost Metzler - *Svein Jarl*.
U.73 – Kptlt. Helmuth Rosenbaum – *Wayngate*. (U.73, still under Rosenbaum, sank the 22,600 ton aircraft carrier HMS *Eagle* in the Mediterranean on 11 August, 1942.)
U.95 – Kptlt. Gerd Schreider – *Cape Nelson*, *Marslew* and *Temple Moat*.
U.96 – Kptlt. Heinrich Lehmann-Willenbrock – *Anglo Peruvian*, *Linaria* and *Sirikishna*.
U.107 – Kptlt. Gűnther Hessler – *Manistee*.
Italian submarine *Michele Bianchi* – C.C. Giovannini Adalberto – *Huntingdon*.
All the boats returned to either Lorient of St. Nazaire.

Ships which survived the attack (*Lost later in the War)

*Aarø (Dan.), *Alex* (Br.), *Bolton Hall* (Br.), *Coracero (Br.), *Duke of Athens (Br*.)*, *Dux* (Nor.), *Ellinoco (Gr.), *Elizabeth Lensen* (Br.), *Empire Cheetah (Br.), *Empire Trust* (Br.), *Evgenia Chandri (Gr.), *Evros (Gr.), *Germanic (Br.), *Harberton* (Br.), *Jessie Mærsk (Br.), *Koumoundouros* (Gr.) *La Pampa* (Br.), *Lista* (Nor.), *Llanashe (Br.), *Matrona (Gr.), *Mount Kitheron (Gr.), *Mount Mycale (Gr.), *Mount Othrys* (Gr.), *New York City* (Br.), *Panaghis* (Gr.), *Papalemos (Gr.), *Rossum* (Du.), *Spar (Du.), *Stylianos Chandris (Gr.), *Tachee* (Br.), *Tennessee (Dan.), *Zephyros* (Gr.).

Wages and War Risk Payments

When a ship was sunk at this stage in the War, the wages of her crew were stopped on the grounds that they were no longer working, and no compensation was paid for loss of effects. This meant, not only that allotments left to families at home ceased, but that, because an Advance of Pay might have been made prior to sailing, they could be in debt to the shipowner.

A War Risk Payment, which seamen called the War Bonus, was introduced on 15 September, 1939. Those over 18 received £3 a month while those under 18 got £1.10/- (£1.50p). Early in 1940, this was increased to £5 and £2-10/- (£2.50p) respectively, and on 1 May, 1942 further increased to £10 and £5. The Payment ended on 31 March, 1947 when it was incorporated into wages.

In Convoy OB.288, therefore, the boys who sparked off this investigation got a bonus of £2.10/- for risking their young lives in the war-torn Atlantic: a fact which reflects badly on successive British Governments which have expressed neither remorse nor shame. The same, however, cannot be said of the Government of Canada, although it took years of pressure for them to make some recompense. On 2 February, 2000, it announced a $50 million tax-free package for Canadian Merchant Navy Veterans (and surviving spouses) who served in the First and Second World Wars and the Korean War.

Maximum payments for 'War-related Service' could be: more than 24 months - $20,000; between 6 and 24 months - $10,000; and between 1 and 6 months, or less than 1 month if captured, killed or disabled - $5,000. An additional 20% to be paid to a seaman who had been a prisoner of war.

When the Canadian announcement was made, there was a deafening silence on this side of the Atlantic.

5. TWO CONVOYS

<u>CONVOY OG.71</u> (OG = Outward to Gibraltar from UK)

Convoy OG.71 sailed from the UK on 13 August, 1941. It comprised 22 merchant ships, bound for Oporto, Lisbon, Las Palmas and Gibraltar. Eight merchants ships and two escorts were sunk.

A German Focke-Wulf Condor sighted the Convoy on the 17th and Heinkel He 111 bombers made an unsuccessful attack on it the next day. But u-boats were now lying in wait.

HNoMS (His Norwegian Majesty's Ship) BATH (LtCdr. Christian F.T. Melsom). This destroyer, proceeding at some distance behind the Convoy, was the first to fall to the u-boats when torpedoed twice by U.204 (Kptlt. Walter Kell) at 1.10am on the 19th, and sank in about five minutes, in approximate position 49°00′N 17°00′W. Most of her complement of 130 were Norwegian. Eighty-three, including 13 RN, died; some when her depth charges exploded as they were swimming in the water. Forty-one were rescued by the corvette HMS *Hydrangea* (Lt. J.E Woolfendon) and the destroyer HMS *Wanderer* (Cdr. A.F.St.G. Orpen), and landed at Gibraltar.

ALVA (Captain C.S. Palmer). Torpedoed and sunk by U.559 (Oblt. Hans Heidtmann) at 1.15am on the 19th , in position 48°48′N 17°46′W. One died, but the other 24 were picked up from lifeboats and rafts – 11 by the *Empire Oak* and 13 by the *Clonlara*.

CISCAR (Captain E.L. Hughes). Torpedoed twice by U.201 (Oblt. Adalbert Schnee) at 3.10pm on the 19th, and sank in position 49°10′N 17°40′W. Thirteen died. Thirty-five picked up by the [10]*Petrel* (Captain J.W. Klemp) and landed at Lisbon.

AGUILA (Captain A. Firth). Torpedoed twice by U.201 at the same time as the *Ciscar*, broke in two and sank within 90 seconds, in position 49°23′N 1756′W. Out of her complement of 69 crew, 84 naval passengers and the Commodore's staff of 8, 152 died, including the entire contingent of 21 Wrens and a nursing sister going to Gibraltar. Ten, including Captain Firth, were picked up from a raft by the corvette *Wallflower* (LtCdr. I.J. Tyson) and landed at Gibraltar. Six were picked up by the tug *Empire Oak*. Captain Firth

---

[10] See Convoy HG.73, page 45.

again survived when he was returning to the UK as a passenger on the *Avoceta*. (See below).

Tug EMPIRE OAK (Captain F.E. Christian). Torpedoed by U.564 (Oblt. Reinhard Suhren) at 10.28pm on the 22nd and sank in seconds, in position 40°43′N 11°39′W. Thirteen, including the 6 rescued from the *Aguila*, died. Nineteen, including the 11 rescued from the *Alva*, were picked up by the corvette HMS *Campanula* (LtCdr. R.V.E. Case), transferred to the destroyer HMS *Velox* (LtCdr. E.G. Ropner), and landed at Gibraltar on the 25th.

CLONLARA (Irish) (Captain J. Reynolds). Torpedoed and sunk by U.564 at the same time as the *Empire Oak*, in position 40°43′N 11°39′W. Nineteen, including 8 survivors of the *Alva*, died. Thirteen, including 5 survivors of the *Alva*, were picked up by the corvette HMS *Campion* (LtCdr. A. Johnson) and landed at Gibraltar on the 24th.

ALDERGROVE (Captain H.W. MacLean). Torpedoed and sunk by U.201 at 2.14am on the 23rd, in position 40°43′N 11°39′W. One naval rating (the only passenger) died. Thirty-eight were picked up from lifeboats by HMS *Campanula*.

STORK (Captain E.A.M. Williams). Torpedoed and sunk by U.201 at the same time as the *Aldergrove,* in position 40°43′N 11°39′W. Nineteen died. Three picked up by HMS *Campion*.

SPIND (Nor.) (Captain Johannes Berg Jonassen). Detached from the Convoy due to having missed a course alteration, and heading for Lisbon when missed by two torpedoes fired by U.552 (Oblt. Erich Topp) shortly before 7am on the 23rd. The u-boat then surfaced and set the ship ablaze by gunfire, before she was forced to dive when the destroyer HMS *Boreas* (LtCdr. D.H.M. Crichton) approached and opened fire on her. Topp made yet another attempt to torpedo the ship, but the torpedo turned out to be a dud. After trying to depth charge the u-boat, the *Boreas* picked up all 25 crew from two lifeboats before making an unsuccessful attempt to extinguish the fire and sinking the ship by shellfire. The survivors were landed at Gibraltar on the 25th. The only casualty was the 2nd Mate who was shot and badly wounded when descending into a lifeboat.

Corvette HMS ZINNIA (LtCdr. C.G. Cuthbertson). Torpedoed and sunk by U.564 at 5.25am on the 23rd, in position 40°25′N 10°40′W. Sixty-eight died when the ship exploded. Seventeen survived, but no other details.

To avoid further carnage, the Admiralty diverted the Convoy into the safety of neutral Portugal, and the remaining 14 merchant ships anchored in the River Tagus on the morning of 24 August.

CONVOY HG.73   (HG = Homeward from Gibraltar)

Convoy HG.73, consisting of 25 merchant ships, sailed from Gibraltar on 17 September, 1941, and was sighted by a German Focke-Wulf Condor when off Cape St Vincent the following day. Nine merchant ships and one escort were sunk.

EMPIRE STREAM (Captain S.H. Evans). Torpedoed twice by U.124 (Kptlt. Johann Mohr) at 7.44am on the 25th and sank in position 46°03′N 24°40′W. Six crew and two stowaways died. Twenty-seven picked up by the corvette HMS *Begonia* (T/Lt. T.A.R. Muir) and landed at Milford Haven on the 30th.

CORTES (Captain D.R. McRae). Torpedoed by U.124 at 2.32am on the 26th and sank immediately in position 47°48′N 23°45′W. Forty died. The Bosun and two Arab firemen picked up by the *Lapwing*.

PETREL (Captain J.W. Klemp). Torpedoed by U.124 at almost the same time as the *Cortes* and sank in position 47°40′N 23°28′W. Twenty-one died, but the remaining 10 were picked up from a raft by the *Lapwing*.

LAPWING (Captain T.J. Hyam). Stopped to pick up the survivors of the *Cortes* and *Petrel* when torpedoed by U.203 (Kptlt. Rolf Mützelburg) at 6.34am, and sank within three minutes in position 47°40′N 23°30′W. Having picked up the men from the *Petrel's* raft and others in the water, the *Lapwing's* lifeboat was returning to the ship when she went down. The boat, which contained 9 from the *Lapwing*, 10 from the *Petrol* and the 3 from the *Cortes*, set sail for the Portuguese coast. After four days sailing, however, and due to a wind change, Captain Klemp of the *Petrel*, who was in charge, decided to make for Ireland, and they landed near Slyne Head, Co. Galway on 9th October. The two Arab firemen from the *Cortes* and a crew member of the *Petrol* died in the boat while the Bosun of the *Cortes* later died in hospital in Clifden. The sloop HMS *Leith* (LtCdr. E.C. Hulton) picked up one other survivor of the *Lapwing*. Twenty-four died.

SIREMALM (Nor.) (Captain Haakon Svendsen). Torpedoed and sunk by U.124 at 11.35pm on the 26th, in position 49°05′N 20°10′W. All 27 died.

AVOCETA (Captain H. Martin). Torpedoed by U.203 at 0031 hours on the 26th, and sank quickly in position 47°57′N 24°05′W. Forty-seven crew and 76 passengers died. Forty picked up by the corvettes HMS *Periwinkle* (LtCdr. P.G. MacIver) and HMS *Jasmine* (LtCdr. C.D.B. Coventry), and landed at Milford Haven on the 30th. Three picked up by the *Cervantes*.

VARANGBERG (Nor.) (Captain E.S. Stenersen). Torpedoed and sunk by U.203 at the same time as the *Avoceta*. Twenty crew and the Chief Engineer of the *Spind* (see above) died. Six picked up from debris and rafts by HMS *Jasmine*.

CERVANTES (Captain H.A. Fraser). Torpedoed and sunk by U.201 (Oblt. Adalbert Schnee) at 2.08am on the 27th, in position 48°37′N 20°01′W. Five crew and 3 passengers died. Thirty-five, including the 3 rescued from the *Avocada* were picked up by the *Starling* and landed at Liverpool on 1st October.

Fighter catapult ship HMS SPRINGBANK. (Captain C.H. Godwin). Torpedoed by U.201 at 2.11am on the 27th. Thirty-two died. Two hundred and one survived; most rescued by HMS *Jasmine* which went alongside the stricken ship and subsequently sank her by gunfire, in position 49°09′N 20°10′W. Others were picked up by HMS *Periwinkle*, while those picked up by the corvette HMS *Hibiscus* (LtCdr. C.G. Cuthbertson) were landed at Gibraltar.

MARGARET (Formerly Finnish). (Captain Holger Pihlgren). Torpedoed and sunk by U.201 at 11.03pm on the 27th, in position 50°15′N 17°27′W. All 34 picked up by HMS *Hibiscus*.

Bibliography
Beyond the Call of Duty by Brian James Crabb
The Fourth Service by John Slader
The Allied Convoy System 1939-1945 by Arnold Hague
www.uboat.net
www.naval-history
www.kentfallen.com
www.warsailors.com

6. THE LOSS OF THE FORT HOWE

By June, 1943, Arthur Owen was an old hand at the game, as, although still in his early twenties, he had been in the Merchant Navy since the beginning of the War in 1939. A 1st Radio Officer employed by the Marconi International Marine Co., he had spent over three years sailing from bases in India and had survived the frightening convoy battle between the u-boats and Convoy SC.121 when he had been on the *Empire Grebe*, carrying high explosives. Now Marconi had instructed him to join the *Fort Howe* in Liverpool, not far from his hometown of Caernarfon.

The *Fort Howe* (Captain William Williams) proved to be a North Sands ship of 7133 grt, built by the Burrard Dry Dock Co, North Vancouver, for the US War Shipping Administration, and less than a year old. Now lend-leased to the British Ministry of War Transport (MOWT), she was operated by F.C. Strick & Co Ltd, London. Arthur was impressed by her and by the up-to-date Canadian Marconi, RCA and Mackay radio equipment which included both MF (Medium Frequency) and HF (High Frequency) transmitters, plus an RT (Radio Telephony) one on Army and Navy channels. There was also a tiny emergency wireless room – on the main deck and well away from the main deck at the after end of the engine room housing. Although only 6′ deep x 4′ wide and likely to have been a converted cupboard, it could prove useful if the main wireless room were destroyed.

As his previous juniors had always been new hands, Arthur was surprised that both had lots of sea-time under their belt and that the 2nd R/O had even sailed as No.1. Normally, his department consisted only of himself and two other radio officers to keep the obligatory 24 hours watch, but now he also had RN and RAF personnel in his charge.

The *Fort Howe* sailed, not only with a military cargo in her holds, but, like many of the ships at that time and as cargo space was precious, with cargo lashed down on her decks. And, although few on board knew it when they left the Mersey, they were in a convoy bound for Loch Long, on the Clyde. The ship's complement of 69 included 20 DEMS (Defensively Equipped Merchant Ships) gunners.

Towards the end of June, the *Fort Howe* sailed from the Clyde in a heavily escorted KMS (United <u>K</u>ingdom <u>M</u>editerranean <u>S</u>low) convoy. As usual, their destination was unknown and, it was some days after entering the Mediterranean that Captain Williams, as instructed, took his sealed orders, and those for the 1st R/O, out of the safe. The ship was taking part in

Operation Husky, the invasion of Sicily, and Captain Williams learned that his destination was a beachhead near Pachino Peninsula, in the southeast of the Island.

When Arthur opened the huge envelope, he had never seen so many detailed instructions in his life; at first glance there seemed to be hundreds of typed pages and that he'd suddenly been chosen as supremo for the entire inter-Services operation! The sheer amount of detail to be absorbed was frightening. He spent days trying to make some coherent sense of it, with all those contingency plans if this, that, or the other went haywire. And, with RN and RAF radio operators as well as his usual Marconi R/Os plus additional gear he had never seen before, he had a somewhat unusual radio department. His best guess was that the *Fort Howe* was a stand-by communications ship. The invasion convoys, from the UK, the US and Egypt, gathered to the south of Malta and, on 9 July, sailed for Sicily. The British Forces headed for the southeast shores of the Island while the United States Forces headed for the southwest. The convoys, sailing in bad weather, experienced no air attacks, and, meeting little opposition, the British rapidly captured Syracuse.

On 12 July, the *Fort Howe* anchored off the designated beachhead as planned and, sometime during the several days she spent there discharging her cargo, an admiral came over to the ship in a fast RN launch. Quite naturally, it was assumed that he had come to see the Master, who came down to welcome him on board, but, after exchanging the briefest of courtesies with Captain Williams, he went straight to the wireless room to consult Arthur about the communications.

With discharging complete, the *Fort Howe* was moved up the coast to a quiet anchorage of her own. She had a destroyer escort all to herself and this destroyer remained with her until the day she left for Algiers.

After loading in Algiers, the ship joined a convoy whose destination was again unknown, but, once the sealed orders, similar to those already described, were opened, they learned that they were now taking part in Operation Avalanche; the invasion of Salerno, on the Italian mainland. Both British and US Forces were again involved. The first troops landed on 9 September; the same day that it was learned that an armistice between Italy and the Allies had been signed. *(Arthur doesn't mention suffering any attacks during either Operation, but, at Salerno, there was heavy opposition from the air and from shore artillery. And it was there that the Germans first used their new glider bombs.)*

Discharging was again carried out from a beachhead and, when it was completed, the *Fort Howe* proceeded to a point off Malta to join Convoy MKS.26 (**M**editerranean to **UK** **S**low) which had originated at Alexandria and consisted of 21 ships.

The night of 30 September was fine, with the wind about Force 4 and a moderate swell running, when Arthur, sleeping in shirt and shorts, was awakened by a loud bang and raced to the wireless room. A torpedo had struck the ship near the mainmast and smashed the propeller shaft. The mainmast whip broke the main aerial and brought the heavy-lift derrick crashing down onto the after end of the boat deck, tragically killing [11]two of the DEMS gunners in an Oerlikon Ack-Ack gun nest. The ship was in position 37° 19'N 06° 40'E, east of Bougie (now Bejaia) in Algeria.

Captain Williams ordered Arthur to send a distress message and, prefixing it with the SSSS signal which indicated an attack by submarine, he sent it several times. Knowing that the main aerial was down and using the doubtful emergency one, he wondered if his transmissions were being heard and received no acknowledgment by the time he decided to leave the largely-wrecked wireless room.

There was nobody about as Arthur, on the bridge, made to leave the listing ship. Only the Master's lifeboat remained, and it was already in the water somewhere down there in the dark. From previous experience, he had learned that hands could be worn red-raw by siding down the falls to a lifeboat so that he always kept a pair of heavy gauntlet gloves attached to his getaway bag. He was the last man to leave and had to jump for the falls; a hazardous job when the ship was listing and the falls swinging further and further away from the ship in the dark.

The 3rd R/O was in the lifeboat which Arthur entered and, after some hours, HMS *Spiraea* (Lt A.H. Pierce), a Flower Class corvette, found them and they were hauled on board from the scrambling nets. The injured men were attended to and a sick berth attendant came up to where Arthur was sitting, drinking rum-laced cocoa, and pointed to his legs. Although he was totally unaware of it, a fair bit of skin had been removed from the insides of his legs by the slide down the falls, and the SBA dressed them.

---

[11] The only casualties and one of whom was 21-year-old Able Seaman Dennis Preston, RN (P/JX 311590) of Leeds.

HMS *Spiraea* landed the survivors at Bougie from where they were taken to Algiers by a military truck. The others were rescued by HMS *Alisma* (Lt G. Lanning RANVR), also a Flower Class corvette, and landed at Algiers. The 2nd R/O, who was in the latter group, had suffered a broken arm earlier in the voyage and, as it was just out of plaster, it caused him to have great difficulty getting off the ship, swimming for ages, and climbing up the *Alisma's* scrambling net. Nevertheless, he was still clutching the lifeboat transmitter when rescued.

In Algiers, the arrangements for DBS (Distressed British Seamen) were very poor indeed. They were billeted in a grotty 5-storey French rooming house in the suburbs and had to walk 2 miles into town for every one of their very poor meals, and back again. Everyone, including Captain Williams, took it up with every authority they could find, but got nowhere. It seemed that the MOWT staff had been the very last outfit to turn up after the liberation of the City, and, by then, the British, US and French Services had collared every hotel, building and facility that was worth having. As usual, there was only rubbish left for DBS. The MOWT had no clout at all in Algiers, and all they could do was to urge them to make a fuss when they got back to the UK.

They all lost a lot of weight during the month they spent awaiting repatriation to the UK, but, fortunately, the weather was warm and mostly sunny. Then, at last, came the great day when they were told to get on board the Cunard troopship, *Franconia*.

They were made very welcome on the troopship which also carried other survivors, including those of the *Fort* Fitzgerald, sunk in Convoy UGS. 18 on 4th October, and sailed to Liverpool in Convoy MKF.25 (Mediterranean to UK Fast).

On returning home to Caernarfon, Arthur spent many hours on the onerous task of compiling a list of all his personal effects that had gone down with the *Fort Howe* as this was required in order to be issued with clothing coupons to buy a complete, new, seagoing kit. Mercantile Marine Offices issued Merchant Navy clothing coupons and there was still a small one in Caernarfon: a legacy of the days when the town had been a thriving port and sailing ships carried Welsh slate all over the world, but now use mostly by those on coasting vessels.

When Arthur took his long list to the Mercantile Marine Office, he had to argue and make a case out for almost every replacement article of clothing that wasn't obviously 100% essential. Nevertheless, his persistence bore fruit as, when he finally emerged and called at the town's biggest tailors and outfitters, to start ordering new uniforms and other clothing, they were so astonished at the number of coupons he produced that the entire staff gathered round to gawp at them. There were more coupons than they had ever seen!

The *Fort Howe* was sunk by U.410, commanded by 25-year-old Oberleutnant-zur-See Horst-Arno Fenski and, although Arthur thought at the time that his was the only ship sunk in the Convoy, the *Empire Commerce* also fell to Fenski.

The [12]*Empire Commerce*, a small tanker of 3750 grt enroute from Bône (now Annaba) to Algiers, was hit just prior to the *Fort Howe* and cut in two. The rear section sank, but the forward section remained afloat. The RN tried to sink it, but, when this failed, it was towed to a beach at Algiers where it was gutted by fire.

According to Fenski, he fired five single torpedoes at Convoy MKS.26 east of Bougie at 0005 hours on 1 October and, when he observed one ship sinking and heard four more detonations, mistakenly thought that he had torpedoed four ships.

On 26 November, 1943, Fenski was awarded the Knight's Cross of the Iron Cross. With great loss of life, U.410 was sunk by US bombs, near Toulon, in position 43°07′N 05°55′W, at 1200hrs on 11 March, 1944. But Fenski died in Hamburg on 10 February, 1965.

Arthur never found out if his distress calls had been heard. Many years later, he learned from men who had been on the two corvettes that, apart from the Senior Officer Escort's ship, none of the RN escort would even have been listening on 500 kcs as they kept watch on only two channels – Admiralty transmissions and the escort's own R/T frequency. It is possible, however, that the calls may have been heard by the commodore's ship and relayed to SOE by VHF R/T.

---

[12] An earlier *Empire Commerce* was sunk by a magnetic mine off North Foreland in June, 1940.

Bibliography:

Arthur Owen's letters to me.
Engage The Enemy More Closely, by Corelli Barnet.
The Empire Ships by Mitchell and Sawyer
www.uboat.net

7. MERCHANT NAVY WOMEN LOST

ALMEDA STAR (Blue Star Line). Stewardess Rose Mary Helena Dawson and Shop Assistant Edith Ellen Dove.

The *Almeda Star* (Captain H.G. Howard) sailed independently for Buenos Aires, from Liverpool, on 15 January, 1941. Torpedoed by U.96 (Kptlt. Heinrich Lehmann-Willenbrock) at 6.45am on the 17th, and sank in 3 minutes, in position 58°40′N 13°38′W, after being shelled and receiving a 4th torpedo at 9.55am. As an SSSS message had alerted the authorities that she was under attack by a submarine, naval vessels were dispatched to the area, but not a trace of her was found. All 165 crew and 194 passengers died.

AMERIKA (A former Danish ship requisitioned by the Ministry of War Transport). Stewardess Else Gantzel and Assistant Stewardess Henriette Gerda-Wischke.

On 14 April, 1943, the *Amerika* (Captain Christian Nielsen) sailed in the Halifax section of Convoy HX.234 which rendezvoused with main New York section on the 15th, bound for Liverpool. In very bad weather when torpedoed twice by U.306 (Kptlt. Claus von Trotha) at 8.50pm on the 21st and sank in position 57°30′N 42°50′W. Eighty-six died. Fifty-four, including 37 RCAF personnel, picked up from lifeboats and rafts by the corvette HMS *Asphodel* (Lt. H.P. Carse) about two hours later and landed at Greenock on the 21st. U.306 also damaged the *Silvermaple* while U.108 (Kptlt. Ralf-Reimar Wolfram) sank the US Liberty Ship *Robert Gray*.

ANCHISES (Alfred Holt & Co.). Stewardess Minnie Beatrice Apperson.

The *Anchises* (Captain D.W. James) was independently bound for Liverpool from Australia and about 120 miles north-west of Bloody Foreland, on the north-west coast of Ireland, in the early afternoon of 27 February, 1941, when bombed by a Focke-Wolf Condor and severely damaged by several near misses. One hundred and thirty-four people, including 5 women and 2 children, left the ship in 6 lifeboats while 34 remained on board in the hope that she might be towed. By 5am the next morning, however, the situation had become so serious that Captain James decided to abandon ship. Flares were burned and rockets fired before the crew began taking to the only remaining lifeboat which, due to the high sea running, had its propeller and most of its oars smashed during launching. As a rocket had been seen by the corvette HMS *Kingcup*, she came to the rescue, but, in manoeuvring alongside, wrecked the lifeboat so that 20 of its occupants were thrown into the water. Captain James and Quartermaster John Sinnott lost their lives in this incident, but the others were saved. The *Kingcup* then began looking for the other boats and succeeded in finding 5 of them before it became dark. A week later, those in the sixth boat were picked up by the Canadian destroyer HMCS *Assiniboine*. According to Admiralty records the *Anchises* sank after being bombed again on the 28th. Fourteen crew were lost, including Minnie Apperson who died in the sixth lifeboat on 2 March and was buried at sea.

ANDALUCIA STAR (Blue Star Line). Stewardess Lily Anne Green.

The *Andalucia Star* (Captain J.B. Hall) sailed independently from Buenos Aires on 26 September, 1942, bound for Liverpool via Freetown. Struck by 2 torpedoes from U.107 (Kptlt. Harald Gelhaus) at 9.45pm on 6 October. All the lifeboats got away except No.2 which became suspended by its after fall, throwing its 40 occupants, including 59-year-old Lily Green, into the sea. Just before the last 2 boats were clear, a third torpedo struck the ship and she sank at about 10.25pm in position 06°38′N 15°46′W. Captain Hall and a few others, the last to leave, launched a raft and jumped into the sea after it. Next morning, the boats set sail for Freetown, but were picked up by the corvette HMS *Petunia* (LtCdr J.M. Rayner) on the morning of the 8th and landed at Freetown that evening. Three crew and 1 passenger died and 251 survived. Lily Green was among those awarded the King's Commendation for Brave Conduct.

APAPA (Elder-Dempster Line). Hairdresser Helen Mona Clifford.

The *Apapa* (Captain E.V. Davies), bound for Liverpool, sailed from Freetown in Convoy SL.53 on 27 October, 1940. At about 9.25am on 15 November, the Convoy was attacked by German Focke-Wulf 200 Condors. The *Apapa* was hit, set ablaze, abandoned, and sank at noon, in position 54°34′N 16°47′W. Twenty-three died. Two hundred and twenty-nine rescued by the *Mary Kingsley*, *New Colombia*, *Boulderpool*, and the corvette HMS *Broke*. Some passengers were able to jump across to the *Mary Kingsley* when her master skilfully brought the stern of his ship close to the stern of the *Apapa*.

ATHENIA (Donaldson Line). Stewardesses Hannah Baird (Canadian), Alison Thornton Harrower, Margaret Dickson Johnston and Jessie Lawler.
The unescorted *Athenia* (Captain James Cook) sailed from Liverpool on 2 September, 1939, bound for Montreal. War was declared at 11am on the 3rd and, at 9.45pm, the ship was torpedoed by U.30 (Oblt. Fritz-Julius Lemp), and sank at 11am on the 4th in position 56°44′N 14°05′W. Of the 1103

passengers and 329 crew, 112 died. Of the survivors, 602 were picked up by the Norwegian ship *Knute Nelson* (Captain Carl Johan Anderssen) and landed at Galway. Two hundred and twenty-three, picked up by the illuminated Swedish motor yacht *Southern Cross*, were transferred to the US merchantman *City of Flint* (Captain J.A. Gainard) and landed at Halifax, Nova Scotia. Four hundred and ninety-five were picked up by the destroyers HMS *Electra* (LtCdr. S.A. Buss) and HMS *Escort* (LtCdr. J. Bostock), and landed at Greenock.

As u-boat commanders were instructed to observe the Hague Convention, which stated that merchant ships were not to be sunk without warning, Lemp contravened the instruction. This infuriated Hitler as many of the *Athenia*'s passengers were American and the sinking might have brought the United States into the War.

AVILA STAR (Blue Star Line). Shop Assistant Gladys Mary Benbow and Stewardess Mary Elizabeth Rowan.

The *Avila Star* (Captain J. Fisher) sailed independently from Buenos Aires on 12 June, 1942, bound for Liverpool via Freetown, from which she sailed on the 28th. Torpedoed by U.201 (Kplt. Adalbert Schnee) at 9.06pm and again at 9.22pm on 5 July, and sank at 10.10pm, in position 38°04′N 22°48′W. Five lifeboats got away. One hundred and ten survivors, from boats 1,4 and 8, were picked up by the Portuguese destroyer *Lima* (Captain Rodriguez) during the late evening of the 8th and taken to Ponta Delgada in the Azores. Twenty-eight in boat No.2 were picked up by the Portuguese sloop *Pedro Nunes* at noon on the 28th and landed at Lisbon the next day. Out a complement of 166 crew and 30 passengers (including 3 survivors of the *Lyle Park* who had been picked up from a lifeboat on 23rd June), 73 died. (Ten died in boat No.2, one on the *Pedro Nunes* and two later in hospital.) Boat No.6, commanded by 1st Mate R. Reid of the *Lyle Park*, was never found.

BORINGIA (Registered in Glasgow but owned by the Danish East Asiatic Co.). Stewardess Meta Nielsen (Danish).

The *Boringia* (Captain Sofus Knolls) sailed independently from Cape Town on 7 October, 1942, bound for Hampton Roads and the UK. Torpedoed by U.159 (Kptlt. Helmut Witte) at 0030 hours on the 8th and, when being abandoned, a second torpedo struck; killing all those in boat No.1 and most of those in boat No.3. The *Boringia* sank at 0036, in position 35°09′S 16°32′E. At 6.30am, the 35 survivors were picked up from two lifeboats by the *Clan Mactavish* (Captain E.E. Arthur) and, although bound for New York, she made for Cape Town. Almost two hours later, the *Clan MacTavish* was herself torpedoed by U.159, and sank in about a minute. At 10am, the 65 survivors, in two lifeboats, were spotted by a plane and, shortly afterwards, were rescued by the *Matheran* which landed them at Cape Town the following day. The *Boringia* had a crew of 60. Twenty-five died when she was torpedoed and a further 7 when the *Clan MacTavish* was torpedoed. Out of the *Clan MacTavish's* crew of 91, 54 died.

BRITANNIA (Anchor Line). Supernumerary Stewardess Mary Bernardine Hine, Stewardesses Annie Seatter and Sarah Struthers, and Chief Stewardess Janet Todd.

Bound for Cape Town, the unescorted *Britannia* (Captain A. Collie) sailed from Liverpool on 12 March, 1941. An unidentified ship was sighted at 7.30am on the 25th, and, when she approached, was seen to be flying the Yugoslavian flag. It was, however, the German raider *Thor* (Kapitän zur See Otto Kähler), and, on seeing her victim attempting to flee, she opened fire. An RRRR message was immediately transmitted. The *Britannia's* guns were no match for those of the *Thor* and, after being hit several times, she surrendered. Kähler waited until all the survivors were off the ship, before he sank her, and aware that the RRRR message would likely result in a warship arriving on the scene, the *Thor* hastily departed. A British warship was sent, but she failed to locate the survivors.

At 9pm on the 29th, the *Cabo Huertas* (Sp.), which had already rescued survivors from a raft and an overturned lifeboat, picked up those in a lifeboat – a total of 77 people. She landed surviving troops at Santa Cruz and passengers and crew at Cadiz, from where they went on to Gibraltar. Sixty-three in another boat were picked up by the *Bachi* (Sp.), and 67 others by the *Raranga*. On 16 April, the remaining lifeboat, commanded by 3rd Mate William McVicar, landed near Sao Luiz, in Brazil. It had originally contained 19 British and 63 Indians. Only 13 British and 25 Indians, in an emaciated state, landed. Out of the 203 crew, and 281 troops and passengers, carried by the Britannia, 122 crew and 127 troops and passengers died.

CARIBOU (Government of Canada). Stewardess Bride Fitzpatrick.

The ferry *Caribou* (Captain B. Taverner) was bound for Port-aux-Basques, Newfoundland, from Sydney, Cape Breton, and in Convoy NL.9, when torpedoed and sunk by U.69 (Oblt. Ulrich Gräf) at 8.21am on 14 October, 1942, in position 47.19N, 59.29W. One hundred and thirty-six, including 57 service personnel, died. One hundred and one were picked up by the minesweeper HMCS *Grandmere* (Lt. J.F.C. Cuthbert) and landed at Sydney the same day. U.69 also sank the *Carolus* (Captain W. Broman) in the convoy.

CERAMIC (Shaw, Savill & Albion Co. Ltd.). Stewardesses Amy Louisa Ellis, Elizabeth Foyle and Ellen Mansell.

The troopship *Ceramic* (Captain H.C. Elford), bound for Sydney, Australia, via St. Helena and Durban, sailed from Liverpool in Convoy ON.149 on 26 November, 1942, and dispersed from it on 2 December. When in position 40°30′N 40°20′W at midnight on the 7th, she was struck by 3 torpedoes, fired in quick succession by U.515 (Kptlt. Werner Henke). With the engines stopped, without lights, in rough seas and in rain, abandoning was difficult. Several boats got away, but some were swamped and others capsized. But the ship did not sink until another 2 torpedoes were put into her three hours later. Of the 657 on board, only Sapper Eric Munday of the Royal Engineers, survived, as he was taken prisoner by the u-boat. More details are given in my article THE FORTUNES OF WAR, published in the July, 2009 issue of the Nautical Magazine.

CITY OF BENARES (Ellerman Group). Assistant Stewardess Annie Bailey, Chief Stewardess Christian Cook, and Stewardesses Margaret Ladyman and Agnes Wallace.

The *City of Benares* (Captain Landles Nicoll) sailed from Liverpool, bound for Quebec, in Convoy OB.213 on Friday the 13th of September, 1940 and was torpedoed and sunk by U.48 (Kptlt. Heinrich Bleichrodt) at 10.8pm, in position 56°43′N 21°15′W, on the 17th: 9 hours after the departure of the RN escort. Those who died, were 123 crew, 51 private passengers (including 4 children), 77 of the 90 children who were been taken to Canada for safety under the government scheme organized by the Children's Overseas Reception Board (CORB) scheme, and 6 of their escorts. One hundred and four survivors were picked up by the destroyer HMS *Hurricane* (LtCdr. H.C. Simms) and landed at Greenock. Forty-five spent 8 days adrift in a lifeboat before being spotted by a Sunderland flying boat. They were subsequently picked up by the destroyer HMS *Anthony* (LtCdr. N.J.V. Thew), but one Indian seaman died before the ship reached Gourock.

The sinking of the *City of Benares* was denounced as a war crime as she was a passenger ship sailing outside the designated 'war zone' and given no warning to allow everyone to leave before she was torpedoed. The Germans, however, disputed this on the grounds that she was armed and in convoy.

CITY OF CAIRO (Ellerman Group). Stewardess Annie Couch and Chief Stewardess Ada Alexandra Taggart.

The *City of Cairo* (Captain W.A. Rogerson) sailed independently from Bombay on 1 October, 1942, bound for Durban, Cape Town, Pernambuco and the UK. Sailed from Cape Town on 1 November and torpedoed twice by U.68 (KrvKpt. Karl-Friedrich Merten) between 8.30pm and 8.40pm on the 6th, and sank ten minutes later in position 23°30′S 05°30′W. The u-boat surfaced, Merten gave the survivors directions and apologized for sinking the ship.

When a count was made the following morning, it was learned that only 6 people were missing so that 292 were distributed in 6 boats. Captain Rogerson ordered the boats to keep together and set a course for St Helena, travelling by day and lying roped together at night. On the 8th, 1st Mate S. Britt, in charge of boat No.1, asked persmission to proceed independently, but it was only after another bad night that Captain Rogerson gave in to Mr Britt's insistance. That same night, Daniel McNeill fell over the side of No. 8 boat when urinating and was lost.

During the night of 12th/13th, boat No.6, with 1st Radio Officer G. Nutter, of the Bibby Line, in charge, drifted away from the group, and at 4.30am on the 19th, when a ship was seen from this boat, flares were sent up and Mr Nutter signalled SOS on his torch. This brought the *Clan Alpine* (Captain C.W. Banbury) to their rescue, boats 7 and 5 were subsequently located and 150 survivors landed at Jamestown, St Helena that afternoon. Those in boat No.8, with 1st Mate T. Green, of BI, in charge, were picked up that same day by the *Bendoran* (Captain W.C. Wilson) and taken to Cape Town.

When it set off on its own, Mr Britt's boat (No.1) contained 54 people, including Annie Couch and Ada Taggart. When it was picked up by the German ship *Rhakotis* (Kapitän zur See Jacobs) on 12 December, only Quartermaster Angus MacDonald, 3rd Steward Jack Edmead, and 21-year-old Diana Jarman (a passenger) remained. Their boat was waterlogged, they had to be hoisted on board, and, when being operated on during the 17th, Diana died. On 1 January, 1943, when the *Rhakotis* was sunk by the cruiser HMS *Scylla* (Captain I.A.P. MacIntyre), Angus and Jack got away in two different lifeboats. Jack's boat was towed into Corunna by a Spanish trawler on the 3rd and he was eventually repatriated to the UK. Along with 79 others, Angus was picked up by U.410 (Kptlt. Kurt Sturm) on the 4th, and landed at St Nazaire. He was released from a German prison camp when the War ended.

Boat No.4, a smaller one, originally contained 17 people, but only 3rd Mate J.A. Whyte and Australian Margaret Gordon (a passenger) remained alive to be picked up by the Brazilian minelayer *Caravelas* on 27 December. After a spell in hospital in New York, Mr Whyte was travelling home on the unescorted *City of Pretoria* (Captain F. Deighton) when she was sunk by U.172 (Kptlt. Carl Emmermann) on 4 March, 1943, and there were no survivors. Out of the *City of Cairo's* original complement of 298, 104 died; 6 when she was sunk, 89 in the lifeboats and 9 after being rescued.

DOMALA (British India Steam Navigation Co.). Stewardesses Martha Alice Elcoat and Violette Hope Wymer.

The *Domala* (Captain W.A. Fitt), which sailed from Antwerp on 29 February, 1940, went aground on Goodwin Knoll, in the Dover Strait, on 1 March. Having been refloated, she was heading for St. Helen's, on the Isle of Wight, but, when off St. Catherine's Point at 5.45am on the 2nd, she was struck by 3 bombs delivered by a German Heinkel III, set on fire and abandoned. Fifty-one and 3 dead were picked up by the small Dutch ship *Jonge Willem*, which herself came under attack, and landed at Newhaven. One hundred and twenty were picked up by the destroyer HMS *Viscount*, and the remainder by shore-based lifeboats. The still blazing *Domala* was towed to Southampton. Many of her passengers were Indian seamen who had served on German merchant ships and being repatriated. One hundred and eight crew and passengers died and 183 survived.

ELYSIA (Anchor Line). Stewardess Catherine McWatt Armstrong.

Bound for Karachi, from Glasgow via Cape Town, the unescorted *Elysia* (Captain D. Morrison) was nearing the southern entrance of the Mozambique Channel on the morning of 5 June, 1942 when intercepted and shelled by the Japanese raiders *Aikoku Maru* and *Hokoku Maru*. Captain Morrison hoisted the signal 'I intend to abandon ship', but the shelling did not immediately stop. When everyone else was off the ship and he was preparing to leave, a small seaplane from the raiders dropped bombs on her and she sank at 9.50am, in [13] position 27°15′S 36°24′E. The raiders departed without attempting to aid the survivors who rescued on the evening of the same day by the hospital ship *Dorsetshire* and the minelayer HMS *Abdiel*. Out of the 136 crew and 58 passengers, 4 European crew, 18 Indian crew and 4

---

[13] A naval source claims that the wreck was sunk by a Japanese submarine on the 9th, in position 27°33′S 37°05′E.

passengers died. Catherine Armstrong was among those commended for their bravery.

GEORGE L. TORIAN (Upper Lakes & St. Lawrence Transportation Co Ltd, Toronto). Second Cook Eileen Pomeroy.

The *George L. Torian* (Captain John Allan) was bound independently for Trinidad from Paramaribo when torpedoed and sunk by U.129 (Kptlt. Asmus Nicolai Clausen) at 1.30am on 23 February, 1942, in position 09°13′N 59°04′W. Fifteeen died. Four were picked up by US Navy flying boat and taken to Trinidad.

GLOUCESTER CASTLE (Union Castle Line). Stewardess Editha Thomas.

Bound for Cape Town, the *Gloucester Castle* (Captain H.H. Rose) sailed from Birkenhead on 21 June, 1942 and in a convoy until it dispersed on 10 July. Sailing independently when shelled by the German AMC *Michel* (Kapitän zur See Helmuth von Ruckteschell) at 7pm on 15 July, and sank within 10 minutes in approximate position 08°00′S 01°00′E. A shell demolished the bridge and radio room, killing all her deck officers except 2nd Mate R. Pargitter, and, as her 3 radio officers also died, no distress message was transmitted. Of the 154 people on board, 93 died, including 6 women, 3 men and 2 children who were passengers. The remaining 61, including a woman, an 18-year-old girl and two young boy passengers, were taken on board the *Michel*, but later transferred to the supply tanker *Charlotte Schliemann*. When the latter eventually sailed, she had some 300 prisoners on board. The women and children were given two cabins, but the others were housed down a small, rat-infested, hold, and all were inadequately fed. The *Charlotte Schliemann* arrived in Singapore on 30 September and 40 prisoners were landed before she sailed for Yokohama, where she arrived on 19 October. But a number of her prisoners did not live to be repatriated at the end of the War. In 1946, Ruckteschell was convicted of war crimes and died in Fuhlbüttel prison, in Hamburg, in 1948, shortly after hearing that he was to be released due to his deteriorating heart condition.

LADY HAWKINS (Canadian National Steamships Ltd.). Canadian Stewardess Lillie Gorbell.

Bound for Bermuda, the *Lady Hawkins* (Captain H.O. Giffin) sailed independently from Boston on 16 January, 1942. Torpedoed twice by U.66 (KrvKpt. Richard Zapp) at 2am on the 19th and sank 20 minutes later, in position 35°00′N 72°30′W. Only 3 lifeboats got away, but 2 of them were never seen again. Of the 76 in the remaining boat, commanded by 1st Mate P.A. Kelly, 5 died while the remainder were picked up towards midnight on the 22nd by the *Coamo* (US) and landed at San Juan, Puerto Rico. Out of *Lady Hawkin's* complement of 109 crew and 210 passengers, 247 died.

NERISSA (Bermuda and West Indies Steamship Co.). Stewardesses Florence Jones and Hilda Lynch.

Bound for Liverpool, the *Nerissa* (Captain G.R. Watson) straggled from Convoy HX.121 which sailed from Halifax, NS, on 16 April, 1941. Torpedoed by U.552 (Oblt. Erich Topp) at 10.34pm on the 30th and being abandoned when two more torpedoes struck. Sank within 5 minutes of being struck by the 3rd torpedo, in position 55°57′N 10°08′W. Alerted by a Whitley bomber, the destroyer HMS *Veteran* (Cdr. W.T. Couchman) arrived and picked up 29 crew and 54 passengers (including 3 Canadian stowaways) who were subsequently transferred to the corvette HMS *Kingcup* (Lt. R.A.D. Cambridge) which landed them at Londonderry. Eight-three crew and 124 passengers died.

ORCADES (Orient Steam Navigation Co. Ltd.). Nursing Sister Kitty Prendergast-Murphy.

Bound for the UK from Suez, the unescorted troopship *Orcades* (Captain C. Fox) sailed from Cape Town on 9 October, 1942. Torpedoed three times by U.172 (Kptlt. Carl Emmermann), between 11.23am and 11.30am on the 10th. Forty-eight people, including Kitty Murphy, died when boat 12a came to grief while being launched, but 20 boats cleared the ship. As the ship was still seaworthy and able to proceed at 5 knots, Captain Fox and 54 crew remained on board in an attempt to save her, but 2 more torpedoes broke her back and she eventually sank in position 31°51′S 18°30′E. The remaining crew then got away in the last 4 boats. The Polish ship *Narwik* had already rescued the other survivors when she approached the 4 boats at midnight, but, as it was dangerous for her to stop, Captain Fox warned her against it. Captain Zarwarda of the *Narwik* ignored the warning, spent an hour picking them up, and all were landed at Cape Town on the morning of the 12th. Forty-eight died and 1026 survived.

RANGITANE (New Zealand Shipping Co.). Stewardesses Catherine Mary de Castella and Jessie Ann Skinner.

Bound for Australia, the *Rangitane* (Captain H.L. Upton) sailed from Liverpool on 25 September, 1940 to join Convoy OB.219. One board were

113 children, and their escorts, being evacuated under the government scheme organized by CORB. However, due to the *City of Benares* having been sunk a week earlier, there was a public outcry, the ship was ordered to return and the CORB passengers disembarked.

Her outward passage to New Zealand was uneventful, and on 25 November she sailed from Auckland, bound for Liverpool. When about 300 miles east of East Cape at about 3.40am on the 27th, her lookouts spotted two ships and, minutes later, she was illuminated by searchlights and warning shots fired across her. And when she transmitted an RRRR message, signifying that she was under attack by an unknown ship, shells began to hit her.

With his ship badly damaged and on fire, and with several people killed, Captain Upton stopped the engines, but the raiders, the *Orion* (Kapitän zur See Kurt Weyher) and the *Komet* (Kapitän zur See Robert Eyssen), continued to fire until they were informed that there were women and children on board. A German boarding party ordered the abandonment of the *Rangitane* and, after everyone was off, they opened the seacocks, but torpedoes and shells had to be put into her before she sank, in position 36°48′S 175°27′W.

The 303 survivors, spread throughout the *Orion*, *Komet* and their supply tanker, *Kulmerland*, were joined by 372 more when the raiders went on to sink the *Triona*, *Vinni* (Nor.), *Komata*, *Triadic* and *Triaster* before heading for Emirau Island, in the Bismarck Archipelago, where 495 were landed. The *Orion*, however, retained 161 white men, including 45 from the *Rangitane* for transportation to Germany. From Emirau, Mr Hopkins, the 1st Mate of the *Rangitane*, and others, went to Kavieng in a motorboat left by the Germans, and the schooner *Leander* then sailed to Emirau where she landed supplies. Some of the survivors were subsequently flown to Australia from Rabaul while the remainder, carried on the *Nellore,* were landed at Townsville on 1 January, 1941.

ST PATRICK (Fishguard & Rosslare Railways & Harbour Co.). Stewardess Jane Hughes.

The *St Patrick* (Captain James Faraday) was on her regular crossing from Rosslare to Fishguard when bombed by a single plane at 4.26am on 13 June, 1941, broke her back and sank seven minutes later, about 12 miles from Strumble Head. The destroyer HMS *Wolsey,* responding to her distress message, arrived at about 5.30am and she, and a patrol boat, picked up 60 survivors and landed them at Milford Haven. Eighteen crew and 11 passengers died.

STENTOR. (Alfred Holt & Co.). Stewardesses Florence May Ball and Florence Denton.

Bound for Liverpool, the *Stentor* (Captain William Williams) sailed from Freetown in Convoy SL.125 on 16 October, 1942. Torpedoed and sunk by U.509 (KrvKpt. Werner Witte) at 7.30pm on the 27th, in position 29°13′N 20°53′W. The explosion caused the bridge area to be showered by burning palm oil. Captain Williams suffered severe burns, Captain R.H. Garstin, the Vice-Commodore, was blinded and Dr. W. Chisholm, the ship's surgeon, sacrificed his life by continuing to administer to the many who were burned. Although the ship sank within 10 minutes, 4 or 5 lifeboats got away, but the remainder of the crew had to jump into the water. At 10.40pm, the corvette HMS *Woodruff* (LtCdr. F.H. Gray) arrived to pick up survivors, but, broke off to hunt a u-boat contact before returning to pick up the others. One hundred, transferred to the destroyer HMS *Ramsey* (LtCdr. R.B. Stannard), were landed at Liverpool while those remaining on the *Woodruff* were landed at Milford Haven. Forty-five, including Captain Williams, Vice-Commodore Garstin and 23 passengers, died. Two hundred and two survived. Eleven other ships were also sunk in Convoy SL.125.

UMONA (Bullard, King Line). Stewardess Hilda Foster.

Enroute from Durban to London, the *Umona* (Captain F.A.B. Peckham) sailed independently from Walvis Bay on 12 March, 1941, bound for Freetown. Torpedoed by U.124 (Kptlt. Georg-Wilhelm Schulz) at 8.15pm on the 30th and, when a second torpedo hit her 8 minutes later, sank within 2 minutes, in estimated position 06°52′N 15°14′W. A young male passenger, DEMS Gunner E. Elliot and 2nd Radio Officer J.E. Hare, succeeded in boarding a small wooden float which was only about 5 feet square, had buoyancy tanks at each corner and became partly submerged under their weight. They had no food or water, but, on 3 April, and by using a cigarette case as a heliograph, managed to attract the attention of what turned out to be the same u-boat which had sunk their ship. Schulz then provided them with water, cognac, biscuits, cigarettes and matches. The radio officer died on the 9th, but the other two were picked up by the *Lorca* on the 12th and landed at Freetown the following day. Only 3 other Indian seamen survived – picked up by the destroyer HMS *Foxhound* (Cdr. G.H. Peters) on the 7th and landed at Freetown on the 8th. Ninety-three, including Hilda Foster, the only woman on board, died.

VIGGO HANSTEEN. 2nd Radio Officer Maude Elizabeth Steane (Canadian).

On 14 August, 1944, the Norwegian Liberty Ship *Viggo Hansteen* (Captain Torbjørn Thorsen) was in Naples when Maude Steane was shot and killed by a crew member, apparently for resisting his advances. The crew member shot himself.

YORKSHIRE (Managed by Bibby Line). Stewardess Helene Reynolds.

The *Yorkshire* (Captain V.C.P. Smalley), bound for Liverpool, sailed from Rangoon on 13 September, 1939 and joined Convoy HG.3 which sailed from Gibraltar on 13 October. Torpedoed three times by U.37 (KrvKpt. Werner Hartmann) at 3.30pm on 17 October, and sank in about 10 minutes, in position 44°52′N 14°31′W. The starboard lifeboats were destroyed and, when one of the portside boats could not be unhooked, most of its occupants drowned. Only 7 boats overcrowded boats were successfully launched. Twenty-four crew and 34 passengers (some of whom were children) died. After about 7½ hours in the lifeboats, in rough seas, 220 were picked up by the *Independence Hall* (US), and, ironically, a u-boat surfaced and thanked her master for rescuing them. Together with the survivors from the *City of Mandalay*, they were landed at Bordeaux on the 21st.

Bibliography
Beyond The Call of Duty by Brian James Crabb
Women Merchant Mariners by Clare Sugrue
A Merchant Fleet in War by Captain S.W. Roskill, RN
The Allied Convoy System 1939-1945 by Arnold Hague
www.uboat.net
www.naval-history
www.warssailors.com
www.caroline.howse.btinternet.co.uk

8. DOUGLAS CAMERON'S ACCOUNT OF VOYAGE 1 OF THE SAMHARLE

(Douglas was a midshipman/deck apprentice with Alfred Holt & Co., owners of the Blue Funnel Line and Glen Line.)

I had a week's leave in Edinburgh before returning to Liverpool. On 9th November 1943, about thirty-eight of us, [14]excluding David Baile and me (the two midshipmen), signed articles for a ship that was yet to be built. A few days later we assembled at the railway station to take a special train to a secret destination. It was intriguing to contemplate the unveiling of this mystery.

The train was blacked out and during the passage through the night it was impossible to tell where we were. The feeble lights in the compartment gave a ghostly atmosphere, too dim for reading. A subdued excitement kept conversation going for a while before everyone dozed off.

Next morning at the destination it was clear that we were in the River Clyde seaport of Greenock. Many other crews of merchant seamen like ourselves came off the train. When we walked out of the station premises there was a murmur from all sides, "It's the Queen Elizabeth." Lying at anchor in the estuary was a large grey-painted passenger vessel slightly dwarfed by the scale of the hills and lochs which formed a backdrop to the scene.
From a loudspeaker, a voice announced, "Queue up at the pier and a tender will take you out to the big ship." 'Big ship' indeed, the QE might as well have been named - it was so well known.

My accommodation was on A-deck, in what may have been termed a 'state-room' in peacetime. For troop carrying, the room was fitted with simple canvas bunks, tubular-framed; five high from deck to deck-head, head to toe right round - no space wasted. Going westbound there were only two tiers in use.

After establishing the position of my room and laying claim to a suitable bed I explored the vessel. There were many decks, but the lifts had notices restricting their use to the higher rank of officer such as 'Major and above.' That was new - a ship with lifts! Down below the waterline aft, near the propeller shafts, were the stewards' cabins; a noisy area where the electric

---

[14] Midshipmen/deck apprentices were named on the articles, but did not sign them as their agreement was with the shipowner and not the Master.

light was on twenty-four hours a day. Further for'ard, at a different level, was the swimming pool, out of use, and lying nearby were several copper coffins supposedly for use if there was a death at sea.

When the time came for our first meal on board, I set out for the first-class saloon. I lost my way and arrived in the galley which was all-shining stainless steel equipment and tables with a different section for each course. Walking through smartly, I came into the saloon and was promptly directed out of another door to join the long queue of officers waiting to get in. The food was astonishing to me in its quantity and quality. I had a quaint notion that in wartime everyone suffered equally. At our table were several American pilots of Air Transport Command who delivered military aircraft to Britain.

A one-page newspaper, the Ocean News, was published on board. I have a copy dated Monday, 15th November, 1943 where the front page headline is 'The 'Eighth Army Takes Atessa'.

On the 19th, the ship docked at Pier 88 on the west side of Manhattan Island. The merchant service personnel were dispersed to various hotels; the other midshipman, David Baile, and I went to Jack Dempsey's Great Northern Hotel in West 57th Street. That same weekend the construction of our new vessel started down south in Baltimore.

My 'New York Handy Guide', published in 1943, quotes the author O. Henry who called the place "Baghdad on the Subway". We were fortunate in having four weeks in New York City - the locals always emphasised the word 'city'. You can have an interesting time in a large city if you have money, but we didn't have very much. My finances amounted to nine pounds sterling per month which didn't go far. The official exchange rate was about four dollars to the pound, but some places tried to give as little as three.

David and I took jobs in Stern's department store on the corner of 42nd Street and 6th Avenue, for four dollars a day. We delivered boxes to the different departments; an undemanding task. Our Chief Officer worked there for one day then gave it up as too demeaning for a person of his rank.

David and I learned quickly, through necessity, the position of all the servicemen's clubs which handed out food and refreshments free of charge. At the Stage Door Canteen, run by the American Theatre Wing, free theatre tickets were made available each afternoon; a fine opportunity which we appreciated. Among several plays we saw were, Arsenic and Old Lace, with

Helen Hayes, and Fanny by Gaslight. David went to a musical and was taken backstage to meet the star Mary Martin. He seemed to have been mesmerised by her and all he could remember was that she had a mole on her left thigh!

The British Apprentice's Club on 23rd Street, run by the wonderful Mrs Spaulding, was a regular haunt. Many of the young ladies who came to the evening dances were daughters of her friends in Greenwich Village. At her request, we gladly volunteered to escort them home on the subway. On one occasion, near Washington Square, the girl I accompanied described a certain restaurant as a 'clip joint'. In those days such American slang seemed outlandish to British ears. Things have changed a bit since then. (Mrs Spaulding later received the O.B.E. for her wartime work.)

You could travel anywhere on the subway for a nickel, five cents. Armed with a subway map and the 'New York Handy Guide' we went round all the sights which were reasonably priced; ice-skating on Rockefeller Plaza, visiting the Statue of Liberty on Bedloe's Island and twice to the top of the Empire State Building.

At the Paramount theatre, a cinema on Times Square, - geometrically not much like a square - we heard Benny Goodman and his band. Times Square was the centre of activity in New York. The sidewalks were always crowded and the striking advertisements on the buildings caught the eye with their flashing coloured lights. An ad. for cigarettes blew giant 'smoke' rings out across the square. At one end was a dance hall with the sign, '10 Cents a Dance'. Hollywood had made a film glamorising its dull reality; bored-looking girls staring glumly into space. Strange to say, although our hotel was next door to Carnegie Hall we were never inside as the tickets were too expensive.

In the last week of our stay, I was told to attend lectures on 'Degaussing and Its Effect on the Magnetic Compass' given by the U.S. Navy at Pier No.1. Apart from that our time was our own.

On the 18th December, our crew met at Pennsylvania Station and took the train to Baltimore; a three-and-a-half hour journey. Again the crew were distributed to different hotels, ours being the Southern Hotel where David and I shared a room with 2nd Radio Officer Hunt.

Baltimore was a Southern town. Before long we were informed about the Mason-Dixon Line which separated North from South. We were in the land of the Confederates where 'dam Yankee' was regarded as one word. The central area seemed a bit shabby and run-down, but the people were more friendly than in New York. The main point of historical interest was Fort McHenry which had been successfully defended against British attack during the War of 1812. During a bombardment in 1814, Francis Scott Key, who was an onlooker, composed the words of the Star-Spangled Banner.'

We enjoyed a lot of hospitality; to describe it all would be tedious. I think we matured a bit during our stay. We met people from a variety of levels in society, most of them outside our previous experience. Well-off business people, who were Republican in their politics, told us that the British Conservative party was tainted with socialism; a bit 'pinko'. They disliked Roosevelt because he had 'used the taxpayers' money to set up projects for the unemployed' - 'using our money to compete with us'. In accepting their kind hospitality, we made no comment - at seventeen, we didn't know much about politics. Others we met lived only for the present or in anticipation of the next party. Again we took the people as we found them and enjoyed their cheerful company.

On one particular visit we were taken to see an old man aged about ninety-five. He was in bed, very frail and saw us, but he didn't speak. Hanging on the wall was the greyish uniform of a Confederate Army officer. The old man had fought in the American Civil War. After a short time of quiet attendance, we left, not fully appreciating the near-reverence displayed by his relatives who had taken us to see him.

At the Bethlehem-Fairfield yard, our ship had been assembled in twenty-three days and launched on the 14th December 1943 as the US ship, *Martha C. Thomas*. Before the launch, a different name was painted on wooden boards each side of the bridge and then they were covered with brown paper. After the launch, the paper was torn off to reveal the new name - SAMHARLE. Under the American lease-lend programme, the ship was handed over to a British authority, the Ministry of War Transport. The MOWT had selected Alfred Holt and Company to 'manage' the vessel, that is, to man her and sail her with cargoes and routes chosen for her by the British Government.

Each day we went down to the ship. These were token visits as there was really nothing we could do while the builders were finishing their work. From my first visit to the shipyard, I retain a vision of a row of ships' bows which formed a receding repetitive pattern along the edge of the creek at Sparrows Point. Around me were large sections of hull, complete deckhouses, machinery and prefabricated sections. These were lifted into place by cranes and welded on to the rest of the structure.

At the Merchant Marine Club, a Scots-American lady gave me two tickets for the train to Washington. It was very kind of her and we enjoyed the visit, but, regretfully, I have forgotten her name. The streets were wide and lined with buildings like Greek temples. It was news to me that the British had been there in 1812 and had burned the White House. The Capitol was interesting. In the room where the President signed important papers, a friendly policeman took us beyond the rope barrier for a better view.

Five days before Christmas 1943, the crew went aboard the ship for her trials in Chesapeake Bay. It was a cold day with thin ice forming in the quieter creeks of the Patapsco River which leads into the Bay. The engines were tried ahead and astern at different speeds, then came the full speed trial over a measured distance. The steering was tested hard-a-starboard and hard-a-port; the anchors were dropped and recovered - equipment tested in all departments. When everything was judged to be satisfactory, the ship was handed over into our care. The paint was still wet in some places, but the ship was now ours to play with. Manuals were supplied with the equipment and we had to study them. One thing we weren't told was how to keep the lifeboats in a swung-out position and this caused us a lot of trouble on our first passage.

What a lot of checking there was in the days that followed! The Chief Officer was astonished, and a little contemptuous, at the range of paint in the lockers. It included 'eggshell' finish which seemed to him to be 'shore-side stuff'. The 2nd Mate appeared happy enough with the chartroom and its three chronometers, which were under his remit. He also found himself in charge of a revolver, handcuffs and leg-irons which were items not usually found in the inventory of British ships.

For David and me, everything was marvellous and luxurious compared to the old Empire Lancer. There were two bunks, with interior spring mattresses on top of box springs, and each one had a bed light! The wash hand basin had hot and cold fresh water and when the plug was pulled out the water ran away down a pipe - no need to empty out a tin receptacle such as we had on the British-built ship. Above the basin, there was a cabinet with a mirror and another light. Along one side, under the porthole, was a green covered settee or day couch and a large wooden locker contained more than enough space for our belongings.

The porthole was the 18-inch size which was wide enough to crawl out of in an emergency. The old standard size of 12-inch diameter was too narrow for most people. The door had kick-panels which could be easily knocked as, when a ship was torpedoed, the doors often jammed.

In the saloon, there was a coffee maker, a toaster and a hotplate. Outside, in the alleyway, was an ice-water tap and hot-water urn for making tea. For food storage there were ample refrigerated lockers as well as ordinary lockers.

On the bridge, there was a twelve-inch diameter signalling lamp as well as the usual, Aldis, hand-held, one. The set of international code flags was conveniently placed so that a hoist could be fastened on to the signal halyard quite quickly. Each flag had a spring-loaded clip. Our chauvinist Chief Officer declared that the spring was a weakness and our British clips (Inglefield type) were superior. He ordered new clips and set the other midshipman and myself the task of replacing the American ones. The latter were really quite good, but they weren't British!

When the ship was launched, it was fitted with a modern 5-inch gun at the stern. The Royal Navy appeared and replaced it with an antique from the First World War; a 4-inch dated 1917. The twelve-pounder at the bow was another obsolescent weapon. The eight Oerlikon 20 cannon had a good reputation for anti-aircraft use. Several Royal Navy DEMS (Defensively Equipped Merchant Ships) ratings joined the ship to service the guns and to form a nucleus for manning them in action.

On the 29th of December, the crew left the hotels to live on board and, on Hogmanay, David and I were at a very pleasant party in some outlying suburb of Baltimore, possibly Tarrytown, when he insisted that we return to the ship to ring 16 bells. This, he said, was an old naval custom, but we were the only ones on board when he did the eight double-rings to welcome 1944.

On the 11th of January, we took our stations for departure. The tugs made fast, the mooring ropes were cast off and we eased slowly out of the harbour on our way to take part in the supply train for the Allied armies in Europe. Although not a problem, the Chesapeake-Delaware Canal was covered with thin ice and after 16 hours we reached Brooklyn.

For the next two weeks, we loaded military stores and Sherman tanks. Some of these were lashed down on deck to large cleats specially welded for the voyage to the Mediterranean. Many wooden boxes containing army stores had the name 'BARI' stencilled on the side. So much for secrecy! Normally we did not know our destination.

When loading was completed at the end of January and we sailed over to the New Jersey side of the Hudson River to have the ship 'degaussed', I thought it ironic that this method of reducing the magnetic field of all Allied vessels should be named after a German scientist (Gauss). The vessel moved into a special berth. All clocks, compasses and instruments which could be affected were taken ashore. Heavy cables were dragged up the side and over the deck to form a series of parallel loops like string round a long parcel. A current was sent through the wire, strong enough to 'wipe' the ship's own 'permanent' magnetic field which could trigger off magnetic mines in shallow waters.

When all was ready, we sailed for Lyneham Roads at Norfolk, Virginia. Norfolk was a large Naval base and, according to an American sailor I met, there were notices in the city's public parks saying, " Sailors and dogs keep off the grass." He then added, keeping a careful eye on me for my reaction, "That's a dam fool notice. What the heck, dogs can't read!"

The times of engine movements and helm orders were recorded by David and me during arrivals and departures. As neither of us owned a wrist watch, we had to rely on an alarm clock which I had bought for $1.65. This 'WARALARM', with its cardboard fibre case, was 'below the counter' and its sale was restricted to war workers. I was able to persuade the shop assistant in a Baltimore store that I qualified.

Convoy UGS.32 sailed for the Mediterranean on the 3rd of February and, like all the other ships, we had our lifeboats swung out, ready for quick lowering in an emergency. Large canvas pads on the end of short channel bars were held against the boats' sides by rope lashings, but, when the convoy ran into a winter gale, the continual movement of the ship soon chafed through the ropes. One night, boat Number 3 swung loose with such violent movements that it was liable to be smashed up. In the panic to make it secure, the Chief Officer switched on the boat deck lights for a short time to let the seamen see what they were doing. In wartime this was really unforgivable and I do not know how he escaped an official reprimand. The solution to the problem lay with channel bars lying on the deck, apparently welded down, but, in fact, stuck with nothing more than paint. Once they were released, they bolted into place and the lifeboats were held as steady as one could desire.

In a gale, the Liberty ship pitched like a bucking bronco and rolled like a cow, as the saying goes. On watch, we stood with feet well astride and held on to the nearest solid support. On the aft side of the compass binnacle, the angle of heel indicator often showed a heel greater than 30 degrees.

If you put aside thoughts of danger, then gales were exhilarating. The seas rushing towards the ship would rise up into hills of turbulent liquid about to engulf us. Usually the ship's buoyancy lifted her up and the wave would roll harmlessly past. At other times, hundreds of tons of seawater poured over the rail and filled the fore deck. For a few moments, the 440 feet long vessel would shudder in her track. As the bow went down, the stern rose up and the propeller raced faster for a few seconds. On deck, the sea swept foaming-white over hatches, winches and deckhouses to fetch up against the for'ard side of the bridge with a hammer-like blow. The swirling confusion of water then streamed to the sides and poured out through the freeing ports in frothy cascades. In the wheelhouse, the helmsman was fortunate if he could maintain the course to within 10 degrees either way.

It was a challenge to take a meal. The stewards sprinkled the tablecloth with water to stop plates sliding and the wooden strips (fiddles) round the edge of the table were raised into place. Only one partly filled plate at a time was handed out. Drinking a cup of tea was like a party trick - swinging to and fro with the movement of the ship. After being thrown out of my bunk on to the deck, I devised a different way of sleeping. I wedged the box mattress so that it tilted towards the bulkhead and slept, arms outstretched, holding the sides of the mattress.

Four large life rafts, which could be released by a sharp blow on a specially designed shackle, were carried on sloping skids. When, during the gale, the Chief Officer noticed that some of the lashings on a raft were coming adrift, David and I were sent down to see what could be done. Climbing up on to the side supports of the raft, making sure of our footholds and handholds, we retied the ropes, keeping in mind the old maxim - 'One hand for the ship and one hand for yourself.'

Most of the crew were in their twenties, but the bosun was older - at least forty. He was a small man with a serious expression, possibly as a result of having been torpedoed. His fear of being trapped made him keep the door open in any room he entered, even the toilet. His hands were large, 'every finger a marlin-spike' but he could play melodious tunes on the mandolin.

After passing through the Strait of Gibraltar, we received a signal ordering our ship to go into Algiers instead of proceeding to Bari. This diversion was strange considering that the battlefront had moved to Italy and the Allies had landed at Anzio a few months earlier. 'Why put tanks ashore in North Africa?' Being a little more cynical in my advanced years, I have wondered if some Army Movements Director (or similar) had noticed that our cargo included several hundred cases of Canadian beer.

Eighteen days after leaving Norfolk, Virginia, the *Samharle* steamed into Algiers Bay. We tied up in the harbour and the Army, using shore cranes, unloaded the tanks. When each one was ashore and released from its sling, soldiers peeled off the waterproof coatings, jumped in, started the engine and drove off. One of the soldiers driving a crane gave me a shot at operating it. The crane swivelled very quickly and I overshot a few times. Before I could improve on my performance, however, an officer shouted up to the soldier and ordered him to stop the teaching-practice immediately.

When we were in the States, believing that we were going to Italy, I had bought an Italian-English phrase book. In Algiers, the stevedores were Arab, their supervisors French and the tally clerks Italian. The latter were now our allies and wore a shoulder flash which was an outline map of Italy. They were friendly and for days I tried to learn some simple Italian phrases from them. They, in turn, were improving their English by speaking to me and, as their need seemed greater than mine, I eventually I gave in and presented them with the phrase book.

As, day after day, David and I had to stand in the cargo holds keeping an eye on the unloading, we could go ashore only after dark. The notorious Kasbah was 'out of bounds', but other parts of the city were still 'creepy'. One evening, we were looking at an Information Office window display which showed photographs of the gallant Allies winning the war! One photo showed a group of British soldiers and I exclaimed to David, "Look at these soldiers. They're carrying Sten guns." A voice from behind whispered in my ear, "Be careful what you say; many of the people here are pro-Vichy." When I looked round a moment later, the speaker had disappeared into the throng.

Wanting to see the town in daylight, I approached the Chief Officer and meekly asked for time off. He brusquely replied, "I didn't get time off when I was an apprentice. Besides, there's no one to take your place in the cargo holds." "What about the radio officers?" I suggested, "They have nothing to do." David and I were given a whole afternoon off, but the radio staff wouldn't speak to us for ages afterwards.

I walked up the steepish streets passing flats built in European style as the French had added a Western city to the Arab quarter. At the top of the hill I found a commemorative bronze plaque to the 'Fort de l'Empereur'. Apparently a handful of French soldiers had successfully fought off hundreds of attacking Arabs, thus gaining a place in history for themselves and their regiment.

Although David and I did not smoke, we collected some of the cigarette ration with a view to barter. Cigarettes were a currency everyone understood. The Frenchman in charge of the stevedores gave me two bottles of fine cherry brandy in exchange for a carton of cigarettes which had cost me two shillings and sixpence (12½p).

After a fortnight of unloading, we sailed for Casablanca - a passage of four days. In the docks were Vichy French warships, destroyed by the Allies to prevent the Nazis from getting them, and the armour-plated foredeck of the battleship, *Jean Bart*, was curled back on itself like the metal on a tin of sardines.

The Moroccan Arabs were a cheerful lot, but we were again forbidden to enter the 'native' area - the Medina. As usual, cigarettes were the common currency of barter, but leather jackets, combs and watches were also sought after. One young Arab held up four notes to pay for some cigarettes, but the suspicious seller/seaman grabbed the hand to reveal only two notes, folded together to look like four! No one seemed to be upset and we all had a good laugh, perpetrator and intended victim, at the unsuccessful attempt at deception. Sand (possibly phosphate) ballast was loaded for the Atlantic crossing and we departed on the 18th March 1944 as part of convoy GUS.33.

In port, the ship's appearance soon became unsightly. As soon as we cleared the land outward bound a general tidy-up commenced. Mooring ropes were neatly coiled and lashed down or stored away. Rubbish was swept up and thrown over the side. Anything liable to move in a seaway had to be fixed in place. The watches were set and we moved into the regular rhythm of sea routine.

My own watch was usually the 12 to 4 with the 2nd Mate. He was a smallish man, slightly rotund. His short pointed beard, which gave him a Captain Kettle look, expressed his own assertive personality. He was the only officer

61

who took an active interest in our learning of the art of navigation. For the enlightenment of David and me, he wrote out some instructions which he called 'Navigation for Tiny Tots'. Like others who had been at sea in the thirties, he had his stories of the dole queues. One of his yarns referred to the time he had made some complaint at the Company head office about unsatisfactory working conditions. He was taken to a window looking down on the street below, "Do you see the queue of men standing there? Any one of them will jump at the chance of getting your job. Now, do you still have a complaint?"

Each day the 2nd Mate calculated the previous day's run. In the scrap log, he pencilled down entries which puzzled me for a while, for example, 'Two hundred and twenty miles nearer Averil.' All was revealed when the weather became warm enough for tropical wear. In his short-sleeved shirt his forearm was exposed showing a tattoo of the word 'Averil'. This turned out to be his wife's name. Such affection!

One night in convoy, a ship in the next column came swinging towards us. I ran through to let the 2nd Mate know, but he was already in the wheelhouse looking at the compass. He shouted at the helmsman that he was right off the course. The seaman replied that he must have fallen asleep. It was our vessel which was the culprit and we were charging towards the column on our port side. There was then some quick manoeuvring, but, fortunately, no collisions.

For a time, I was on the 4 to 8 watch with the Chief Officer. He was a quietly spoken, honest, straightforward man, but, on rare occasions, he could get worked up and would throw down his cap on the deck to express his feelings. As befits the rank of Chief Officer, he was more restrained than the 2nd Officer in his yarns about times gone by.

Round about 6 to 6.30 am, I would go down to the galley to make tea for the two of us and one morning I walked in to find smoke creeping out from the edges of the oven door. Inside the oven were trays of bacon being grilled for the crew's breakfast. The galley boy opened the door and immediately the smoke turned into flames. The bacon and the fat in the trays were on fire! I looked round for a foam extinguisher or a bucket of sand. The galley boy had gone out to the alleyway and leapt back with a bucket of water which he threw on the flames. There was an explosion and the room filled with rolling clouds of smoke and soot. I dropped to the deck and was unscathed, but the galley boy lost his eyebrows and the hair at the front of his head. A sheaf of menus on a hook turned into black carbon and it was a dramatic demonstration of the danger of using water to put out a fire of oil and fat.

On 4th April, we docked at Hoboken, New Jersey, where military stores were loaded, including Grumman Avenger aircraft and bow-doors for landing craft. Opposite Manhattan, Hoboken is on the west side of the River Hudson and a short journey on the subway took us, once again, to the entertaining diversions of New York City.

Armed guards watched over the ships in port in case of attempts at sabotage by IRA sympathisers and, as tensions between Ireland and England are not new, some of our English seamen got into a fight with Irish-Americans somewhere in New Jersey.

The loading was carried out by gangs of stevedores of mixed national origins. In the cargo hold, where I was supervising, the ganger was Irish, aggressive and very muscular. One day he got into an argument with a Polish member of his squad. The altercation went as follows:
"You Polacks are useless. The Germans knocked out your country in less than a fortnight!"
"That's not true. Besides, what about you Irish? The English have got you right under their thumb."
"What! We've been fighting the English for six hundred years and we're not finished yet!"
Knowing that I was a Scot, the Irish ganger turned to me and said, "The English are rotten. You don't like them, do you?"
"No, not at all," I quickly replied. After all, he was a brawny individual with large muscles and discretion is the better part of valour!

Two and a half weeks later we were outward bound with more military supplies in convoy UGS.40, 81 ships not including escorts. The meeting point was at Hampton Roads, Virginia from where we took a southerly route across the North Atlantic. The Strait of Gibraltar was passed through on the 9th May with Gibraltar abeam at 1244.

Our American escorts were always busy, turning the sea into frothy turbulence as they raced along the convoy perimeter. The waters of the Mediterranean had a reputation for producing false echoes on the Asdic. Sometimes an escort would hoist the black pennant for a suspected submarine contact and post-war German reports indicate that U-616 and U-967 tried to make contact with the convoy but failed.

Identification of aircraft is often difficult and there is seldom enough time for a change of mind. Somewhere along the African coast, I was on watch on the upper bridge, enjoying the afternoon sunshine. The Chief Officer had gone below to the chartroom to do some calculations. While scanning the horizon I listened idly to the chatter of our escort vessels coming over the VHF transceiver which hung in a corner of the bridge. Someone spoke with an urgent ring in his voice. "Joe. Do you see that aircraft approaching? Did he give a recognition signal?"
"I didn't see one, but he must be O.K. The guys in the outer screen let him go by."

To the front of the convoy a twin-engined aircraft in desert-type camouflage was flying diagonally across our course about 100 feet above the water. It could have been a Beaufighter or a Junkers 88, but no one seemed to know! A few seconds later, the plane was out of sight and the matter had no more importance. (From a comment in the Convoy Commodore's report, it seems more than likely that the plane was a Ju88.) On the following day, 11th May, the convoy was attacked by 62 enemy aircraft in the area of Cape Bengut.

The Geneva Convention allowed merchant ships to have defensive armament. A large gun for surface firing was a usual feature at the stern, but never at the bows where an anti-aircraft gun could be installed as it was a defensive weapon. As previously mentioned, we had an ineffective twelve-pounder at the bow and a 4-inch, of 1917 vintage and with a range of about 1200 yards, at the stern. A few yards from it was the 'pillar box' - a rocket-firing device which could fire twenty, two-inch, rocket projectiles in banks - but our main A.A. defence was the eight excellent Oerlikon 20 mm cannon. The ship's plating was hardly thick enough to stand up to cannon fire or even machine gun bullets although the bridge had some protection which looked like tarmacadam and was called 'plastic armour'.

About 9.15 pm, David Baile and I were sitting talking to the Naval Yeoman of Signals when the alarm bells sounded the attack warning - short-long, short-long - AAA in Morse code. We ran to our room, collected our steel helmets and lifejackets, then went smartly up the ladder to the bridge deck above and our gun stations. I was No.2 on a bridge Oerlikon and the No.1, DEMS Gunner A.B. Hunt, was already getting into the harness. The convoy was between Algiers and Bougie Bay and, as it was not long after sunset and there was still a glimmer of light on our port quarter, the convoy would be silhouetted against the western sky.

Guns were being fired from all round the convoy, but not, as yet, from our vessel. There appeared to be a bit of wild firing at nothing in particular. Once Hunt was in the harness, I stood on the right side of the gun and fixed the intercom phones over my helmet as best as I could. The 2nd Mate stomped up and down in his capacity as our Gunnery Control Officer, shouting out directions. 'Tracers' were flying all over the place - some uncomfortably close. They emerged from the gun muzzles a white colour, quickly changing to red. Some rockets went off with a 'whoosh' of flame. On the starboard beam, I saw an aircraft low over the water travelling very quickly and shouted to Hunt. He opened fire and the other guns followed. The noise was intense and thudded into my ears. The effective range for the Oerlikon was about 1000 yards and the plane passed out of range. Although lots of other ships were firing at targets which we couldn't see, there was a lull for us. An explosion, about half a mile away to our rear, caught our attention. Red-hot fire blazed on the water for a second or two before eclipsing into darkness. It was an enemy aircraft, burning briefly on the surface before sinking.

Ahead of us, the naval escort opened up. The sky was filled with the colours of fireworks. We spotted a plane coming from the opposite direction to the first. Like an orchestra given its cue, all our guns opened fire. About ten feet away from our gun, tracer bullets were flying across the width of the ship from an over-enthusiastic gunner on the port side of the bridge deck. This dangerous action should not have been possible. Limiting rods were in position at every gun pit, but ours were ineffective because the flame guards had been removed from the ends of the gun barrels. The guns could thus be rotated or elevated to any direction. There was a sudden explosion close to the ship and I saw some splashes on the surface of the water near the starboard side. Our 'pillar box' had fired its rockets at a low angle of depression and some of the 2-inch projectiles had struck the water. The plane passed behind some ships and we had to cease firing. Hunt told me to put on a fresh magazine - each one holding about 60 rounds. Again, at some distance, we saw some red fire on the water. It was quickly extinguished and, after some time of inactivity, it was clear that the raid was over.

The next day at daylight, we found the results of the wild shooting. Our galley funnel, at the rear of the bridge, had a hole in it and, aloft, some of the wire rigging had been cut by the fire of our own guns. During the action, the twelve-pounder was not used, as there were not enough men to man it, and one Oerlikon gun had not been fired - the seaman in charge of it claiming that there had been a fault, but the truth being that he had forgotten to take the safety catch off the trigger. In the next column, the U.S. Liberty Ship *James*

W. Fannin, found an aircraft torpedo in her anti-torpedo defence nets. They lowered the nets back into the water and were diverted to Malta to have the torpedo removed. That was my only 'action' of the war and I was fortunate not to be involved in anything worse.

At the time, we were told that five enemy aircraft had been shot down and no ships lost. More details are given in the publication, Chronology of the War at Sea by Rohwer and Hummeichen: 'On May 9, the convoy UGS 40 with 65 ships ([15]80 had sailed from the USA with 3 returning) passes through the Straits of Gibraltar. Escort [16]TF60 (Cdr Sowell USCG) with the cutter CAMPBELL, USS destroyers DALLAS, BERNADOU, ELLIS, BENSON, the DE's EVARTS, DOBLER, DECKER, SMARTT, WYFFELS, WALTER S. SCOTT, BROWN & WILHOITE. In addition, there are the British AA cruiser CALEDON, the French DE TUNISIEN, the French submarine chaser CIMETERRE and the US minesweepers SUSTAIN & STEADY. U 967 & U 616 fail to make contact with the convoy.

On the evening of 11 May, 62 aircraft of I and III/K.G. (Kampfgeschwader-Battle Squadron) are deployed against the convoy. British Beaufighters flying from Sardinia intercept some of the attackers, and lose two aircraft; the remainder attack in four waves in the area of Cape Bengut. The pilots believe that they have sunk a destroyer and seven freighters and damaged many others. In fact, no ship is hit and [17]19 aircraft are lost.'

In his book, The Atlantic Battle Won, Samuel Eliot Morison gives another account:
'UGS 40 ......inflicted heavy loss on the attacking German aircraft and got through with hardly a scratch. Both escorts and merchantmen put on such a superb performance that an effort has been made to preserve this convoy's composition.'

On 19th May, the low-lying land of the Nile delta was sighted and before long we were all at our stations as, with a pilot on board, we entered Port Said. The statue of Ferdinand de Lesseps, complete with cloak and cravat, stood loftily on the breakwater with its inscription APERIRE TERRAM GENTIBUS (To Open the Land to the Nations). Port Said had no tall buildings, but unfortunate eye-catching features of the scene were several over-large advertisements for Scotch Whisky.

---

[15] It was 81.

[16] It was TF61.

[17] It was 17.

After a short time at anchor in Port Said harbour, a Suez Canal pilot boarded, together with two Arabs. Two mooring boats were hoisted on board and the Arabs could be lowered in them to take our lines ashore if we were required to moor in order to allow a north-bound vessel to pass. A searchlight was compulsory for night passages. Its large square housing was hung at the bows and, in action, it hissed away as its carbon electrodes wore down.

The distances from Port Said were marked every one-fifth of a kilometre. At intervals were signalling stations such as Gare de Kabret, Kantara and Tineh. At Ismailia, a pretty little place, pilots were changed. They were of various nationalities; British, French and Greek. From Ismailia, on the west side of the Maritime Canal, lay the Sweetwater Canal - a misleading name as, according to what we were told by soldiers of the Eighth Army, anyone who fell into *that* canal was immediately given injections to prevent typhoid and fever! The ground in the vicinity was irrigated and intensely cultivated. Beyond this bright green strip the land was barren and, at points along the banks of the Suez Canal in this area, local people put up signs asking passing ships to throw them firewood - a very scarce commodity.

After two days at anchor in the Gulf of Suez, we headed off, independently, down the Red Sea. Not needed on the bridge, David and I worked on deck - doing the usual humdrum tasks under a blistering sun when the motion of the ship neatly cancelled out a northerly breeze so that she moved as if in still air.

Four days took us to Aden and we managed to get leave to go ashore in that barren place where grass did not grow on the reddish-coloured rocks as rain seldom fell. We went to the cinema - arriving after the film had started. The Arab projectionist had mixed up the reels and we saw the last reel before the middle one! From time to time, a lizard crawled across the screen and, at the end of the performance, we all stood for God Save the King. While standing to attention, some specks of light in the ceiling caught my eye and it was a few seconds before I realised that there was, in fact, no ceiling or roof and the specks of light were the stars!

When we left Aden on 28th May, for Colombo, Ceylon (Sri Lanka), we again sailed independently, but as enemy submarines were known to operate in the Indian Ocean, we had the choice of sailing directly, with our anti-torpedo nets streamed, or following a zigzag course. The disadvantage of streaming the nets was the speed reduction from 11 knots to about 8½. On the other hand zigzagging was of doubtful merit.

There was a book of recommended zigzags for merchant ships and post-war reports indicate that every U-Boat had a copy. The pages of possible patterns indicated the percentage lost in distance steamed. A pattern was chosen and the wheelhouse zigzag clock had its adjustable edge markers moved to the minutes indicated on the plan. The minute hand of this special clock carried a springy extension on its tip and, when this touched each marker, a circuit was closed and a bell rang to change course.

The south-west monsoon was prevailing when we arrived in the roads off Colombo, Ceylon where several ships were at anchor waiting for a berth to unload. The day after our arrival was D-Day in Normandy, but we had little news about the landings. In the Mercantile Marine Office back in Britain, we had all been asked if we were willing to take part in D-Day. Each man's identity card was stamped with a V to show he had volunteered to take part. This was a strange request considering that we went into areas of equal or greater danger without being asked if we agreed. It was said that American seamen were paid extra in dangerous zones, but British pay was the same no matter where we sailed.

From deck level to the surface of the water was only about ten feet - our freeboard when loaded. Rope ladders and a cargo net were rigged over the side for bathers, but we came out of the water with red weals on the skin, caused by small jellyfish with long thread-like stinging tendrils. Local people came out in fragile-looking canoes, to sell coconuts and bananas and their simple craft of logs lashed together were nearly awash. One afternoon, some American seamen swam over from their ship, about quarter of a mile away. Swimming through a moderate swell, they were good and confident swimmers.

After waiting about a fortnight, and as Colombo had no quays, we moored to buoys in the large harbour where the upper-works of Blue Funnel's *Hector*, were a constant reminder of the Japanese bombings of 1942. By mid-1944, however, our air defence had greatly improved and Colombo had become the headquarters of South East Asia Command (SEAC). The only threat now was from enemy frogmen and mini-subs and, to discourage them, naval craft dropped small depth charges at random through the night.

Our cargo was discharged into barges, but, as the Grumman Avenger aircraft proved too wide to pass through the dock gates, they were returned to the barges and taken round the end of the perimeter fence. Another consignment we carried were large bow doors for landing craft - all part of the build-up for the offensive against the Japanese.

Several US and British aircraft carriers lay near us, including *Illustrious* and *Victorious*, together with large warships such as the battleships *Queen Elizabeth* and *Valiant*, and their presence sharpened up the 8 a.m. and sunset flag ceremonies. Exactly on the dot of the hour, our ensign was smartly hoisted, often under the sharp eye of the Chief Officer. On the naval vessels, the British and American armed guards vied with each other in polished ceremony. At the end of the day, the time of sunset had to be calculated in advance from the data in the Nautical Almanac and we prided ourselves on getting it right each time. (On 25th July, the warships carried out an attack on Sabang in Sumatra).

Gunnery training was given to the crew during our stay and we went to a coastal site where a drogue, towed by an aircraft, provided the target. Clay pigeon shooting was also practiced with a shotgun as the principle of 'aiming-off' was supposed to be similar for aircraft and clay pigeons.

We had all done gunnery courses in the UK. I did mine at Longniddry, near Edinburgh, where the excellent facilities included a simulator known as the 'dome'. A mock-up of a gun and its harness was in the centre of the hemispherical-shaped building. Once you were in the harness, the instructor started up a cine-projector to display the image of an attacking aircraft on the inside of the concave roof. As the 'aircraft' approached, you kept it in your 'gun' sights and, when it came within range, you opened fire, with the realistic noise of gunfire provided from a record. When the trigger of the dummy gun was pressed, a yellow spotlight, not visible to the gunner' because he looked through a yellow filter, showed the instructor where the trainee was aiming. Another training device was a simple fairground gun which fired a steady stream of small, steel, ball bearings at wooden models sliding down a wire towards the operator.

A hard-working man, always busy with maintenance, our Petty Officer, in charge of the six RN DEMS gunners, was painting a gun mounting and its shield. Using the standard low-visibility grey paint, he carried on, with a display of zeal, to paint the tower on which the gun was carried. The latter, however, was regarded by the Chief Officer as part of the ship and, as he had been watching disapprovingly from the bridge, he called to the PO to come up to him. "Why did you paint the gun tower when it's not your job?" he asked. "But I thought…" began the PO. "You're not here to think, you're here to do what you're told," was the brusque reply.

Twice we went south, by train, to Mount Lavinia where we swam and rode surfboards through the heavy swell. When the waves finally carried us to the sand, there were a few desperate moments hanging on against the fierce undertow of water running back down the steep beach and, during the time of our stay, two servicemen were drowned. The pair of ebony elephants on my bookcase were bought in Colombo after much agonising and counting of rupees. Unlike India, which had 16 annas to the rupee, Ceylon had 100 cents to the rupee.

After eight and a half weeks at Colombo, we sailed for Durban, Natal, at 1130 hours on the 6th of August, and, when the equator was crossed during the passage, there was no ceremony. The 16th of August, 1944 saw us in a position south-east from the island of Madagascar, within four days' steaming distance of Durban, and at 10pm that same day, my previous ship, the *Empire Lancer*, was torpedoed in the Mozambique Channel when on passage from Durban to Majunga, in Madagascar. All the deck officers and midshipmen were lost. A few survivors reached the African coast in one lifeboat and Angus Wilkieson, the Chief Engineer who had befriended me and was the officer-in-charge, was awarded the OBE.

As we approached Durban, the motion of the sea changed to a long rolling swell with about a quarter of a mile between the crests. The ship seemed to toil up one slope and to slide down the next. Once we were through the narrow entrance, the harbour at Durban opened up into a fine broad sheltered anchorage. There wasn't a lot of shipping in port, but one vessel worthy of mention was the 1892, Dundee-built, 4-masted sailing ship *Lawhill* which seemed small compared to the Liberty Ship. Although the days were past when troop transports called in at Durban on their long way, round Africa, to the Middle East, a few canteens still hung on in town to welcome the occasional serviceman.

As apartheid existed, the Post Office displayed a 'Nie Blanke Nie' sign - presumably an inverted way of keeping black people in a queue of their own. In the streets, the Zulu rickshaw 'boys' plied their trade although 'boys' was a misnomer as they were men of fine stature who pulled two persons in their carriages compared to one in most other countries.

Our new vessel had been free from insect life, but weevils, brought on board in the fresh supplies of flour and other commodities ordered by the Chief Steward, now appeared in large numbers. They were in the cocoa and had to skimmed off the top before the beverage could be drunk. At breakfast, cornflakes had to be examined, flake by flake, and black spots in the bread represented their remains. Complaints to the stewards brought only the standard trite retort, "What's the matter? Don't you like fresh meat?" In our rooms, cockroaches challenged us for the right to eat sandwiches set out for those on watch during the night. Then there were steam flies....! But the people were very friendly and we received, much appreciated, gifts of 'comforts'.

A day's run from Durban brought us to Lourenço Marques (now Maputo), in Portuguese East Africa, to load coal. But, although survivors from the *Empire Lancer* were reputed to be in the town, nobody made contact. As high-level religious delegates from Portugal were expected, bunting and flags hung from every post and pole and, as the country was neutral, our DEMS gunners had to go ashore in civvies. They borrowed these from the rest of the crew so that it appeared as if they had robbed a washing line. The beer ashore was voted to be good stuff. Everyone memorised the Portuguese word 'cerveza' and it's amazing how far you can travel without knowing any more than one or two foreign words and pointing or miming for the missing vocabulary. A favourite 'watering hole' was the Café Penguin where the amiable proprietor produced a spare jacket for any one in shirt sleeves wishing to dance.
Alongside the palm trees on the platform of the railway station, stood a splendid locomotive. Built in Schenectady, N.Y., it was the classic engine of the Western movie, with cowcatcher, bell and large headlight.

The African workers loved to work in unison. Each afternoon they removed the loose coal from the deck, swinging their shovels in time together and chanting a rhythmic song. How I missed having a camera as, with coal dust everywhere, 'before and after' shots of our crew, at the beginning and end of each day, would have made good black and white studies.

We left our berth at the coal wharf on 3rd September, 1944, the fifth anniversary of the outbreak of war, sailing independently for Aden. And, as U-Boats had sunk the *Teucer* as well as the *Empire Lancer* since our departure from Colombo, the horizon was scanned very carefully indeed as we worked our way up the African coast.

At Aden, we found some of the crew of the *Teucer* waiting for a passage home and were delighted that we could accommodate them on our vessel. During our short stay, the 2nd Mate negotiated with an Arab for the purchase of a monkey and, having acquired this 'pet', he made a corner for him on the boat deck. We now began to realise the full meaning of the phrase 'monkey tricks'. His first move with a bowl of food was to turn it upside down. At the slightest chance he would race away and I prize the memory of the sight of half the crew charging up and down trying to coax him out of the rigging.

71

He would leap through an open porthole in a flash, grabbing anything he fancied and, if anyone found a half-chewed packet of cigarettes, they knew whom to blame.

From Aden, we headed up the Red Sea and, after two days at anchor at Suez, entered the Canal at 1400 on the 25th to arrive at Port Said at 0400 the next day. Our friends from the *Teucer* left us here for transfer to a ship to the UK, but, although they made light of their ordeal, I wondered if we had heard the whole story. Now on our way to Sicily with our 10000 tons of coal, we took the temperature of each hold every day to be sure that spontaneous combustion was not setting the cargo on fire. As, on the boat deck, the monkey was looking really miserable due to the drop in air temperature, the 2nd Mate fashioned a kind of woolly vest for him from an old sock.

A pilot boarded to take us into the small port of *Catania*, dominated by Mount Etna to the north, and our Captain put a challenging question to him as soon as he reached the bridge - "This ship is loaded to a draft of 27 feet 9 inches and the Sailing Directions say that *Catania* can only take vessels of up to 26 and a half feet." Boldly putting his arm across our senior officer's shoulders, the pilot replied, "Not to worry, Captain!" and gave the order to proceed. We were about ten feet from the quay when we ran aground, but, undaunted, the crew were set to work taking the gear off our derricks. Long baulks of timber were obtained ashore and strongly lashed to the end of each jib in order to make them long enough to reach the quay. The running gear was put back and unloading commenced. After a few hundred tons had been taken out the vessel floated high enough to be warped alongside. A steam-driven pleasure craft with a 1930-ish appearance lay at a nearby berth. It was said to be Tito's yacht, but there was no sign of him or anyone else on board.
During our stay of only three days, the Chief Officer showed his usual reluctance before agreeing to my request to go ashore. As I walked along the quay, I saw the 2nd Mate making a deal with a Sicilian who wanted to buy the monkey and it was just as well that the deal went through so that the creature was not taken any further north into colder climes.

The British controlled this area and, on looking for the soldier on duty at the harbour gate, I saw him sitting in a nearby wine shop which was dominated by an enormous barrel. With his rifle between his legs, he looked up at my call and shouted, "Aye, Aye, mate!" and waved me on. A few yards further on, I was surrounded by about twenty children all holding lira notes and shouting for cigarettes. I had gone ashore with a carton of 200, which I eventually sold for two thousand lire, and, after that, I was free from harassment. Walking through the dark streets, I heard the sound of pleasant singing coming through the closed shutters of a house and, later, the melodious strumming of a mandolin helped to make up my mind as to what to do with the money. The mandolin I bought cost me the equivalent of three shillings and sixpence (17½.p), but I never did learn to play it properly, even though the bosun gave me some lessons.

Catania had been occupied by the Germans the previous year and when I picked up a guidebook in German at a bookstall, the stallholder quickly removed it from my grasp and substituted it with one in English. Some shops had souvenirs, in aluminium supposedly obtained from crashed aircraft, and I have an ashtray and a model Stuka made from the metal.

The bulk of the cargo was to be discharged at Palermo and, as we coasted north towards the Strait of Messina, we had a fine view of the landscape. The Americans held the Palermo district and the harbour was filled with their landing craft and other naval vessels. The buildings of the harbour area had been devastated by Allied bombing and, when we tied up in a space behind a sunken vessel, we were the only merchant ship in the port.

When discharging commenced, Sicilian stevedores, in the holds, shovelled the coal into large iron skips which were lifted up and their contents emptied on to the quay. The coal was then shovelled into straw baskets and loaded onto small, beautifully carved, horse-drawn carts. The latter, with Biblical scenes painted on their sides, made a steady procession as they cleared the fuel from the quayside. As, once again, I went ashore with a carton of cigarettes tucked into my jacket, ready for bartering with the locals, two iron-faced US soldiers, with carbines at the ready, stopped me at the dock gate. One of them covered me with his gun while the other searched me and, although I was allowed to pass, it seemed to me that the security angle was overdone. Unlike Catania, there was little to buy in Palermo so that some of the crew changed their Italian lire into 'Invasion dollars' which they had learned could be converted into US dollars. The Americans - dedicated souvenir hunters - had swept the place clean. Bottles of the syrupy Marsala were available, but it's not a wine that travels well.

Food riots broke out while we were in the harbour, but we saw nothing of the disturbance as our shore leave was suspended for several days until they were under control. The Americans kept us diverted by showing up-to-date films in a makeshift outdoor cinema on the quay. All we had to do was to bring down chairs from the ship and make ourselves comfortable. The October temperature in Palermo was comparable to a British summer evening. They also arranged for transport to take us to a local stadium where baseball equipment was provided, but there were few takers among the British crew. Soft drinks and candy were freely available. The Americans were good at this kind of welfare for the 'boys' in the Services.

Our 3rd Mate was a pleasant, well-mannered, chap from Somerset who had been on one of the last vessels out of Singapore in 1942. During our stay in Palermo, he had a notion to paint a water line right round the vessel; a job usually done in dry dock. The other middy and I were told to carry out this cosmetic exercise although the impracticality of the task and its unnecessary nature made me question our junior officer's fundamental wisdom. The part of the ship against the quay could not be touched at all, but we did what we could from a ship's lifeboat bobbing up and down in waves produced by the frequent passage of small naval craft. Once the cargo was unloaded we sailed for Oran in North Africa; about three day's run.

In Oran, the ships were anchored at equal distances apart with their sterns made fast to mooring buoys. Shortly after our arrival, the US Liberty Ship in the next berth made a move to leave by letting go aft and heaving up the anchor. When their anchor windlass jammed, they tried to contact the Shore Signal Station by lamp, but we were in the way. One of their signalmen called us up by semaphore and I read the message while the other middy took it down. All this time the American vessel was drifting down on us while, on the decks of both ships, seamen ran to place fenders against the inescapable collision. When the ships came together, I walked to the wing of the bridge and handed our written copy of the signal to the American. He confirmed that it was correct so we went to the other side and sent off the text using our own twelve-inch lamp. That was the only occasion in my seafaring career when semaphore came near to being useful.

On the last day of October, we left Oran for Casablanca - about two days run for our eleven-knot vessel. Near our destination, we were overhauled by a French cruiser and, in port, we loaded sand ballast. Nothing had changed much since our previous call in March. Cigarettes were still the main currency and bartering took place in every street. An international boxing match was advertised and we went along in the evening to a theatre to see the contest between USA, France and Britain. The auditorium was filled with many soldiers, and some sailors, while GIs, armed with carbines, were on duty to suppress any partisan display by the audience.

On the eleventh of November, we left in convoy GUS.57 for the States. Not far from the land, four waterspouts could be seen in the distance. Through binoculars, a mist of spray was visible at the base of each whirling vortex and the top of each column broadened out where it touched the clouds.

In these warmer waters, flying fish were abundant - rising out of the sea and gliding along on the crests of the wavelets until they sank back under the surface. Many landed on the main deck, but one even reached the boat deck - more than thirty feet above the waterline. A young seaman collected a number and offered them to the cook, but he firmly refused the offer, claiming that they were bony fish with little edible value.

When we were eleven days out and in position 33°29′N 49°39′W, a signal was received to detach from the convoy and proceed independently to Panama. The Mona Passage was our route - through the curving string of islands which encloses the Caribbean Sea. After going through the passage, we turned back to go to San Juan, in Porto Rico, and arrived there on the last day of November. Morro Castle guards the narrow entrance which opens up into a spacious harbour and our vessel tied up with its bow overhanging what seemed to be a main street. Young ladies waved up to us with friendly greetings which was quite gratifying to many of the crew who could hardly wait to get their shore leave. Above the beautiful bay, US Navy blimps hovered - excellent support aircraft for anti-submarine work as long as there was air supremacy.

We had called to replenish our bunkers, but, for a day, nothing happened and the rumour was that the supplier had confused Alfred Holt and Company with Lamport and Holt who had defaulted on payment for oil some years previously. But, as oil was supplied to us on the second day and the Lamport and Holt Line was an equally reputable British company, the rumour is likely to have been false.

Meantime, a few members of the crew had been busy ashore drawing money out of their US Post Office accounts. Somehow or other they had managed to deposit 'invasion' dollars while we were in the Med., but were now withdrawing ordinary dollars which were acceptable everywhere. The streets were teeming with American sailors and young females of quite a forward disposition. Places of entertainment had shows which seemed daring at the time, but would no doubt raise only a yawn nowadays. When in one of them, we spotted the Chief Officer and departed quickly. A couple of weeks later, when we were in the Pacific, he remarked to me that he didn't think the other middy and I should have been in a place like that!

Four days after leaving San Juan, we arrived at Colon in the Panama Canal Zone and, as this was a busy place, it was over a week before our turn came to go through. I was greatly surprised to see our elderly Chief Engineer going ashore as he usually stayed on board in port after port because he said he had been to them all several times before. When I questioned him, he replied that he had certainly been to Panama before, but the Canal had been built since then and he wanted to see the changes. And he was probably right to expect changes between 1914 and 1944!

The local entrepreneurs were working hard to satisfy the demands of American servicemen. Every few yards there was an 'alehouse'. Bordellos were numerous and, outside one, I counted about fifty or so US sailors standing in line.

The Canal, approximately fifty-one miles long, lies in a NW to SE direction and, from the Atlantic end, three locks at Gatun lift vessels 85 feet above sea level. The Gatun Lake is used for some part of the way then comes the Galliard Cut which took six years to construct. At the Pacific end, one step down is made at the Pedro Miguel Lock and then two steps down at the Miraflores Lock.

When we left Colon about 7.30 in the morning, armed American marines, with impassive faces turned yellowish through taking the anti-malaria, Mepacrine, pill, kept a close eye on our manoeuvres. They ran their own telephone line from the bridge to the engine room and made a separate check on each engine movement. It takes about twenty minutes to pass through each lock and ship's engines are not used. Electric traction engines, known as mules, haul the vessel through and we had three on each side.

In one lock, an iguana was swimming and one of the winchmen lassoed it - supposedly with the intention of eating it. Most of the banks of the Canal were green with all sorts of vigorous-growing plants and, near the Gaillard Cut, high-pressure water jets were tearing away unwanted banks of earth.

In this area, I experienced the heaviest rainfall of my life. Great torrents fell as if they were being poured out of buckets and, in moments, the decks were awash because the scuppers couldn't cope. Water cascaded in waterfalls from each deck to the next below, but, fortunately, it didn't last long. About 3.15 p.m., the Canal was cleared. The marines departed and, in Balboa Bay, pelicans flew low above the water as we steamed out into the Pacific.

It's a long haul from Panama to British Columbia, over three thousand miles, and it took us fifteen days. Off the coast of Mexico, tunny (tuna) boats were numerous, but other merchant ships were scarce. The sea abounded with schools of dolphins which rolled up to the surface and under again in never-ending undulations. Los Angeles was abeam on Christmas Day, but well below the horizon.

On the 29th, we passed the fir-clad headland of Cape Flattery, then Victoria and on up the Fraser River to New Westminster. In early maps of Western Canada, the city of New Westminster appears as the most important town on the mainland of British Columbia. Vancouver came into prominence with the advent of the railroad in the latter part of the nineteenth century.

It was in British Columbia that the 2nd Mate had his beard shaved off. A soft baby-skinned face was revealed and the part of his status which depended on image was lost. If a man's image demands a beard then he should stick with it.

As our movements back and forward between New Westminster and Vancouver are now a bit of a mystery to me, they are noted without explanation.

JANUARY 1945

6th   Depart New Westminster at 0900; arrive North Vancouver at 1500. Enter dry dock. Move to West Indies Pier.

12th   Depart West Indies Pier, North Vancouver at 0800. Arrive New Westminster on the Fraser River at   1230.

15th   Depart New Westminster at 1300. Arrive La Pointe, Vancouver at 1800.

17th   Depart Vancouver at 1800.

18th   Arrive Victoria at 0100.

19th   Depart Victoria at 1630.

20th   Arrive Port Alberni, Vancouver Island at 0330.

Going down river from New Westminster, there was a panic when the steering gear jammed hard-a-starboard and the ship headed towards the bank. The Captain shouted from the bridge to let go the anchor and hold it at one shackle. Chippy, the Carpenter, struck at the brake handle with a sledgehammer and, after two or three blows, the anchor went out at a run. When fifteen fathoms had run out, that is to say one shackle, he hammered the brake back on. The vessel swung round in the current and then its whole weight came on to the anchor which held fast on the bottom. The shock made the anchor chain jump out of its patterned recesses on the windlass. Sparks, rust and mud flew and the anchor gang took cover until the leaping chain fell back and was firmly gripped.

The incident did not ruffle our Captain who maintained his usual air of detachment. The 3rd Mate was the only officer who seemed able to jolly him along into a sustained conversation. As regards David and me, it has to be said that he was polite but distant. He wasn't interested in us as individuals and spoke to us only when giving commands.

Chippy was a young Welsh-speaking chap from a small port in Wales. There was another Welsh speaker among the ABs and the two of them would often talk together in their mother tongue, but always broke off and went back into English if any one came near. Chippy was a good friend and we had many a good yarn with him.

Vancouver Harbour is entered through the Narrows then the bay opens up into large creeks with the city on the southern side. To the north, the horizon is filled with a range of mountains and, while the city itself was not inspiring in either layout or architecture, the setting was magnificent.

Victoria is the capital of the province although it is on an island in the south-west corner of BC - hardly central. The bay is a good anchorage and the town has a quiet charm. After a brief stay, we moved round to the west coast and sailed up the narrow fiord which has Port Alberni at its head. There was just enough room for us to go alongside the timber berth where we loaded ten thousand tons of wood in various bundles and sizes and, when the holds were full, the remainder was stacked up on the deck. People were very welcoming in the village, which was a short distance away and where, apart from the post office, all the buildings, including the hotel, were made of wood.

On the long run back to Panama, the Master was concerned at the large volume of deck cargo and he considered the vessel to be overloaded for the passage across the North Atlantic in winter. On the 9th of February, we tied up in Colon and unloaded 500 tons of timber which altered the draft about ten inches. Departing from Colon on the 11th, we reached New York on the 19th and anchored in the lower harbour. And, although our Coast Guard identity cards were renewed, there was no shore leave during our four-day stay

In convoy HX.340, to the UK, we were the last ship on the port column. Our Chief Officer thought this was a vulnerable spot and, when he came on watch at 4 a.m., he would let the speed drop to a point where we were a mile or so astern. As daybreak approached, he would increase speed and be back in position before full daylight. One morning, when we were well out of position, one of the US escort ships came up and signalled, "Do you wish to stay with this convoy or do you intend to start one of your own?" I stood, Aldis lamp in hand, waiting for the Mate to compose a forthright and witty reply. Alas, he just grunted and said nothing.

After an uneventful trip across the Western Ocean, we arrived in the Bristol Channel in thick fog and anchored off Portishead. Two days later, on the 12th March 1945, we entered Avonmouth and rang 'Finished With Engines' for our last time on the *Samharle*.

Postscript: In 1947, Holts bought the Samharle and operated her as the Troilus until they sold her in 1958. She then became the Green River and was scrapped in Osaka in 1963.

Author (left) with Douglas Cameron and his wife, Lilian, Scottish War Memorial, Edinburgh Castle, May, 1998.

EPILOGUE

Although the civilian Merchant Navy suffered a higher percentage loss than any of the Armed Services in the Second World War, there is no memorial to it within the Scottish War Memorial in Edinburgh Castle as that which is deemed to represent it bears the incorrect title 'The Mercantile Marine'.

Due to the good service given by the Mercantile Marine in the First World War, George V conferred the title Master of the Merchant Navy and Fishing Fleet on the Prince of Wales in 1928. From that date, therefore, the correct title has been HM Merchant Navy and the silver lapel badge given to all of us, and which we proudly wore, bore the letters MN.

In case this should be regarded as pedantry, I would point out that the name change of our military air service was recognized as there is a memorial to 'The Royal Air Force' under that of 'The Royal Flying Corps'.

When, in 2000, I requested the Trustees of the Memorial to rectify the omission, they declined to do so on the grounds that their predecessors of 1945 had taken the decision not to make any changes. They did, however, agree to add a Red Ensign to the colours, but while pleased about this, it does not make up for the lack of a memorial to the Merchant Navy.

DANGEROUS VOYAGING 2

- in the Merchant Navy

Ian M. Malcolm

1. CARLTON

CARLTON. (Captain W. Learmont). Bound for Buenos Aires from Newport, Mon., sailed in Convoy OB.260 which left Liverpool on 16 December 1940 and dispersed on the 19th. Torpedoed and sunk by the Italian submarine *Pietro Calvi* (Capitano di Corvetta Giuseppe Caridi) on the 20th in position 55°18′N 18°49′W. Twenty-nine died and 4 survived.

The above paragraph gives the bare facts; now here is the grim account given by George Robinson, the ship's 30-year-old 1st Mate.

In that uncertain light between dark and dawn on a cold Atlantic winter morning, I was more than halfway through my watch as Chief Officer of a merchant ship bound south.

We had been in convoy up to noon the previous day, 19th December 1940, then the convoy was dispersed, every ship for itself and Heaven help the hindmost.

Turning from the wheelhouse to walk to the port wind of the bridge I sighted the shape of a submarine close under my port bow, apparently recharging batteries before daylight. I yelled out "Action Stations. Hard-a-port. Submarine." The lookout man sounded the klaxon while I turned the port Hotchkiss machine gun and opened fire upon the conning tower of the sub. By this time we were alongside the sub and the Captain of this ship I was serving on was beside me at the gun. "What is it?" he yelled. (*It may seem strange that Mr Robinson does not name the ship or the Captain, but the War was in progress when he wrote this account and secrecy was paramount.*)

"Submarine now on our port bow, sir." I turned on the gun again and at once we could see the tracer bullets fly into the air from her hull. "By God, it is too," said Captain L. "What nationality?" "I haven't asked him yet," I replied quite truthfully. I had never thought a submarine could crash dive so quickly as that one did! Within seconds we lost sight of her, without having the chance to use our 4" gun aft.

Our next duty was evasive action, 'Full Speed' and every zigzag in the boat, hoping against hope that in the last hour of darkness we could get away from the sub. What a hope, seven knots against twelve and we had the seven.

From that time until 11.30am we ran at full speed, zigzagging, guns crew at station and lookouts posted forward, aft and amidships.

I decided to shave before lunch and had actually lathered my face when six short blasts on the steam whistle – this is it, torpedoes, I ran for the top bridge. When I got to the top of the ladder we were hit amidships, it was raining Welsh coast from our cargo, the ship listed heavily over to starboard. Captain L. turned to me with the order, "Dump the confidential papers, Mr Robinson." This I did by merely dropping them over the side in their weighted canvas bag.

"Books have sunk, sir," I reported. "Very well, we will abandon ship Mr Robinson. "Aye, aye, sir."
I was given these orders by Captain L. as coolly as he would have asked the steward for an extra cup of tea.

The entire ship's company was taken off, half in the starboard lifeboat with Captain L., and the other half in the lifeboat with me. The weather was moderate to fresh, and really cold, the date being 20th December 1940. (When checking the lifeboats before sailing from the UK, Mr Robinson had found them unseaworthy and had had them replaced.)

After a very short conversation with the commander of the submarine who again submerged, I sailed my boat towards the Captain's and brought up a few yards distance. "Any further orders, sir?" I asked.
"Usual thing, out sea anchor and wait for twenty-four hours on the hope that some bright radio op. may have heard our very brief message and the ship might proceed to this position. "Very good, sir," I replied.

Captain L. then shouted, "Good luck, lad. I hope we both make the Pilot Station." "And to you, sir, " I replied. This was the last conversation I had with him. He was by no means a young man. This was to have been his last voyage before retirement. It *was* his last voyage!

In my boat among the men I had an AB named James Patterson. During the short time he had served under me I recognised him as a very capable seaman. He would be about 40 to 45 years of age, and as I was later to find out, very, very tough. Splitting the boat's company into two watches, I took command of one, the 3rd Mate and Patterson in charge of the other.

The boat lying to anchor, head to wind and sea, I told the men to settle down for the night - one watch below, close together and covered, the other around the boat - four hours on, then four hours below.

Before settling down, we opened the bundle of grey service blankets to cover the men. Patterson came aft to me and said, "Oh sir, if you don't mind, can I wet these blankets first?" "Whatever for?" I asked. "They'll soon be wet enough."

"That's right, sir, but a wet blanket will stop the wind cutting through." How right he was, not only in this, but in a great many other things too. I thank God to this day for the fact that Patterson was with me throughout this ordeal, otherwise this would never have been written.

Between dark and dawn of the next day, the weather worsened to a fresh gale. With very heavy seas running, our sea anchor carried away and we had to take to the oars. At daybreak, we were alone. Of the Captain's boat there was no sign. They had gone the first night. From now on, we were on our own – a fight to live in and through some of the worst weather I myself had ever experienced then and since.

Our food supplies consisted of, at the beginning of the trip, some tinned milk, biscuits and a five-gallon cask of water. From the first day, I put everyone on the strictest of rations – one half of a dipper of water twice a day, at daylight and at dark. The rationing of this water was given to Patterson to dole out an equal to every man. He also watched that cask at all times until it was no longer needed. There was nothing left!

Whenever a rainsquall passed over the boat I ordered "Out sail" then we all sat around the side thwarts with the sail between us catching the rain. I can say right now, it takes a lot of rain water to remove the salt from the canvas of the sail.

Again Patterson came out with his ideas, two strands of rope-yarn tied on the spool down the mast, with the loose end at the bottom dipped into a tin also tied to the mast. In this method he supplied us with a lot of drinking water.

The weather was very cold, we were at times washed with green seas breaking over the boat and making bailing practically continuous.

Patterson by this time always relieved me at the sheet and tiller, the 3rd Mate having very wisely given way to a wiser and more experienced man.

Christmas Day arrived and strange to say the weather eased a little, and the sun shone, spirits rose too!

After our morning ration of water, Patterson said, "After this trip, sir, I shall never drink another pint of beer." "Why not, Jock? Going teetotal," I asked. "Och no, sir," said Jock, "I'll have mine in a bucket after this, to make up for what I've missed." "Well Jock, when we get ashore, I shall buy you the largest whisky and the largest beer we can find." How little we knew of the future.

That Christmas Day, although it was the one and only day that we were not struggling to keep the boat right side up, was the turning point of resistance, both mentally and physically.

That night, December 25th 1940, saw the first one of the boat's company to die. I have no intention giving actual names, to do so would be to revive those memories that are best forgotten.
During the night it was reported to me that one of the men was moaning. I had the man laid in the bows under cover to see if anything could be done – there was nothing – he died. As we put the man over the side, I repeated all I could remember or the burial service, I'm afraid it was very little.

In a newspaper clipping, it states that it was a 63-year-old seaman who went mad and jumped overboard after pulling the plug out of the bottom of the boat. While others replaced the plug, Mr Robinson rescued the man who died about an hour later. It also states that, between Christmas Night and New Year's Day, another seven died and were put over the side.

From that day I had the task of keeping the men occupied, pulling at the oars, bailing, singing, even go washing the inside of the boat – any occupation I could think of. The weather was bitterly cold and getting colder, as near as I could estimate as we travelled more to the north westward with drift and leeway than we had sailed south eastwards.

Patterson every day would strip off his boots and socks, then with his wet woollen socks massage his feet, legs, arms and even his feet and chest, saying to me, "Getting nippy now, sir!" I couldn't agree more. What a man, if there was a job to do, he was there. His boyhood had been spent in the Western Isles of Scotland, his ambition at this time was that we would eventually land there with the boat so that he could claim the boat for his for a fishing craft. He certainly worked hard to bring this about.

Day after day, night after night, we sailed and drifted, company getting less each day, burial party every morning.

New Year's day 1941, there was only seven of us remaining as I sat at the tiller and looked around at the men. I wondered if I looked as they did. Eyes sunken in their cheeks, beards, and very little life left. One of these men had recently been rescued by the Royal Navy from one of the German prison ships that attempted to reach Germany. Three of my company were boys 16-17 years of age; boys in years – men in experience of life and death at sea in wartime – seamen – but men! Never a whimper even when dying, maybe an occasional, "Do you think we'll make it, sir? " Is there a man strong enough not to have that thought sometimes? I don't think so.

From the 20th of December 1940 until the 8th of January 1941, we were adrift, travelling where the wind and sea took us. Towards the end of that time, I knew only too well that the watches Patterson took were of much longer duration than those I stood. Upon being relieved by myself, he would cover himself with the blankets, fold his arms across his chest and fall instantly asleep; wakening up as quickly when I tapped his shoulder and said, "Your turn, Jock." "Aye, Aye, sir!"

Then when I lay down he would cover me up, grasp the tiller and the last thing I would see would be his hard stern face watching the Pole Star.

Morning watch, 8th January 1941, with Patterson at the tiller, myself lying down forward, the other remaining men, Pearson and Morris, lying amidships. Suddenly Patterson let out a yell, "There's a ship! Look over to starboard."

I shouted back, "You're mad, there is no ship!" Just then the boat lifted on the wave crest and we could see her, steaming towards us. Never in my life will I be able to put into words the feeling that I had at that moment – RESCUE.

For several days we had not moved much, we did now. Morris and I put out an oar each and started rowing. Pearson tightened up the sail and Patterson steered – where that strength came from I shall never know.

We must have asked Patterson a thousand times, "Can you see her? Has she seen us?" I was trying to row and blow my whistle at the same time. Pearson was waving frantically, Patterson was solidly at the tiller. At last we were around her lee quarter and alongside. SS ANTIOPE – never will I ever forget that name, although she herself was lost next voyage.

The crew on deck threw down lines, we made fast fore and aft, then next came a rope ladder. Like a monkey, Patterson was up that ladder, halfway stopped and returned to the boat. "Och I've got to have a souvenir." He grabbed the drinking dipper and then up that ladder. The remaining three of us were hauled aboard by the crew who had to do so as we could not make the ladder.

Upon reaching the upper deck, I said to the seaman holding me, "Don't stand me on my feet for God's sake. Carry me. Me feet have given out on me!" I was carried amidships to the saloon, we had at last been rescued.

How many of that ship's company are alive today? I have no means of knowing, but to them all I say, "Thank you", the brotherhood of the sea is stronger than ever. I knew even then that they had all taken upon themselves an additional and greater risk to stop their ship to pick up four survivors. Whilst stopped, she was perfect sitting duck for any u-boat commander.

The Antiope was bombed and sank, in position 53°13′12″N 1°08′18″E, on October 27th, 1941, when on passage from London to New York. One died.

We were landed in Halifax, Nova Scotia, Canada, on 21st January 1941, one month and a day since being torpedoed. We were rushed to hospital; four living skeletons, so the papers wrote – at least we were living!

In an article in the Southampton based Southern Daily Echo, George Robinson said that he and two of his three companions were in a very bad state. Their arms and legs were frozen, their tongues were about four inches thick for want of water, their mouths were "like a furnace", and that he himself had lost 8½ stones in weight.

Three of us were put to bed, but Patterson, still going, had spotted a bathroom. No nurse was going to bathe him – they had quite a job persuading him to get out of that bath.

Three days afterwards, in the evening, there was a knock at my room door. When the nurse opened the door, in walked Patterson, all dressed up in his shipwrecked seaman's outfit – one of everything.

"Good evening, sir, how are you doing?" he greeted me.

"All right, Jock, how are you?" I could even at that distance smell the heather or something Scotch from his breath.

After some of the usual conversation, he said, "Can you get rid of the wee lassie for a while?"

I asked the nurse to leave as my friend had something he wished to speak of privately. Although reluctant, she did so. No sooner was the door closed behind her than – "Remember, sir, all our talk about the biggest whisky and beer when we got ashore?" I laughed and said, "Oh yes, here we are ashore."

"Well," said Jock, "I couldna get any whisky, but I've got some gin. Just open your mouth, sir." From under his coat he produced a bottle of gin – he had fulfilled another promise.

The following evening, Patterson paid another visit, this time to say goodbye. He had joined a ship that morning, having had his fill of life ashore. He was rather peeved during his first day on board his new ship. At the usual lifeboat drill before sailing, he had been told by the boatswain that he (Patterson) appeared to know little about lifeboats. Life's like that.

I have never seen Patterson again since. Through a mutual acquaintance, I have heard that, despite all the Nazis' efforts to stop the Merchant Service, Patterson did not swallow the anchor until 1947. I am also led to believe that he is still attempting to quench the thirst he developed in 1941.

(Signed) Geo. Wm. Robinson OBE LSM
Master Mariner

Due to frostbite, John Morris and George Robinson had both legs amputated below the knees. On his return to the UK, and when he had recovered, Mr Morris became a spot welder in a Birmingham war factory. Mr Robinson, left Halifax in early November 1941, followed by many months in Dunston Hill Hospital in Gateshead. With artificial legs fitted, he wanted to go to sea again, but as the authorities wouldn't allow it, he took a touring job which involved explaining to workers what the Merchant Navy was doing. He did, however, return to sea after the war and commanded his own ship until leaving the sea in 1950. And Isobel Morison, who had nursed him in Halifax, was his wife.

S S CARLTON

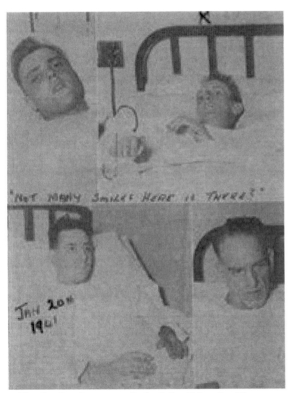

Clockwise from top left. John Morris, George
Robinson, AB Patterson and OS Pearson.
Halifax Hospital.

'BADER OF
THE M.N.'

Capt. George Robinson,
of Gosforth, was awarded
the O.B.E. and Lloyds
War Medal for "bravery
at sea, inspiration and
outstanding powers of
organisation and seaman-
ship," after the rescue.

Both his legs were
amputated, but he went
back to sea as a captain—
the "Bader of the Mer-
chant Navy."

He spent over two years
in hospital and married
the Canadian girl who
nursed him.

Morris lost both his legs
and became an aircraft
worker; Pearson, in hospital with frostbite and exposure, went to America.

And Patterson, who
complained only of being
tired, went back to sea a
few days after the rescue
ship landed them.

Sunday Sun, Merchant Navy
Parade, Newcastle, 1944.

Captain Robinson, with walking stick and standing left of the Lord Mayor, was presented with a sword.

All the above information, including photographs, was given to me by Captain Robinson's son, also called George.

2. INDUNA

The *Induna* (Captain W.N. Collins) Sailed in Convoy PQ.13 which departed from Loch Ewe on 10 March, 1942 and then from Reykjavik on the morning of the 20th, bound for Murmansk.

On the night of 25/26 March, they lost the convoy due to bad weather, but met two other ships and the small ex-whaler HMS *Silja*, being delivered to the Soviets. Later that day, the group was attacked by a single plane. No damage was done and, towards evening, another three ships joined them. At 9.30am on the 28th, they were attacked by dive-bombers. Again, no damage was done, but a single plane returned in the afternoon and damaged two ships. At midnight on the 28th, they sailed into ice, and by morning, it became so thick that they had to stop. The *Silja* had now run out of fuel and requested a tow and that 16 men she had rescued from a lifeboat be taken on board. The men walked across the ice to the *Induna* before she successfully turned round and began the tow. In heavy seas, a gale force wind and snow falls, the tow rope parted at 8pm on the 29th and, as a search for the *Silja* proved futile, they headed alone for Murmansk; the other ships having left when they were in the ice field.

At 7.20am on the 30th, the *Induna* was in position 70º 55′N 37º 18′E, northeast of Kola Inlet, when torpedoed on the starboard side of No. 5 hold. The hold contained cans of aviation spirit, and, as there was an explosion and the after end of the ship was set ablaze, the order was given to abandon ship. The *Induna* had two lifeboats and a small jolly boat. The former two got away, but those in the port lifeboat saw that the falls of the jolly boat had fouled and the men trying to clear them were never seen again. A second torpedo struck the ship and she went down stern first at about 8am. The u-boat surfaced when the lifeboats when standing off the ship. Its number could not be discerned, but it was U.376 (Oblt. Friedrich-Karl Marks).

The two lifeboats became separated and it was 7.30pm on Thursday, 2nd April, before the starboard boat was seen by Soviet planes, and half-an-hour later they were rescued by a Soviet minesweeper. There had been 32 in the boat at the outset, but several had died from exposure; particularly those who had drunk a surfeit of whisky on the first night. The 9 men remaining in the port lifeboat were picked up by the same minesweeper during the same night, but the 16-year-old Steward's Boy and an American died later in hospital, as did others from the starboard boat. And, as all suffered from frostbite, none was able to walk when rescued and several had feet and legs amputated. The survivors remained in the hospital at Murmansk until they could walk reasonably well, and were brought home on HMS *Liverpool*. Thirty-one died and 28 survived.

Other ships sunk in PQ.13

Raceland (Panamanian flag, but not a Panamanian on board.). (Captain Sverre Brekke). Bombed and sunk on 28th. Thirty-two died. Twelve became prisoners of war.
Empire Ranger (Captain M.E. Sadler). Bombed and sunk on the 28th. All 55 became POWs.
Bateau (Pa.) (Captain Johan A. Haltlid). Sunk by the German destroyer Z26 on the 29th. Thirty-nine died and 7 became POWs. Z26 was subsequently sunk by the cruiser HMS *Trinidad* (Captain L.S. Saunders).
Effingham (US) (Captain C.H. Hewlett). Torpedoed and sunk by U.435 (Kptlt. Siegfried Strelow) on the 30th. Twelve died and 31 survived.

Due to frostbite, many of those who survived had limbs amputated. For example, six of the survivors of the *Raceland*, lost both legs. Fourteen ships reached Murmansk, but the *New Westminster City*. (Captain W.J. Harris) and the *Empire Starlight* (Captain W.H. Stein) were bombed and sunk in the port on 3 April. Two died and 50 survived on the *New Westminster* and 1 died and 67 survived on the *Empire Starlight*.

3. MAIDEN VOYAGE OF THE CAPE HOWE (II)

Sailed from the Clyde on 13 February 1943 to join Convoy ON.166, but returned to land an injured seaman the next day. A few days later, sailed in Convoy ON.169 which, with the Norwegian ship *Geisha* as Commodore, contained 37 ships and left Liverpool on the 22nd. (Fifteen ships were subsequently lost in Convoy ON.166.)

The following information was given to me by Stan Mayes, an AB on the Cape Howe who is now deceased.

From the first day, we experienced atrocious weather of gales and blizzards and, on the fourth day out we became a straggler during the hours of darkness. Later, the *Baron Kinnaird* also became a straggler and was sunk by U.621 with the loss of all hands. We in *Cape Howe* (Captain P. Wallace) received a radio message to proceed to Canada independently. We sailed north towards Iceland, until we entered slush ice where u-boats could not operate, and then to a westerly course for many days until we became frozen in within sight of the coast of Labrador. It was impossible to use the protection nets during this time. About three days later we seen by a patrolling Catalina flying boat and after an exchange of signals it flew away. Next morning a Canadian corvette arrived to assist us, tossing a depth charge onto the ice it then steamed clear until detonation. This procedure was repeated until our ship was freed from the ice and we could sail clear. The corvette then escorted us to Halifax arriving on 16th March. Our ship was leaking due to the crushing ice and series of explosions so we entered a drydock for repairs.

Sea water had mixed with the old mortar in the ballast rubble and it was a difficult job to discharge it as it had hardened and set. It had taken 30 days Clyde to Halifax. A few days in drydock and we then moved to a wharf and here we loaded Army tanks into the lower holds – these were sealed and covered with tarpaulins and then 8000 tons of grain was loaded into the same holds. Loading completed we went to anchor in Bedford Basin to await assembly of a UK bound convoy.

On 8th April we sailed with other ships and rendezvoused with Convoy HX.233 from New York making a total of 51 ships – *Devis* was Commodore ship. A few days later we met a blizzard and lost touch with the Convoy - sailing independently we came across a New York bound convoy ON.177 on 16th April and joined them but diverted in St John's, NFL next day. Moored to buoys in St John's harbour was a Dutch ship *Madoera* and we berthed alongside her. *Madoera* was a survivor from ON.166, our first convoy. A huge hole was in her bows caused by a torpedo from U.653 on 24th February.

On 22nd April we sailed from St John's and later rendezvoused with Convoy HX.235 from Halifax. The Convoy had 40 ships and 19 escorts. It was a reasonable uneventful voyage to the UK with the occasional sound of detonating depth charges and approaching the Scottish coast *Cape Howe* and a few other ships diverted into Loch Ewe on 3rd May. Next day a convoy of 35 ships, WN.423, left Loch Ewe for Methil and arrived on the 6th. On 7th May we sailed in FS.1109 six ships for the Thames and arrived London on 9th May and berthed in Millwall Dock. Paid off the following day. Research has shown that the *Cape Howe* as a straggler from two convoys in the North Atlantic for many days had sailed thousands of miles of u-boat infested ocean. It is incredible that our ship passed through operations areas of 40 u-boats and came through unscathed.

4. CONVOY SL.76

(SL = Freetown to UK)

DJURDJURA. (Captain P.E. De La Rue). Sailed in Convoy SL.76 which left Freetown on 31 May 1941, bound for the UK. Torpedoed by the Italian submarine *Brin* (Capitano di Fregata Luigi Longanesi-Cattani) on 13 June when in position 38°53′N 23°11′W. Thirty-two died and 5 rescued.

EIRINI KYRIAKIDES (Greek). Torpedoed by the *Brin* at the same time and in the same position as the *Djurdjura*. All 31 died.

CATHRINE. (Captain Johannes Teng). Straggling from the Convoy and in position 49°09′N 25°05′W, about 600 west of Cape Clear, southwest of County Cork, Ireland, when torpedoed twice by U.43 (Kptlt. Wolfgang Lüth) at 3.15pm on 17 June. Broke in two and sank within two minutes so that that there was no time to send an [18]SSSS message and survivors had to jump into the sea. As they clung to floating debris, rafts and an upturned lifeboat, the u-boat surfaced and Lüth asked if they were all right – a stupid question which no-one deigned to answer. After the u-boat left, four men clinging the upturned boat lost their grip and drowned before it was eventually righted and baled out.

At about sunrise on the 20th, the lifeboat, and shortly afterwards a raft, was spotted by U.204 (Kptlt. Walter Kell). Those in the lifeboat asked Kell for water, but his answer was "We have no water for Britishers."

During the last eight days in the lifeboat, they had no food and very little water so that when a convoy was sighted, they were too weak to try to attract its attention. Seven died of starvation and exposure and when they were rescued by the trawler *Boreas* on 19 July, only three remained alive to be landed at Valentia and taken to hospital. They were the only survivors out of the crew of 27.

CALABRIA. (Swedish). Captain John G. Olsson. Also straggling from the Convoy, and in position 55°57′N 9°15′W, when torpedoed by U.141 (Oblt. Philipp Schüler) at 3.29am on 22 June. Three engine room staff were killed and all the survivors, including four injured, left in the port lifeboat as the starboard one had been damaged. While making for the Irish Coast, they saw an outward bound convoy and a plane, but were unable to attract attention.

---

[18] I am being attacked by submarine.

Eventually, they *were* seen by a plane which alerted the destroyers HMS *Cossack* (Captain P.L. Vian) and HMS *Sikh* (Cdr. G.H. Stokes). At 11pm on the 23rd, when about one-and-half miles from Inishtrahull Island, County Donegal, they were picked up by HMS *Sikh*, subsequently transferred to the netlayer HMS *Guardian* (A/Captain H.A.C. Lane) and landed at Londonderry. Three died and twenty-one survived.

5. CONVOY HG.76

(HG = Homeward from Gibraltar)

Composed of 32 ships, Convoy HG.76 sailed from Gibraltar on 14 December 1941, bound for the UK, and because previously convoys had suffered at the hands of the enemy, it was escorted by 17 warships. The Convoy Commodore, Vice-Admiral Sir Raymond Fitzmaurice, was on the *Spero* and the Senior Officer Escort, Commander Frederick John (Johnny) Walker, was on the sloop HMS *Stork*.

Although Spain was technically neutral, its Fascist government sympathised with the Nazis so that German spies in Algeciras, across the bay from Gibraltar, and on Gibraltar itself, notified the BdU about all convoys sailing from, arriving in, or passing Gibraltar. The U-Boat Command was therefore informed as to the composition and departure time of Convoy HG.76 and u-boats were positioned across its path.

On 16 December, the Convoy was sighted and its position reported by a Focke-Wulf Condor patrolling from Bordeaux, which guided U.108 (KrvKpt. Klaus Scholtz) to the convoy and to report its position to other u-boats. During the night of 16/17 December, the wolf pack closed in and by morning on 17 December, the convoy passed beyond the range of Gibraltar-based aircraft.

Merchant ships sunk

RUCKINGE. (Captain William A. Ross). Torpedoed and damaged by U.108 at 6.15am on the 19th, in position 38°20′N 17°15′W, and subsequently shelled and sunk by the corvette HMS *Samphire* (LtCdr. F.T. Renny), as the wreck was a danger to navigation. Out of her complement of 37 crew, 3 DBS (men whose previous ships had been sunk) and 1 stowaway, 3 crew died – Galley Boy Sidney T. Coulman and Firemen Trimmers David Norwood and Joseph Townsley. Survivors were picked up by the *Finland* (also in the Convoy) and by HMS *Stork* which eventually docked in Devonport.

ANNAVORE. (Norwegian). (Captain Gerhard Reichelt). Torpedoed by U.567 (Kptlt. Engelbert Endrass) at 7.23pm on the 21st in position 43°55′N 19°50′W and, with a cargo of iron ore, sank almost immediately. Thirty-four died and 4 survived – 2 engineers and 2 ABs.

Royal Navy ships sunk

HMS STANLEY. Destroyer. (LtCdr. D.B. Shaw). Torpedoed twice by U.574 (Oblt. Dietrich Gengelbach) at 4.15am on the 19th, in position 38°12′N 17°23′W. One hundred and thirty-six died and 25 picked up by HMS *Stork* and HMS *Samphire*.

HMS AUDACITY. A merchantman converted into an Escort Carrier. (Cdr. Douglas William MacKendrick). At 9.37pm on the 21st, struck by 3 torpedoes fired by U.751 (Kptlt. Gerhard Bigalk) and, 10 minutes after the third hit, sank in position 43°45′N 19°54′W. The survivors were picked up by the corvettes HMS *Convolvulus* (Lt. R.S. Connell), HMS *Marigold* (Lt. W.S. Macdonald) and HMS *Pentstemon* (LtCdr. J. Byron). I have failed to obtain details of the casualties, but it seems that over 70, including Cdr. MacKendrick died.

U-Boats sunk

U.127 (KrvKpt. Bruno Hansmann). On the 15th, seen on the surface by the Australian destroyer HMAS *Nestor* (Cdr. George S. Stewart) and dived when attacked. Depth charged by the *Nestor* and sunk in position 36°28′N 9°12′W. All 51 died.

U.131 (FrgKpt. Arend Baumann). On the 17th, detected by a Martlet plane from HMS *Audacity* and forced to dive. Depth charged by HMS *Pentstemon* and forced to resurface. Shot down an attacking Martlet while trying to escape, but scuttled by her crew, in position 34°12′N 13°35′W, after being hit by several shells from HMS *Stork*. All 47 taken prisoner.

U.434 (KrvKpt. Wolfgang Heyda). On the 18th, depth charged and sunk by the destroyers HMS *Blankney* (LtCdr. Philip Frederick Powlett) and HMS *Stanley* (LtCdr. David Byam Shaw). Two died and 42 taken prisoner.

U.574 (Oblt. Dietrich Gengelbach). On the 19th, rammed and depth charged by HMS *Stork*. Resurfaced and scuttled by Engineer Officer Oblt. Lorentz, in position 38°12′N 17°23′W. Twenty-eight died and 16 taken prisoner.

When interrogated, the prisoners claimed that Gengelbach wanted to resurface in order to save lives. Lorentz, however, did not agree and it was only after a furious argument that he obeyed the order; and shot himself immediately after doing so. After surfacing, Gengelbach appeared briefly on the bridge, before descending from it and going down with his boat.

U.567 (Kptlt. Engelbert Endrass). On the 21st, and just 3 hours after sinking the *Annavore*, depth charged by HMS *Deptford* (LtCdr. Hugh Robert White), and sunk in position 44°02′N 20°10′W. All 47 died.

On the 23rd, Donitz, staggered by the losses and the lack of ships sunk, and with the Convoy now having continuous air support, recalled the remaining boats to Bordeaux.

6. VYNER BROOKE

The following is a direct quote from Wikipedia.

On 12 February 1942 the Sarawak royal yacht *Vyner Brooke* left Singapore just before the city fell to the Imperial Japanese Army. The ship carried many injured service personnel and 65 nurses of the Australian Army Nursing Service from the 2/13th Australian General Hospital, as well as civilian men, women and children. The ship was bombed by Japanese aircraft and sank. Two nurses were killed in the bombing; the rest were scattered among the rescue boats to wash up on different parts of Banka Island. About 100 survivors reunited near Radjik Beach at Bangka Island, in the Dutch East Indies (now Indonesia), including 22 of the original 65 nurses. Once it was discovered that the Island was held by the Japanese, an officer of the *Vyner Brooke* went to surrender the group to the authorities in Muntok. While he was away nurse Irene Melville Drummond suggested that the civilian women and children should leave for Muntok, which they did. The nurses stayed to care for the wounded. They set up a shelter with a large Red Cross sign on it.

At mid-morning the ship's officer returned with about 20 Japanese soldiers. They ordered all the wounded men capable of walking to travel around a headland. The nurses heard a quick succession of shots before the Japanese soldiers came back, sat down in front of the women and cleaned their bayonets and rifles. A Japanese officer ordered the remaining 22 nurses and one civilian woman to walk into the surf. A machine gun was set up on the beach and when the women were waist deep, they were machine-gunned. All but Sister Lt Vivian Bullwinkel were killed. Wounded soldiers left on stretchers were then bayoneted and killed.

Shot in the diaphragm, Bullwinkel lay motionless in the water until the sound of troops had disappeared. She crawled into the bush and lay unconscious for several days. When she awoke, she encountered Private Patrick Kingsley, a British soldier that had been one of the wounded from the ship, and had been bayoneted by the Japanese soldiers but survived. She dressed his wounds and her own, and then 12 days later they surrendered to the Japanese. Kingsley died before reaching a POW camp, but Bullwinkel spent 3 years in one. She survived the war and gave evidence of the massacre at a war crimes trial in Tokyo in 1947.

Vivian Bullwinkel/Mrs Statham, died of a heart attack at the age of 84 in Perth, Western Australia, on 3 July, 2000.

7. IMPERIAL TRANSPORT

The *Imperial Transport* (Captain Walter Smail) was bound for Trinidad in ballast when torpedoed by U.53 (KrvKpt. Harald Grosse) on 11 February 1940 in approximate position 59°N 12°W. Broke in two and abandoned, but the stern section was later reboarded and, after waiting two days for the weather to moderate, she got underway again. Late on the 14th, she encountered four destroyers and HMS *Kingston* (LtCdr. Philip Sommerville) stood by her as she proceeded to port. As the weather deteriorated on the morning of the 15th, the tanker, doing only four knots, was unable to make any headway. HMS *Kingston* attempted to tow her, but when this failed, she took off the crew.

The tug HMS *Buccaneer* and the destroyer HMS *Forester* arrived, but as the weather was too bad to board the stern section, the surviving crew were transferred to the *Forester* and landed at Scapa Flow on the 17th.

Two more tugs, HMS *St Martin* and HMS *Englishman* arrived, and the stern section towed to the Firth of Clyde with ten men from the *Forester*, who had boarded to assist with the towing operation, still on board.

From the 20th to the 23rd, HMS *Mohawk* (Cdr. J.W.M. Eaton) screened the salvage operation and, on the 26th, the stern section, escorted by HMS *Gleaner* (LtCdr. H.P. Price) was beached at Kilchattan Bay, in the Isle of Bute. A new forward section was subsequently fitted to the ship and she returned to service in June 1941.

Two died - Richard Edwards, Pumpman, and Jack Williams, Cook, were both drowned when abandoning the ship on the 11th.

U.53 was depth charged and sunk on the 24th by the destroyer HMS *Gurkha* (Cdr. A.W. Buzzard) when in position 60°32'N 06°14'W. All 42 died.

Second Incident

Bound for Trinidad in ballast, sailed in Convoy ON.77 which left Liverpool on 17 March 1942. Struck by two torpedoes fired by U.94 (Oblt. Otto Ites) at 6.16am on the 25th when in position 46°26'N 41°30'W. This stopped the engines and put the steering gear and wireless equipment out of action. With the ship beginning to have a list, the crew abandoned her in four lifeboats, but were soon picked up by corvette FFL *Aconit* (Lt. Levasseur) of the Free French Navy, and her doctor attended to two injured men.

When, at 11.30am, Captain Smail and Mr Swanbrow, the Chief Engineer, reboarded to access the damage, they found the fore deck awash and a large hole in the port side. And after spending about an-hour-and-a half on board, they again left the ship.

At 6pm, the Canadian corvette HMCS *Mayflower* (LtCdr. G.H. Stephen), sent a party on board and there was a failed attempt to pass a hawser over in order to try towing the damaged ship. They were joined by the Master, Chief Engineer, Mr Broom, the 2nd Engineer, Mr Malins, the 4th Engineer, and Donkeymen Peter Andrea and George Coles who, after succeeding in getting the engines going again, returned to the *Mayflower* with her boarding party.

With 45 of the *Imperial Transport*'s crew still on board, the FFL *Aconit* set out for St John's, Newfoundland, the following morning while the skeleton crew returned to the stricken tanker. Steam was raised again, she was brought back on to an even keel, and using her emergency steering gear aft and escorted by the Mayflower, she got underway at 8.30pm. The weather, although fine at the outset, was bad during the next two days. Nevertheless, she averaged 5.8 knots and arrived in St John's on the 30th.

After temporary repairs were made, she left St John's on 24 August and sailed, unescorted, to New York, via Halifax, arriving in New York on 5 September. And, after being permanently repaired in Hoboken, returned to service in February 1943.

All 51 survived.

8. AUSTRALIND

Unescorted and bound, via the Panama Canal, for the UK from Adelaide, when intercepted by the German raider *Komet* (Kapitän zur See Robert Eyssen), disguised as a Japanese ship, and sunk in position 4°13′S 91°03′W, off the Galapagos Islands on 14 August 1941. Captain Walter J. Steven, Senior 4th Engineer Douglas B. Beardsall and 4th Engineer Thomas E. Curran died from their injuries, and the remaining crew of 43, including one of the aforementioned who was severely injured, taken on board the Komet before their ship was sunk.

When the Australind did not stop after intercepted, the Komet fired two warning shots, and when she began transmitting an [19]RRRR message and manned the 4-inch gun at the stern, shells were pumped into her, killing two of the three men mentioned above.

The prisoners were well treated on the Komet, and when the injured man died soon after being taken on board, he was buried at sea with full honours.

---

[19] Being attacked by a Raider.

9. EMPIRE SONG

Bound for Alexandria and loaded with 10 Hurricanes and 57 tanks, sailed in Convoy WS.58 which left the Clyde on 28 April, 1941. The Convoy consisted of only four other ships – *Clan Chattan*, *Clan Lamont*, *Clan Campbell* and *New Zealand Star*.

About 45 miles west of Pantelleria when struck by two mines, only minutes apart, shortly after midnight on 8 May. Captain W. Jennings gave the order to abandon ship, but asked for volunteers to remain on board in an attempt to save the ship. Seven, including L/Cpl. G.R. Myers of the Royal Tank Regiment, answered the call, but two hours later, the situation had deteriorated to such an extent that they had to slip into the sea from the badly listing and burning ship.

The destroyers HMS *Fortune* (LtCdr. E.N. Sinclair, RN) and HMS *Foresight* (Cdr. J.S.C. Salter, RN) were standing by, and a whaler from the latter containing both RN and MN volunteers whose intention was to save the ship and her badly needed cargo, was approaching her when she blew up and sank, in position 37º9′N 11º01′E. Bits of the ship, tanks and other debris were thrown into the air, and the whaler was sunk with the loss of one man. Ordinary Seaman Albert Howarth, D/JX. 229949, who had been in the whaler, was subsequently awarded the Albert Medal as, although his right foot had been blown off, he kept a shipmate afloat for ten minutes until a lifebelt was thrown to him. Nineteen-year-old B.S. Evenden, her 4th Mate, and 17 Indian seamen died. One hundred and twenty-eight were rescued by HMS *Foresight* and taken to Malta.

Minutes before the *Empire Song* was struck, a mine exploded in the paravane of the *New Zealand Star*, but caused only minor damage.

10. CONVOY SC.1

Departed Sydney, Cape Breton, on 15 August 1940, bound for the UK.

HMS PENZANCE (Cdr. A.J. Wavish). The sloop was one of the six escorts when torpedoed by U.37 (Kplt. Victor Oehrn) in position 56°16′N 27°19′W, southwest of Iceland, at 8.38pm on the 24th. Broke in two and, when the stern section sank, some of the survivors in the water were killed. Twelve men were picked up by the *Fylingdale*, but an injured man died and was buried at sea, and seven others were rescued by the *Blairmore*.

BLAIRMORE (Captain Hugh Campbell). Torpedoed and sunk by U.37 in position 56°00′N 27°30′W, southeast of Cape Farewell, at 1.46am on the 25th. Five died and 36, including the 7 survivors of HMS *Penzance*, picked up by the Swedish ship *Eknaren* (Captain Erik Kallstrom and landed at Baltimore, Maryland.

EVA (Nor.) Captain Ingvald Vaage). Due to unsuitable coal, had been straggling shortly after departure from Sydney and, at 4.03pm on the 27th she was torpedoed in position 57°48′N 11°51′W, about 60 miles east of Rockall, by U.28 (Kptlt. Günter Kuhnke). The crew, three of whom were injured, abandoned the ship in three lifeboats and made landfall at Boligarry, Isle of Barra, on the 30th. One man died and 17 survived.

Due to her cargo of timber, the vessel did not sink, so that the u-boat surfaced and, after firing shells into her, she eventually caught fire and was left in a sinking condition.

As an SSSS message, sent by the *Eva*, had been heard, a plane, HMS *Hurricane* (LtCdr. H.C. Simms, RN) and HMS *Havelock* (Captain E.B.K. Stevens, RN) were sent to assist. HMS *Hurricane* arrived that night and found no survivors, but, after extinguishing the fire, LtCdr. Simms requested a tug, as he thought the ship could be saved. It was, however, washed ashore and wrecked one mile from the Butt of Lewis Lighthouse.

ELLE (Finnish) (Captain Werner Öjst). Torpedoed by U.101 (Kptlt.Fritz Frauenheim) at 4.25am on the 28th when in position 57°43′N 12°18′W. Two died and 27 picked up by the sloop HMS *Leith* (Cdr. G.R. Waymouth, RN) which scuttled the ship by gunfire, and landed the survivors at Greenock on the 30th.

11. CONVOY UGS.7

The letters UGS stood for <u>U</u>SA to <u>G</u>ibraltar <u>S</u>low, a series of convoys initiated at the time of the Allied invasion of North Africa (Operation Torch) in November, 1942. The author was 3rd Radio Officer of the *Samite* in Convoys UGS.18 and UGS.38. Both convoys were attacked by the Luftwaffe when off the coast of Algeria, and the details are given in his book Life Aboard a Wartime Liberty Ship.

Convoy UGS.7, consisting of approximately 72 ships and 9 escorts, sailed from Hampton Roads on 1 April 1943.

JAMES W. DENVER (US) (Captain Everett W. Staley). The Liberty Ship on her maiden voyage and bound for Casablanca, straggled from the Convoy due to engine trouble and was torpedoed by U.195 (KrvKpt. Heinz Buchholz) at 8.41pm on the 11th, in position 28°52′N 26°30′W.

When the ship took on a heavy list and settled by the head, bringing the propeller out of the water, the crew abandoned her in five lifeboats. The one with a motor capsized during launching, but all its 18 occupants were taken into the other four boats. Captain Staley, who remained on board for an hour after his crew had left, then descended into a lifeboat, and while the boats lay off the stricken ship during the night, the u-boat sank her with another torpedo.

The four boats set together sail for the African coast, but became separated during the second night. At 10.43pm on the 13th, one of the boats was seen by U.159 (Kptlt. Helmut Witte) who questioned its occupants before departing.

After seven days afloat, the 11 in one boat were picked up by the *Cabo Huertas* (Sp.) and landed at Las Palmas on 21 April. After 13 days, 15 in another boat were picked up in position 22°42′N 35°05′W by the *Campana* (Sp.) and landed at Aruba on 3 May. On 6 May, 13, including Captain Staley, landed about 90 miles north of Port Etienne, Rio de Oro. The terrain was inhospitable desert in which they might have died, but, three days later, they were spotted by a British patrol plane which dropped food and medical supplies to them. And the next day, they were picked up by the submarine chasers *PC-2040* and *PC-1041* and landed at Port Etienne on 11th. After 23 days at sea, 11 were rescued by the steam fishing trawler *Albufeira* (Port.) in position 21°55′N 17°10′W and landed at Lisbon on 10 May, but the second engineer died of exposure and was buried at sea. The remaining 19 survivors in the last boat were rescued after 35 days by the sailing ship *Juan* (Sp.) near

Belle Nassent and taken to La Aguerrio, Rio de Oro, but an oiler later died in a hospital at Gibraltar. Two died and 67 survived.

At 7.52am on the 20th, U.565 (Kptlt. Wilhelm Franken) fired torpedoes at the Convoy when it was about 60 miles west of Oran, Algeria, and sank the *Michigan* and the *Sidi-Bel-Abbès* in position 35°59′N 1°25′W. The ships stations were 8.1 and 8.2 respectively i.e. the first and second ship in column eight.

MICHIGAN (US) (Captain Birger Jacobsen). Began to settle by the bow and abandoned in two lifeboats and three rafts in ten minutes although was an hour later before it sank. The survivors were picked up by the ASW trawlers HMS *Stella Carina* (Lt. J.V. Lobb, RANVR) and HMS *Foxtrot* (Lt. J.B. Bald, RNVR), but transferred to the minesweeper HMS *Felixstowe* (T/Lt. C.G. Powney, RNVR) which landed them at Oran. All 61 survived and were repatriated to New York on the *Delnorte* (US).

SIDI-BEL-ABBÈS (Fr.) Bound for Oran from Casablanca with a complement of 1287, including 907 Senegalese troops, when torpedoed and sunk in an enormous explosion at the same time as the *Michigan*. Four hundred and fifty-three, including those wounded and burned, were picked up by the British escorts, assisted by lifeboats from the *Michigan*. Eight hundred and thirty-four died.

12. MENDOZA

Mendoza (Captain B.T. Batho), a captured Vichy-French ship managed for the MOWT by Alfred Holt & Co., sailed independently from Mombasa towards the end of October 1942, bound for Durban. At 3.33pm on 1st November, she was torpedoed by U.178 (Kpt. Hans Ibekken), when in position 29°20´S 32°13´E, about 70 miles east-north-east of her destination.

When Captain Batho ordered 'Emergency Stations', the crew and passengers assembled at the lifeboats while Mr G.B. Crossley, the Chief Engineer, went below to assess the damage. The engines had been stopped on orders from the bridge and water was pouring into the engine room from fractured pipes. He shut the necessary valves, started the pumps on the bilges and, after seeing that everyone was out, joined the Master on the bridge. And when it was found that both propellers and the rudder had been blown off, the order was given to abandon ship.

Two lifeboats had been destroyed, but the other ten got away. However, Captain Batho, Mr Crossley, Mr D.B.L. Grew, the 1st Radio Officer, three deck officers and several European crew were still on board when a second torpedo struck. Mr Grew later reported that, when standing beside Captain Batho, smoke and flames shot up just aft of them, wreckage rained down on them and they could see only a foot or two in the smoke.

The ship was listing heavily to port when the men who had remained on board had to jump into the sea. Mr J.D. Weir, the 1st Mate, Mr F. Crooks, the 3rd Mate, and Mr Grew were severely burned and Captain A.F. Barclay, the Staff Captain, was so badly injured that he later died.

When a plane arrived and signalled that help was on the way, Captain Batho waited until dusk before ordering the boats to make for the coast. Soon after daylight, however, the *Cape Alva* (US) was sighted and, although she carried explosives and it was dangerous to stop, she did so and picked up the occupants of the boats. Regrettably, when Midshipman I.K. Gray was assisting Captain Batho on to the jumping ladder, the lifeboat rose on the swell and crushed the Captain between the boat and the ship's side. Three US sailors climbed down the scrambling to try to get a line round him, but unable to help himself, he drifted away and was lost. The *Cape Alva* landed the survivors at Durban.

In 'A Merchant Fleet in War ', the wartime history of Alfred Holt & Co. by Captain S.W. Roskill, RN, only the *Cape Alva* is recorded as having rescued the survivors. The u-boat net, however, states that the South African minesweeping whaler HMSAS *Nigel* also took part in the rescue and landed survivors at Durban.

The u-boat net also states that the master 19 crew, 3 DEMS gunners and 3 passengers died and that 127 crew, 3 gunners and 250 passengers were saved. On the other hand, South African History Online states that 'A total number of 150 people died including the captain, crew and service personnel.'

13. TURAKINA

The *Turakina* (Captain James Boyd Laird), bound independently for Wellington from Sydney, Australia, when intercepted by the German Raider *Orion* (KrvKpt. Kurt Weyher) at 5pm on 20 August, 1940 when about 260 miles west of Taranaki. Set ablaze by gunfire before being sunk by torpedoes in position 38°33′S 167°12′E. Thirty-six died. Twenty-one, including wounded, taken prisoner by the *Orion*.

The following is the personal story of Edward Sweeney.

"On the 20th August 1940, I was a 20-year-old member of the crew of the refrigerated cargo vessel, the SS *Turakina*, owned by the New Zealand Shipping Company. We were sailing from Sydney to Wellington, in the Tasman Sea, when attacked by a German converted Merchant ship, the Raider *Orion*. She was disguised as a Japanese vessel, the *Tokyo Maru*. I was a member of the gun crew, and after an uneven battle firing our single 4.7" gun, we were torpedoed, shelled and soon ablaze, after continuous bombardment. 19 members of our crew of 57 were rescued by the *Orion*, the remainder killed. Our attackers praised our courage for fighting against overwhelming odds, but considered us mad English. I was rescued by our attackers and eight months later, after being imprisoned on another German ship, the *Altmark*, we safely docked in Bordeaux, France. I had no money or belongings, as everything went down with the ship.

After imprisonment in a transit camp, we were eventually entrained for Germany. Although armed guards were in our carriage, I escaped by diving from the train 20 miles from Paris, in occupied France. After some hair-raising experiences, I escaped from a concentration camp in Argeles-sur-Mer, Southern France. I crossed the Pyrenees into Spain, and was arrested and jailed by the Civil Guard for not having papers to prove my identity. After a spell in filthy jails, I was imprisoned in a labour concentration camp at Miranda de Ebro, in Northern Spain, carrying a large basket of stones on my back, helping to build a new major road.

Fifteen months after my leaving England, I was eventually released, reaching Glasgow, via Gibraltar, none the worse for my adventures. Apart from a newly shaven head just before we left, I was quite fit, and glad to be back home in familiar normal surroundings."

Consisting of 36 merchant ships and 6 escorts, departed Liverpool on 15 August 1942 and dispersed on 3 September. The Commodore, Captain S. White, RNR, was on the *Athelprince*.

The BdU (the u-boat command) had sent 13 boats to locate the Convoy, but when first sighted by U.705 (Kptlt. Karl-Horst Horn) on 23 August, the ensuing attack was repelled by the escort. However, at 9.25am on the 24th, it was again located, this time by U.660 (Kptlt. Götz Baur), and, at about 1.30am the next day, the 3 u-boats on the starboard side began their attacks with the following result.

EMPIRE BREEZE (Captain Robert Thomson). Bound for New York and Baltimore when torpedoed twice by U.176 (Kptlt. Reiner Dierksen) at 1.57am. Fireman and Trimmer Doaley Yuset was killed and the 3rd Mate badly injured when blown off the bridge and into No.3 hold. This was where the torpedoes had struck and he was able to swim through the gaping hole in the ship's side. Three of the 4 lifeboats had been successfully lowered and he was picked up. The rescue ship *Stockport* (Captain Thomas E. Fea) tried to locate the boats, but was unable to do so because of fog. As the ship remained afloat, the crew reboarded her the next day, her radio officers succeeded in repairing the damaged equipment and sent distress messages. This resulted in the dispatch of the tug HMS *Frisky* from St. John's, NF, and the corvette HMCS *Rosthern* (Cdr. P.B. Cross) which was part of the Convoy's escort. By the time they arrived, however, there was no sign of the ship. During the foggy night of 26/27 August, the remaining 48 crew were picked up by the *Irish Willow* which landed them at Dunmore, Ireland, on 1 September. As No.1 hold was slowly flooding when the ship was finally abandoned, Captain Thomson thought that she had foundered shortly afterwards in approximate position 49°45′N 35°10′W. KATVALDIS (A Latvian ship commandeered by the MOWT.) (Captain Ints Lejnieks). Bound for Cape Breton and Clarke City, Quebec, when torpedoed by U.605 (Kptlt. Herbert-Viktor Schütze) at about 2am on the 25th. Rolled over to port and sank, bow first, within two minutes, in position 48°55′N 35°10′W. Three lifeboats were lowered, but one overturned and the other two narrowly escaped being hit by deck ballast thrown into the air. Three died and 44 picked up by the *Stockport* within an hour, and landed at Halifax, NS, on 1 September.

SHEAF MOUNT (Captain Ralph S. De Gruchy). Bound for Botwood, Newfoundland, when torpedoed by U.605 at the same time and in the same position as the *Katvaldis*. Caught fire and sank within two minutes. As all the lifeboats were dragged down with the ship, survivors clung to wreckage until picked up some two hours later by he *Stockport*. Thick fog hampered the rescue operation, but the red lights and whistles attached to the life jackets were a great help. Twenty-five died and 26 or 27 survived.

TROLLA (Nor.) (Captain Ole Grande). Bound for Sydney, Cape Breton, when torpedoed by U.438 (Kptlt. Rudolf Franzius) at 2.01am on the 25th and sank within a minute in the same position as the *Katvaldis* and the *Sheaf Mount*. The survivors, who had abandoned the ship in one lifeboat and a raft, were spotted by the Norwegian corvette HNoMS *Eglantine*, but she had to leave them when the image of a u-boat was seen on her radar. Due to the fog, the *Stockport* was unable to find them, but while searching for a u-boat, the Norwegian corvette HNoMS *Potentilla* (LtCdr. C.A. Monsen) came across them at 5am. It was a risky to stop to pick them up so that all were anxious as they were taken on board and the search for u-boats resumed.

When the *Potentilla* arrived in St. John's, NF, on the 27th, four badly injured men were taken to the hospital, but the 44-year-old Chief Engineer, Oscar Julius Næss, died the next day. Six, including the Chief Engineer, died.

U.705, which had first spotted the Convoy, was depth charged and sunk by an RAF Armstrong Whitley off Cape Ortegal, Spain, on 3 September 1942 with the loss of all 45 on board.

15. STONEGATE

Homeward bound from South America and sailing unescorted when intercepted by the German Pocket Battleship *Deutschland* at about 11.15am on 5 October 1939, 600 miles east of Bermuda. The crew were told to take to the lifeboats before she was sunk by gunfire and they were taken on board the warship. Although confined to cabins on a lower deck and allowed only half-an-hour's exercise at dusk, they were well treated and had plenty of food.

On the 9th, the US ship *City of Flint* (Captain Joseph H. Gainard) was intercepted by the *Deutschland*, and 3 officers and 14 men boarded to inspect her manifests, as they suspected that she had goods for Britain in her cargo.

The 37 crew of the *Stonegate* were transferred to the *City of Flint* where they were herded into the forecastle and had to sleep in the cold on the wet deck. The Americans were, of course, also prisoners, but were given complete freedom and did their best to provide the British seamen with food and clothing. A prize crew was placed on board and with Lt. Hans Pussbach in command, they sailed for the Norwegian port of Tromso where, on arrival on the 22nd, the *Stonegate*'s crew were put ashore.

For some unknown reason, the *City of Flint* was then taken to Murmansk before returning to Tromso where fresh water was procured. Although the United States was neutral, the Captain had been told that his ship was considered to be a German prize, but when it left the port, it was stopped by two Norwegian destroyers. This part of the story is taken from Captain Gainard's account which is somewhat confused, but, outside Bergen, they met up with the *Schwaben* and orders were shouted across to Lt. Pussbach to take the ship to Haugesund. However, Norwegian officers boarded, the Germans were taken off, and the ship handed back to the Americans.

On 30th October, the crew of the *Stonegate* arrived home on a Norwegian ship.

16. CONVOY HX.112

Consisting of 41 ships, sailed from Halifax, Nova Scotia, on 1 March 1941, bound for the UK, but only 36 were present when attacked. The Commodore was Rear Admiral F.B. Watson on the *Tortuguero*. The Escort consisted of the destroyers HMS *Walker*, HMS *Vanoc*, HMS *Sardonyx* and HMS *Scimitar*, and the corvettes HMS *Bluebell* and HMS *Hydrangea*. The Senior Officer Escort (SOE) was Captain Donald G.G.W. Macintyre on HMS *Walker*.

Shortly after midnight on the 15th, the Convoy was spotted by U.110 (Kptlt. Fritz-Julius Lemp). Lemp reported the contact to the BdU, before firing three torpedoes at the Convoy, but only one found a target; the tanker *Erodona* when she was in position 61°20′N 17°00′W.

The explosion broke the ship in two, the stern section sank and the crew abandoned ship. A tank in the bow section was on fire, but when the fire burned out and the section remained afloat, it was towed to Edisvik, near Reykjavik, by the rescue tug HMS *Thames*. As the damage was extensive, it was August 1942 before she was towed to Blyth, Northumberland, where a new stern section was fitted, and she returned to service in February 1944. Thirty-six died and 21 survived.

The only other u-boat to have success that night was U.99 (Kptlt. Otto Kretschmer) which torpedoed the following ships on 16th March.

BEDUIN (Nor.) (Captain Hans Hansen). Broke in two, and the bow section shelled and sunk by a British armed trawler on the 19th. On the 18th, the stern section was taken in tow by the tug HMS *St. Olaves*, but sank on the 20th in position 61°07′N 10°50′W. Four died. Twenty picked up by the trawler *River Ayr* on the 18th and landed at Thorshaven, Faroe Islands, the following evening. Ten landed at Fleetwood by the Icelandic trawler *Hilmir* on the 23rd.

FRANCHE COMTE (A French tanker commandeered by the MOWT.) (Captain Leslie C. Church). Damaged in position 61°15′N 12°30′W, but no details.

J.B.WHITE (Canadian) (Captain J.W.R. Woodward). Torpedoed twice and sank in position 60°57′N 12°27′W. Two died. Thirty-eight picked up by HMS *Walker* and landed at Liverpool on the 21st.

KORSHAMN (Swed.) (Captain S. Lantz). Sunk in position 61°09′N 12°20′W. Twenty-four died and 12 survived.

VENETIA (Captain Alexander Mitchell). Sunk in position 61°00′N 12°36′W. All 40 picked up by HMS *Bluebell* (LtCdr. Robert E. Sherwood) and landed at Greenock.

FERM (Nor.) (Captain Bernt A. Thorbjørnsen). Torpedoed in position 60°42′N 13°10′W. Taken in tow the next day, but sank on the 21st. All 35 picked up by HMS *Bluebell*.

U.99 had slipped inside the Convoy while the escort was chasing U.100 (Kptlt. Joachim Schepke). Due to the vigilance of the escort, the u-boat had been unable penetrate the screen and, at 1.30am on the 17th, HMS *Walker* located her on its ASDIC. HMS *Walker* and the destroyer HMS *Vanoc* (Lt Cdr. James G.W. Deneys) then depth charged U.100 until she was wrecked. Schepke chose to surface rather than sink and as soon as she popped up, HMS *Vanoc* rammed her. Schepke was pinned against the periscope and the u-boat plunged to the bottom. Thirty-eight died, including Schepke, and six rescued.

While the above action was taking place, U.99, with all her torpedoes gone, was preparing to return to Lorient, her home port. Unfortunately, she first had to circle the Convoy and, in the darkness, arrived at the very spot where U.100 was being attacked. HMS *Walker* picked her up on its ASDIC and dropped six depth charges which put all her lights and she plunged to 700 feet before sufficient air could be blown into the tanks to stop her descent. As his boat was so damaged, Kretschmer brought her to the surface where she was fired upon, with little affect, by the *Walker* and the *Vanoc*.

Kretschmer got hold of a torch and signalled, "Please save my men. Boat is crippled." "Don't scuttle the boat," came the reply. "What does scuttle mean?" he asked. But before he and his crew jumped into the sea, he sent a short explanatory message to BdU and scuttled the boat. Three died and the other 40 were picked up by the *Walker* where they were put into the crew's mess beside merchant seamen rescued by the destroyer. Their reception was therefore a frosty one and, when they disembarked at Liverpool, the Army had to protect them from a stone-throwing crowd.

Kretschmer spent almost seven years as a prisoner-of-war in England and Canada. On returning home, he joined West Germany's Navy, served with NATO and retired a Flotilla Admiral. He died in a boating accident on the Danube in 1998, aged 86.

17. EMPIRE METAL

The *Empire Metal* (Captain Selwyn Law) was an 8201grt tanker built by Harland & Wolff Ltd., Govan, completed in September, 1942, and operated by the British Tanker Co. on behalf of the Ministry of War Transport. Her crew joined in late September and she sailed in Convoy ON.135 which departed Liverpool on 2nd October and arrived, unscathed, in New York on the 21st.

Having loaded, she sailed from New York on 19 November in Convoy HX.216, bound for the UK. At 2.30pm on 1 December, in position 57° 07′N 20°16′W, the *Empire Metal* and the *Empire Airman* detached from the Convoy and proceeded to Manchester under escort. The *Ocean Crusader* (Captain Ellis Wynne Parry), on her maiden voyage and a straggler from the Convoy due to the bad weather, was torpedoed and sunk on the 26th by U.262 (Oblt. Heinz Franke) when in position 50°30′N 45°30′W, and all her 50 crew died.

Sailed in Convoy KMS.5G which left the Clyde on 11 December 1942 and arrived in Bône, Algeria, on the 27th. Since the Allied invasion of North Africa, in November, 1942, all convoys had to be fought through the Mediterranean, and Bône, the main supply base for the U.S. First Army, suffered from incessant air raids. There was, however, a lull over the Christmas period, but this ended on New Year's Day 1943 when the *Novelist* and *Harpalyce* were both damaged.

Shortly after 7am on 2 January, German fighters launched a diversionary attack on the aerodrome, at some distance from the port. This was almost immediately followed up by Junkers 87s attacking the shipping, with the British shore batteries, naval vessels and the merchant ships putting up a tremendous barrage. Just as the Stukas were departing, two Fokker-Wulf 190 fighter planes roared in at mast height. The *Empire Metal,* discharging petrol into the storage depot, was hit in the bows; there was a terrific explosion, and flames shot high into the air. The tanker burned for four days, although she was shelled by a destroyer to prevent further explosions. Six died, including her Master and Joseph Halligan, her 16-year-old Deck Boy.

The *St. Merriel* was also sunk, and, by rolling over, put her berth out of action for some considerable time. Five died. The *Dalhanna*, the *Melampus*, and the cruiser HMS *Ajax*, received minor damage, when an ammunition dump blew up.

Postscript: In August, 1949, the *Empire Metal* broke in two when she was being raised. In May, 1950, her stern section was beached at Grenouillère, near Bône, for demolition on site. In August, 1950, her bow section was taken to Savona to be broken up for scrap, but her machinery was removed, reconditioned and installed in the Mohawk Navigation steamer *Captain C.D. Secord*, trading on the Great Lakes, in 1954. The *St Merriel* was also raised, in 1950, but sank off Cape Noli, on the north-west coast of Italy, when under tow and on her way to be scrapped.

18. ROOSEBOOM

Prior to surrender of Singapore to the Japanese on 15 February 1942, there was a mass attempt to escape from the Island. Vessels of all descriptions were employed and, as Sumatra was still held by the Dutch, many made for Sumatra.

The *Rooseboom* (Captain Marinus C. A. Boon), a 1035-ton KPM (Koninklijke Paketvaart-Maatschappij (Royal Packet Navigation Company) ship which normally ran between Sumatra and Java, sailed from Tanjong Priok (the port for Batavia/Djakarta) on 22 February, bound for Padang on the west coast of Sumatra. And, after embarking a large number of military and civilian refugees, including women and children, she sailed for Colombo on the 27th. The number on board is not known, but it is likely to have been in the region of 500.

Towards midnight on 1 March the *Rooseboom* was about halfway to Colombo when she was torpedoed by the Japanese submarine I-59 (LtCdr. Yoshimatsu) in position 00°15′N 86°50′E. On the 11th, two Javanese seamen were rescued by the Dutch ship *Palopo* and landed at Colombo on the 14th and, until the end of the War, it was assumed that they were the only survivors.

WALTER GIBSON'S STORY

Walter Gibson, a regular in the Argyll and Sutherland Highlanders, who had crossed to Sumatra in a sampan, joined the *Rooseboom* at Padang. Due to the excessive number of passengers, the troops slept on deck and were packed together like sardines.

On being torpedoed, the vessel capsized and sank rapidly. One lifeboat got away and, although designed to hold only 28, it contained 80, including Gibson who had been pulled on board after clinging to wreckage for about an hour. Fifty-five others were in the water, either clinging to the boat or to floating debris, or just floating. Several were wounded: Gibson had a burst eardrum, his collarbone was broken, and a piece of metal was lodged in his shin. At the stern of the boat were three women: Mrs Gertrude Nunn, the wife of the Director of Works in Singapore, who always remained cheerful and did her best to support those in pain, the wife of the Dutch mate of the ship, and Doris Lim, a pretty Chinese girl dressed in a coloured skirt and shirt, but with bare feet.

Although the lifeboat had been well stocked with food and water, most had floated away due to it being damaged and overloaded so that it had almost foundered. The lack of water was, of course, a main problem as was the tropical sun which took its toll on barely covered bodies and drove some to acts of madness.

Some experienced hallucinations and the 1st Mate, saying that he was going for help, jumped overboard and swam into the darkness. Captain Boon was stabbed and killed by one of his own engineers who, while being apprehended, jumped overboard and swam away. Officers of the Argylls and others died, and five young soldiers murdered people, in order to drink their blood, until they, themselves, were set upon and put overboard.

Twenty-six days later, when only the emaciated Walter Gibson, Doris Lim and three Javanese remained in the lifeboat, it drifted onto coral off the island of Sipora, the smallest of the Mentawai Islands, west of Sumatra. One of the Javanese perished in the surf, but all the others succeeded in landing safely.

The surviving Javanese were never seen again, and after two days on their own, during which they drank copious amounts of fresh water, Walter and Doris were found by Malays. After wrapping them in sarongs, the Malays carried them to their village where they remained for six weeks, regaining their strength, until the Japanese arrived and took them prisoner. And when they were taken to Padang on 18th May, it was 79 days since they had left there on the *Rooseboom*. Walter saw Doris only once after arriving in Padang. This was when he was being interrogated by the Japanese and later, when in hospital, he was told that she'd been shot. This, however, was not true. She married a poor Chinese farmer and was murdered by him.

In June 1944, and having spent two years in a POW camp in Medan, Walter, and 743 POWs, boarded an old rat-infested ex-Dutch ship called the *Van Wyck*, bound, they thought, for Thailand. The *Van Wyck* was in a convoy when torpedoed, but Walter was rescued by a tanker and taken to Singapore where he remained a prisoner until the Japanese surrendered in August 1945. He returned to Edinburgh, but subsequently emigrated to Canada.

The full account of Walter Gibson's experiences is given in his book, *The Boat*.

EPILOGUE

Although the civilian Merchant Navy suffered a higher percentage loss than any of the Armed Services in the Second World War, there is no memorial to it within the Scottish War Memorial in Edinburgh Castle as that which is deemed to represent it bears the incorrect title 'The Mercantile Marine'.

Due to the good service given by the Mercantile Marine in the First World War, George V conferred the title Master of the Merchant Navy and Fishing Fleet on the Prince of Wales in 1928. From that date, therefore, the correct title has been HM Merchant Navy and the silver lapel badge given to all of us, and which we proudly wore, bore the letters MN.

In case this should be regarded as pedantry, I would point out that the name change of our military air service was recognized as there is a memorial to 'The Royal Air Force' under that of 'The Royal Flying Corps'.

When, in 2000, I requested the Trustees of the Memorial to rectify the omission, they declined to do so on the grounds that their predecessors of 1945 had taken the decision not to make any changes. They did, however, agree to add a Red Ensign to the colours, but while pleased about this, it does not make up for the lack of a memorial to the Merchant Navy.

FORTUNES OF WAR

Ian M. Malcolm

INTRODUCTION

The first part of the book tells what happened to the numerous ships listed in Volume XIV of *The Marine Observer* of 1937.

In the second part, Douglas Cameron describes three of his wartime voyages. Douglas and Ian joined the Blue Funnel Line at the same time (he as a midshipman/deck apprentice and Ian as a radio officer), but didn't meet and become good friends until they had both retired from teaching. Douglas and Ian had several holidays together, including spending a week manning a wireless museum in Orkney, and were about to embark on a trip to Liverpool (principally to visit the Maritime Museum) when he collapsed and died in April 1999. Ian, now 90, still misses him.

IAN WITH DOUGLAS (LEFT), RRS DISCOVERY, DUNDEE, 1997.

THE FORTUNES OF WAR
Ian M Malcolm

Many years ago, I was browsing through books in an Edinburgh junk shop when I came across a copy of Volume XIV of The Marine Observer of 1937 and gladly stumped up the £3 asked for it. On the inside of the front cover an attached label states - 'AWARDED by the METEOROLOGICAL COMMITTEE to Mr. A. Molineux S.S. "Cairnglen" As an acknowledgment of his valuable voluntary meteorological work at sea for the year ended 31st March, 1938.' Although, over the years, I have dipped again and again into this interesting book, it occurred to me only recently to try to trace the Second World War histories of the host of ships whose officers submitted information, including, of course, that of the *Cairnglen*. And here is the result.

HMS AJAX – Participated in many engagements, but best known for her involvement in the Battle of the River Plate which led to the scuttling of the pocket battleship *Admiral Graf Spee* (Captain Hans Langsdorff) in Montevideo harbour in December, 1939. Sold for scrap in November, 1949.

ALYNBANK (Bank Line) – Requisitioned by the Admiralty and became an Armed Merchant Cruiser (AMC). On Russian Convoys and sunk off the Normandy beachhead in June, 1944 to form part of the Mulberry Harbour. Salvaged in 1945 and scrapped at Troon.

ARIGUANI (Elders and Fyffes) – Requisitioned by the Admiralty and used first as a Fighter Catapult Ship. Escorting Convoy HG.75 (Homeward from Gibraltar) on 26 October, 1941 when damaged by a torpedo fired by U.83 (Oblt. Hans-Werner Kraus), in position 37°50′N 16°10′W. Abandoned, reboarded and towed to Gibraltar. Returned to owners in 1946.

ARLANZA (Royal Mail Line) – (Scrapped in 1938.)

ASTURIAS (Royal Mail Line) – Requisitioned by the Admiralty. Used as an AMC and later as a troopship. Became a state-owned emigrant ship in 1945 and scrapped in 1957.

ATHENIA (Donaldson Line) – Unarmed, unescorted and bound for Montreal from Glasgow when torpedoed and sunk by U.30 (Oblt Fritz-Julius Lemp), in position 56°44′N 14°05′W; only hours after war was declared on Sunday, 3 September, 1939. Of the 1103 passengers and 315 crew, 112 died. As Lemp contravened the rules by torpedoing the *Athenia* without allowing her passengers to leave, and as 28 US citizens lost their lives, Hitler had the news suppressed.

ATHLONE CASTLE (Union Castle Line) – Requisitioned as a troopship. Returned to Company service in 1946 and broken up in Taiwan late 1965.

AUSONIA (Cunard White Star Line) – Requisitioned by the Admiralty. An Armed Merchant Cruiser (AMC) before being converted into a repair ship in 1942. Decommissioned in 1964 and scrapped in Spain in 1965.

AUSTRALIA STAR (Blue Star Line) – Damaged by incendiary bombs in Liverpool on 3 May, 1941. Scrapped in 1964.

BEAVERBURN (Canadian Pacific Railway) – Bound for Saint John, New Brunswick, in Convoy OA.84 (Thames to Liverpool with an Atlantic element) which sailed from Southend on 2 February, 1940 and dispersed on the 5th. Torpedoed and sunk at about 1pm on the 5th by U.41 (Kptlt. Gustav-Adolf Mugler) when in position 49°20′N 10°07′W. One died out of her crew of 77. Survivors picked up by the tanker *Narragansett* and taken to Falmouth. U.41 sunk that same day by destroyer HMS *Antelope* (LtCdr. T. White).

BERWICKSHIRE (Turnbull, Martin & Co. Ltd.) – Bound for Tamatave, Madagascar, and in Convoy DN.68 (Durban northwards to dispersal) when torpedoed and sunk by U.861 (Kptlt. Jürgen Oesten), in position 30°58′S 38°50′E at 0038 hours on 20 August, 1944. Eight died. Ninety-four picked up by the *ASW trawler HMS *Norwich City* (Lt. R.A. Groom) and landed at Durban. *Anti-Submarine Warfare.

BRITISH ADMIRAL (British Tanker Co.) – The report was dated 8 September, 1936 and she was sold for scrap in December.

BRITISH CORPORAL (British Tanker Co.) – Torpedoed by Schellboot (E-boat) S.26 on 4 July, 1940 and again on the 5th. Badly damaged, but towed to port and, after being repaired by the Ministry of War Transport (MOWT), renamed *Empire Corporal*. Sailed in Convoy TAW.12 (Trinidad-Curacao-Key West), bound for Key West from Curaçao, when torpedoed and sunk by U.598 (KrvKpt. Gottfried Holtorf) shortly before midnight on 11 August, 1942, in position 21°45′N 76°10′W. Six died and 49 taken to Guantanamo Bay, Cuba, by the destroyer USS *Fletcher* (Cdr. W.M. Cole).

BUTESHIRE (Houston Line) – Scrapped in 1948.

CAIRNGLEN (Cairn Line) – On 22 October, 1940, when nearing the end of her passage from Montreal, via Leith, to the Tyne and proceeding slowly through fog, she struck a reef near Marsden, drifted, and broke her back on rocks. Twenty men reached the shore in a ship's lifeboat and the remainder rescued by Bosun's Chair.

CAPE OF GOOD HOPE (Lyle Shipping Co. Ltd.) – Unescorted and bound for Abadan from New York when torpedoed and sunk by gunfire by U.502 (Kptlt. Jürgen von Rosenstiel) at 7.43pm on 11 May, 1942, in position 22°48′N 58°43′W. All 37 crew survived. The Master's boat, carrying 18, reached the Virgin Islands on the 24th and the 1st Mate's boat, carrying 19, reached the Dominican Republic on the 29th.

CARTHAGE (P & O Steam Navigation Co. Ltd.) – Requisitioned by the Admiralty on 7th September, 1939 and converted to an AMC. Transferred to the MOWT on 30 December, 1943 and used as a troopship until returned to P & O in 1948.

CERAMIC (Shaw, Savill & Albion Co. Ltd.) – Requisitioned as a troopship in February, 1939. Bound for Sydney, Australia, via St. Helena and Durban, she sailed from Liverpool in Convoy ON.149 on 26 November, 1942, and dispersed from it on 2 December. When in position 40°30′N 40°20′W at midnight on the 7th, she was struck by 3 torpedoes, fired in quick succession by U.515 (Kptlt. Werner Henke). With the engines stopped, without lights, in rough seas and in rain, abandoning was difficult. Several boats got away, but some were swamped and others capsized. But the ship did not sink until another 2 torpedoes were put into her three hours later.

On reporting the sinking to BdU (Commander U-boats), Henke was ordered to seek out the Master and find out the destination of the ship. It is reported that he was shocked by the horrific scene around him as he attempted to do this at noon on the 7th, but, unable to locate Captain Elford, he picked up Sapper Eric Munday of the Royal Engineers and took him prisoner. Of the 657 on board the *Ceramic*, only Eric Munday survived. Among those who died were Queen Alexandra nurses, adult civilians and 12 children.

Henke, who was taken prisoner when U.515 was sunk on 9 April, 1944, was shot and killed while slowly climbing the perimeter fence of the interrogation center at Ft. Hunt, Virginia on 15 June, 1944. As he ignored the warnings given by the guards, it is thought that he deliberately committed suicide in the belief that he would face trial as a war criminal.

CHINESE PRINCE (Furness, Withy & Co. Ltd.) – Bound for Liverpool from Port Said via the Cape and sailing unescorted when torpedoed and sunk by U.552 (Oblt. Erich Topp) in position 56°12′N 14°18′W at about 4.15am on 12 June, 1941. Forty-five died and 19 picked up and taken to Londonderry by the corvettes HMS *Arbutus* (Lt A.L.W. Warren) and HMS *Pimpernel* (Lt F.H. Thornton).

CITY OF EXETER (Ellerman City Line) – Scrapped in 1950.

CITY OF ROUBAIX (Ellerman City Line) – Damaged during an air raid on Liverpool on 20 October, 1940. Damaged and then sunk during an air raid on Piraeus on 6 April, 1941. The *Clan Fraser*, with explosives among her cargo, was hit by 3 bombs which killed 7 of her crew and set her on fire. The vessel was then abandoned and, at 3.30am on the 7th, she blew up; sinking the *City of Roubaix* and wrecking the harbour. No lives were lost on the *City of Roubaix*.

CITY OF TOKIO (Ellerman City Line) – A naval stores ship in Freetown from 1940 until 1941. Scrapped in 1951.

CLAN MACWHIRTER (Clan Line) – Bound for Hull from Bombay, the *Clan MacWhirter* sailed from Freetown in Convoy SL.119 on 14 August, 1942. When straggling from the Convoy, she was torpedoed and sunk in position 35°45′N 18°45′W at 1am on the 27th by U.156 (Kvkpt. Werner Hartenstein). Eleven died. Seventy-five picked up by the Portuguese sloop *Pedro Nunes* and taken to Funchal, Madeira.

CLYDEBANK (Andrew Weir's Bank Line) – No information other than she was not a war casualty.

DORIC STAR (Blue Star Line) – Sailing alone and bound for the UK from Sydney, Australia, when intercepted by the *Admiral Graf Spee* in position 1915°′S 05°05′E on 2 December, 1939. All taken on board the *Graf Spee* before sunk by gunfire.

DURHAM (New Zealand Shipping Co.) – Damaged by a mine on 28 August, 1941. Damaged by Italian assault craft on 20 September, 1941. Survived the War.

EASTERN COAST – No information.

ERIN (Standard Fruit Co.) – Sold to Elders & Fyffes in 1947 and renamed *Manistee*.

FORDSDALE (Shaw Savill & Albion) – Sold in 1952 and scrapped in Taiwan in 1959 when called the *Jui Yung* and owned by the Chinese Maritime Trust.

FRANCONIA (Cunard Line) – Became a troopship. Together with the *Alcantara* and the *Empress of Canada*, sailed from Gibraltar on 2 September, 1939, bound for Malta. Collided with the *Alcantara* and seriously damaged. On 5 October, 1939, suffered bomb damage when off the west coast of France with 8000 troops on board. Assisted in the evacuations of Norway and France April-June, 1940. Served as the HQ of Mr Churchill and his staff during the Yalta Conference in February, 1945. Broken up at Inverkeithing, Fife, in 1957.

GLENGARRY (Alfred Holt & Co.'s Glen Line) – Renamed *Glenstrae* in March, 1939 to release the name for a new ship being built in Copenhagen. Damaged by a bomb during an air raid on London Docks on 7 September, 1940. Transferred to the Blue Funnel Line in February 1949 and renamed *Dolius*. Broken up at Briton Ferry in 1952.

HARMONIDES (Houston Line) – Bound for Lourenço Marques, from Calcutta via Trincomalee, when torpedoed and sunk by Japanese submarine I-165 (Cdr. Torisu Kennosuke) on 25 August, 1942, in position 01°47′N 77°27′E. Fourteen died.

HMS HERALD (Sloop) – Scuttled at Seletar, Singapore Island, during the Japanese invasion in February, 1942. Raised by the Japanese, renamed *Heiyo* and sunk by a mine in the Java Sea on 14 November, 1944.

INANDA (T & J Harrison) – Bombed and sunk in London Docks during an air raid on 9 September, 1940, but refloated, repaired and renamed *Empire Explorer*. Sailed from Trinidad on 8 July, 1942, bound for Barbados and the UK. At about 2.45am on the 9th, torpedoed and sunk by gunfire by U.575 (Kptlt. Günther Heydemann) when in position 11°40′N 60°55′W. Out of her complement of 78, 3 died. Survivors picked up by HMS *MTB-337* and landed at Tobago.

IXION (Alfred Holt & Co.'s Blue Funnel Line) – Sailed from Glasgow, bound for New York, on 2 May, 1941, and joined Convoy OB.318 (Liverpool outward). Torpedoed by U.94 (Kptlt. Herbert Kuppisch) shortly after 11pm on the 7th, in position 61°29′N 22°40′W. Abandoned, but did not sink until 2.45am the next day. All 105 survived. Eighty-six picked up by the *Nailsea Moor* and taken to Sydney, Cape Breton. Nineteen picked up by the corvette HMS *Marigold* (Lt. WS Macdonald) and taken to Greenock.

AS JOHN WILLIAMS V (London Missionary Society) – No information.

MADURA (British India S.N. Co.) – Assisted in the evacuation of Singapore, February, 1942. Scrapped in 1953.

MAKURA (Union S.S. Co., New Zealand) – (Believe scrapped in 1937.)

MALDA (British India S.N. Co.) – Recently converted to a troopship and bound for Colombo in a convoy of 7 ships when sunk by Japanese warships in the Bay of Bengal on 6 April, 1942. Twenty-five died. Survivors picked up by the *Indora* which was herself sunk that same day. One lifeboat landed on coast of Orissa.

MAHRONDA (Thos & Jno Brocklebank) – Damaged in an air raid on Liverpool during the night of 21st/22nd December, 1940. Torpedoed and sunk by Japanese submarine I-20 (Cdr. Yamada Takashi) on 11 June, 1942, in position 14°37′S 40°58′E. Five lifeboats got away and landed at Mozambique. All survived.

MAIMOA (Shaw Saville & Albion) – Sunk in the Indian Ocean on 19 November, 1940 by the German raider *Pinguin* (Captain Ernst Kruder). Crew taken on board the *Pinguin*, but transferred to the captured Norwegian tanker *Storstad* which landed them in Bordeaux the following year.

MARON (Blue Funnel Line) – Carried troops and equipment of the British Expeditionary Force to French ports during September/October, 1939. Took part in the invasion of North Africa (Operation Torch) and, having discharged most of her cargo in Algiers, sailed from the port in a convoy of 4 ships on the evening of 12 November, 1942. Torpedoed at 3pm the next day by U.81 (Kptlt. Friedrich Guggenberger) and sank within 15 minutes, in position 36°27′N 00°55′W. As the boats were already swung out, all 81 crew got away. They were picked up by the corvette HMS *Marigold* (Lt J.A.S. Halcrew) and taken to Gibraltar, from where they were repatriated to the UK on the *Mooltan*. (In 'A Merchant Fleet in War', Captain S. W. Roskill claims that the *Maron* was sunk by U.431.)

MASHOBRA ((British India S.N. Co.) – Requisition by the Admiralty. Bombed and damaged at Gansaas, Halstad, Norway on 25 May, 1940. Beached and destroyed during the evacuation to prevent her being used by the Germans.

MATHERAN (Thos & Jno Brocklebank) – Sailed from Halifax on 8 October, 1940 in Convoy HX.79 (Halifax to UK). Torpedoed and sunk by U.38 (Kptlt. Heinrich Liebe) at 10.15pm on the 19th when in position 57°N 17°W, about 120 miles west-southwest of Rockall. Out of her complement of 81, 9 died and 72 picked up by the *Loch Lomond* which was herself sunk by U.100 (Kptlt. Joachim Schepke) at 7.20am the next day. All the survivors of the *Matheran* survived the second sinking, but 1 crewman of the *Loch Lomond* died. Survivors of both ships picked up by the minesweeper HMS *Jason* (LtCdr R.E. Terry) and taken to Methil, Fife.

MONGOLIA (P & O Steam Navigation Co. Ltd.) – Chartered to the New Zealand Shipping Co. from 1938 till 1950 and sailed as the *Rimutaka*. Sold to Incres S.S. Co., Panama, in 1950 and renamed *Europa*. Scrapped in 1964.

MOOLTAN (P & O Steam Navigation Co. Ltd.) – Requisitioned by the Admiralty, converted to an AMC and based at Freetown. Returned to P & O in January, 1941 and converted to a troopship. Took part in Operation Torch. Resumed service as a passenger liner in 1948 and broken up at Faslane, on the Gare Loch, in1954.

NALDERA (P & O Steam Navigation Co. Ltd.) – (Broken up at Bo'ness in 1938.)

NATIA (Royal Mail Lines) – Bound for Buenos Aires from London when sunk by the German raider *Thor* (Captain Otto Kaehler) off Fortaleza, Brazil on 8 October, 1940. Out of her complement of 85, 1 man died and another wounded. Survivors taken on board the *Thor*, but transferred to the supply ship *Rio Grande* which reached Bordeaux on 13 December.

OPAWA (New Zealand Shipping Co.) – Sailing unescorted and bound for the UK from Lyttelton, New Zealand, when torpedoed, shelled and sunk by U.102 (Oblt. Hermann Rasch) during the afternoon of 6 February, 1942, in position 38°21′N 61°13′W. Out her complement of 71, 56 died and the 15 survivors picked up and taken to New York by the Dutch ship *Hercules*.

ORARI (New Zealand Shipping Co.) – Struck in the stern by a torpedo from U.43 (Oblt. Wolfgang Lüth) at about 8.45pm on 13 December, 1940, in position 49°50′N 20°55′W, but succeeded in reaching the Clyde under her own power. Missed by torpedoes fired by Italian submarine *Luigi Torelli* (C.C. Antonio de Giacomo) at 1am on 11 Mar, 1942, in position 13°N 57°W. Damaged by a mine when half-a-mile from Valetta harbour on 16 June, 1942, but 1 of the 2 ships, out of convoy of 6, which reached the port after 2 days of continuous air attacks. Sold to 'Capo Gallo' Cia. di Nav, Palermo, in 1958 and renamed *Capo Bianco*. Scrapped in 1971.

ORDUNA (Pacific Steam Navigation Co.) – Became a troopship in February, 1941. After the surrender of Japan in August, 1945, brought home, from Rangoon, 1700 servicemen who had been prisoners of the Japanese. Broken up in Dalmuir in 1951.

PORT AUCKLAND (Port Line) – Sailed in the Halifax section of Convoy SC.122 on 9 March, 1943, bound for Avonmouth from Brisbane. Struck by 2 torpedoes from U.305 (Kptlt. Rudolf Bahr) shortly after 11pm on the 17th and sunk by yet another torpedo from the same u-boat about half-an-hour later, in position 52°25′N 30°15′W. Out of the 118 on board, 8 died and 110 picked up by the corvette HMS *Godetia* (Lt A.M. Larose) and taken to Gourock. Forty-three u-boats were involved in the simultaneous attacks on both SC.122 and Convoy HX.229, also bound for the UK and travelling on the same course some hours behind. A total of 9 ships were sunk in SC.122 and 13 in HX.229. The u-boats were eventually driven off on the night of the 19th by RAF Liberators, one of which sunk U.384.

PORT BOWEN (Port Line) – Ran aground near Wanganui, New Zealand, on 19 July, 1939. Became a total loss and dismantled where she lay.

PORT DENISON (Port Line) – Sailed from Methil in Convoy OA.220 on 26 September, 1940, bound for New Zealand. Bombed by a single aircraft that same evening when north-east of Peterhead and sank in the early hours of the 27th. Sixteen died and survivors rescued by the anti-submarine trawler HMS *Pentland Firth*.

PORT FREMANTLE (Port Line) – Broken up at Osaka, Japan, in September, 1960.

PORT GISBORNE (Port Line) – Bound for Cardiff from Auckland and in Convoy HX.77 which sailed from Halifax on 30 September, 1940. Torpedoed by U.48 (Kptlt. Heinrich Bleichrodt) shortly after 10pm on 11 October and eventually sank in position 57°02′N 17°24′W. Three lifeboats were launched, but one capsized and its occupants drowned. Survivors in 1 boat picked up by rescue tug HMS *Salvonia* (Lt G.M.M. Robinson) on the 22nd. Those in the other boat rescued by the *Alpera* on the 24th and landed at Greenock. Two other ships were sunk in the Convoy.

PORT WELLINGTON – (Port Line) – In the Indian Ocean, bound for the UK from Adelaide, when, on 30 November, 1940, she was captured by the German raider *Pinguin* (Captain Ernst Kruder). On fire and scuttled by a boarding party after 81 crew and 7 women passengers had been transferred to the raider. (This includes the wounded Master who died on the *Pinguin*.) On 9/10 December, the *Pinguin* and the raider *Atlantis* were refuelled by the tanker *Storstad* which took over 400 prisoners from the former and over 200 from the latter before sailing for Bordeaux. During the passage, more prisoners were collected from the cruiser *Admiral Scheer* and she arrived in Bordeaux on 4 February, 1941.

RANGITATA (New Zealand Shipping Co.) – Requisitioned as a personnel carrier in December, 1939. Carried evacuee children to New Zealand and sailed from Liverpool in Convoy OB.205 on 29 August, 1940. At midnight on the 30th when in position 56°04′N 09°52′W, narrowly missed by a torpedo from U.60 (Oblt. Adalbert Schnee) which damaged the Dutch vessel *Volendam*, also carrying evacuees. Converted to a troopship in 1941, returned to the Company in 1946 and broken up at Split, Yugoslavia, in September, 1962.

SAN ADOLFO (Eagle Oil Shipping Co.) – Requisition by the Admiralty in November, 1939 and employed as a fleet oiler. On Russian convoys and in Operation Torch. Scrapped in 1957.

SAN ALVARO (Eagle Oil Shipping Co.) – In Convoy PA.69 (Persian Gulf to Aden) when torpedoed and set on fire by U.510 (Oblt. Alfred Eick) on 22 February, 1944. Abandoned and sunk, in position 13°46′N 48°55′E, by HMAS *Tamworth* (Lt. F.E. Eastman) which picked up the survivors and landed them at Aden the next day. One gunner died out of the 53 on board.

SCYTHIA (Cunard Line) – Converted to a troopship at the beginning of the War. Carried troops to the Middle East in November, 1940, and then evacuee children to New York. Damaged by an aerial torpedo near Algiers on 23 November, 1942 when engaged in Operation Torch. Five died out of the 4300 on board. Returned to Cunard in 1950 and scrapped at Inverkeithing, Fife, in 1958.

SOMERSET (Federal Steam Navigation Co. Ltd.) – Bound for Liverpool from the River Plate and sailed from Freetown in Convoy SL.72 on 17 April, 1941. Bombed by a solitary Focke-Wulf when off Achill Head, County Mayo, Ireland, on 11th May. Abandoned and broke in two. Stern half sank, but forepart remained afloat until sunk by the escort. All crew picked up by the corvette HMS *Alisma*.

STRATHAIRD (P & O Steam Navigation Co. Ltd.) – Requisitioned as a troopship in September, 1939. Brought in the region of 7000 out of Brest during the Dunkirk evacuation in June, 1940. Returned to P & O at the end of 1946 and scrapped in Hong Kong in 1961.

TAIROA – (Shaw Saville & Albion) – Bound for London from Brisbane when, on 3 December, 1939, intercepted and sunk in the South Atlantic by the *Admiral Graf Spee*, after crew taken off. The latter were on board the *Graf Spee* during the Battle of the River Plate, but landed in Montevideo before she was scuttled just outside the harbour on the 18th.

TANDA (Eastern & Australian Steam Ship Co. Ltd.) – Unescorted and on passage from Melbourne to Bombay when torpedoed and sunk in position 13°22′N 74°09′E by U.181 (FrgtKpt. Kurt Freiwald) on 15 July, 1944. Nineteen died out of complement of 216. Survivors picked up by the minesweeper HMIS *Bihar* (Lt W.L. Deeble) and the corvette HMS *Monkshood* (Lt G.W. McGuinness) which landed them at Colombo on the 18th.

TANTALUS (Blue Funnel Line) – With her engine room machinery dismantled, left Hong Kong under tow by the tug *Keswick* on 5 December, 1941, bound for Singapore. The Japanese attack on Pearl Harbour took place on the 7th, and, when Japan declared war on Britain as from 6am on the 8th, all British ships in the area were instructed to find refuge where they could. Captain R.O. Morris decided that, as the speed on the tow was only 5 knots, his best bet was Manila, where they arrived on the evening of the 11th. As the port was continually being bombed by Japanese planes, Captain Morris thought it safer to move the ship to nearby Bataan, but although she had not been hit, he realized the situation was hopeless and took all his crew ashore early on the 26th. And it was as well that he did so as, from the beach that day, they saw the *Tantalus* capsize and sink after receiving direct hits. When Manila fell to the Japanese on 3 January, 1942, all were taken prisoner. T.H. Fletcher, the 3rd Mate, and H.E. Weekes, an A.B., were later executed because they were caught trying to escape.

TARANAKI (Shaw Saville & Albion) – Scrapped in Aioi, Japan, in September, 1963.

THISTLEGLEN (Allan, Black & Co.) – Bound for Glasgow, sailed in Convoy SC.42 from Sydney, Cape Breton, on 30 August, 1941. Torpedoed and sunk at about 4.45pm on 10 September by U.85 (Oblt. Eberhard Greger) when in position 61°59′N 39°46′W. Three died out of complement of 49. Survivors picked up from lifeboats and rafts and taken to Belfast by the *Lorient*. Nineteen u-boats attacked the Convoy from the 9th till the 16th, sinking 16 ships and damaging 2 others.

TITAN (Blue Funnel Line) – Bound, in ballast, for Sydney, Australia, from London and joined Convoy OA.207 after bunkering at Methil on 31 August, 1940.Torpedoed and sunk by U.47 (Kptlt. Günther Prien) at 0040 hours on 4th September when in position 58°14′N 15°50′W. *Six died. Twenty-four Europeans and 66 Chinese picked up from two lifeboats by the corvette HMS *Godetia* and the Canadian destroyer HMCS *St. Laurent* (Cdr. H.G. DeWolf). *In 'A Merchant Fleet at War', Roskill states, 'it appears that no lives were lost'.

TONGARIRO (New Zealand Shipping Co.) – Scrapped in August, 1960.

TUDOR STAR (Blue Star Line) – Broken up at Hendrik-Ido-Ambacht, Netherlands, in 1950.

TYNEFIELD (Tanker) – Struck a mine and sank at the southern end of the Suez Canal on 5 October, 1941. One source states 8 died while another states 4.

VANCOUVER CITY (Reardon Smith & Sons Ltd.) – Unescorted and on passage from Suva, Fiji, to the UK when torpedoed and sunk at 10am on 14 September, 1939, by U.28 (Kptlt. Günter Kuhnke), in position 51°23′N 07°03′W. Three died. Thirty rescued and taken to Liverpool by the Dutch tanker *Mamura*.

FC (Fisheries Cruiser) VIGILANT – No information.

WESTMORELAND (Federal Steam Navigation Co. Ltd.) – Unescorted and on passage from Wellington to London when torpedoed and sunk by gunfire by U.566 (Kptlt. Dietrich Borchert) during the forenoon of 1 June, 1942, in position 35°55′N 63°35′W. Out of her complement of 68, 3 died. Forty-five survivors picked up and carried to Halifax by the Canadian ship *Cathcart*.

Twenty picked up and carried to New York by the U.S. troop transport *Henry R. Mallory*.

RRS (Royal Research Ship) WILLIAM SCORESBY (Falkland Islands Dependencies Survey) – Requisitioned by the Admiralty and served as a minesweeper. Returned to normal service after the War.

WORTHING (Southern Railway) – Carried men of the British Expeditionary Force to France in 1939 and brought out wounded during the Dunkirk evacuation. Requisitioned by the Admiralty in 1940. Named changed to HMS *Brigadier* and served as a Landing Craft Infantry ship. Returned to the Newhaven-Dieppe cross Channel service after the War. Sold to John Latsis, Piraeus, in 1955, renamed *Phryni* and broken up in 1968.

Bibliography:

U-boat website
Red Duster website
The Fourth Service by John Slader
A Merchant Fleet in War by Captain S.W. Roskill, RN
The Allied Convoy System by Arnold Hague

THE EMPIRE LANCER
(Douglas Cameron's story)

In 1939, when the Second World War started, I was thirteen years old. Three years later, I took the Higher Leaving Certificate which was the necessary 'ticket' for entry to college or university. During these years we became accustomed to being at war. Personal decisions were dominated by the war. My aim, on leaving school, was to join either the Royal Navy or the Merchant Navy. My parents would not hear of my going to sea at the age of sixteen and so, on leaving Boroughmuir High School, I went to Leith Nautical College for their one-year cadet course. During that year, I applied to over thirty shipping companies for a position as an apprentice and eventually was accepted by the company known as the Blue Funnel Line. The account of my first trip is based largely on notes made at the time.

The 4th of July 1943 was the day of my departure from Edinburgh to Liverpool. Father gave me some old-fashioned advice, "If you have to abandon ship get out as quickly as you can and don't turn back for personal belongings."

My father had ordered a taxi to take us to the railway station. My farewells to my mother and sister were made in the house. My sea-going gear was packed in a steel sea-chest and a canvas sea-bag. I wore my brand-new uniform with its brass buttons showing the badge of the shipping company, Alfred Holt & Company.

The train left about 1030 from the old Caley (Caledonian) station at the west end of Princes Street in Edinburgh. Many passengers were in uniform. On the journey, there were long unexplained stops between stations and it was nearly 7 p.m. before I reached the Midshipmen's Hostel in Riversdale Road in Liverpool. The hostel was a Victorian dwelling-house, some of its rooms converted into small dormitories.

The next day, Monday, I had to report at 9.15 to the administrator for midshipmen, Mr. Pierce, in his office at Birkenhead. A suburban railway station was near the hostel and trains reached the centre of Liverpool in a short time. This line was the overhead railway which was elevated on a continuous bridge-like structure along the length of the docks' area. From the train there was a good view of the city. Many buildings had been destroyed or damaged by German air raids. Alfred Holt and Company had been bombed out of their main office in India Buildings and had moved to Ullet Road.

Near the River Mersey were the Liver buildings with their sculptures of mythical birds - the Liver birds. In front of the Liver block was a large space, the Pier Head, where all the trains started, and finished, on their circuit journeys. Not far away was the floating landing--stage for the river ferries which crossed and re-crossed the Mersey all day long.

The Liverpool natives are known as 'scousers'. They have a distinctive accent and some words of their own - not enough to be called a dialect. Blue Funnel ships were crewed either by scousers or Chinese.

While waiting for a ship the midshipmen were expected to attend daily at the company office to do 'school' lessons. A spare 2nd or 3rd mate usually took the class. Their lack of enthusiasm was shared by the middies. Written assignments were given out to be completed at sea. For some of us, these were a bore because they went over topics already covered in the cadet course of a nautical college. My previous year had been spent on such a course at Leith where, if I may lay modesty aside for a moment, I was first student in the class of thirty-six.

Before the war, the Alfred Holt company had a fleet of about of seventy-five ships, one of the largest
shipping companies in the U.K. Correspondingly they had about 250 apprentices whom they called midshipmen.

The group included companies which Holts had taken over such as the China Steam Navigation Company and the Glen Line. Most of their ships had names taken from Greek mythology, for example, *Agamemnon, Hector, Teucer, Menestheus, Troilus, Alcinous, Tyndareus* (inevitably known as Tin Drawers) *Bellerophon* (Billy Ruffian) and so on. Holt's, like many other shipping companies, managed ships for the Ministry of War Transport. These ships were mainly wartime-built for the MOWT and had names beginning with Empire, Ocean, Fort or Sam. After the war, some of them were bought by these companies who renamed them in their own fleet style.

In the afternoon of that first day at the office I went down to the Mercantile Marine Office with Donald Leech to register my indentures - the apprenticeship document or contract. It was not necessary for an apprentice to sign the ship's articles as he was already bound to the owners by his indentures, in my case, for three and a half years. The crew signed on for a nominal two year voyage.

My indentures are dated 5 July 1943. They are printed on linen paper measuring 16 inches by 11.5 inches. There is a centuries-old ring in the wording; 'the said Apprentice will faithfully serve his said Masters….nor frequent Taverns or Alehouses, unless upon their business….the said Masters….will and shall use all proper means to teach the said Apprentice….the business of a seaman, and ….of a ship's officer.'

The document ends by stating that I would be paid as follows:

> £4.10 for the first six months.
> £12.00 for the first year.
> £15.00 for the second year.
> £24.00 for the third and last year.
> A total of £55.10 for the 3½ years.

In addition to this, there was my £5 per month War Risk Money although those over 18 received £10. I made out an allotment note for £3 a month in favour of my mother.

Donald, the senior middy, came from Blackpool. His manner was cheerful, chatty and confident - a pleasant chap to sail with. His father owned a fleet of fishing trawlers sailing out of Fleetwood. At this time he was about 20 years old and had nearly finished his time as an apprentice. Four years' foreign-going sea time was a standard requirement for entry to sit the examination for 2nd Mates.

Soon after we had met for the first time he asked me to hand him my cap. Inside my new cap there was a cane grommet to keep the shape round. Donald removed the grommet then squashed the cap several times. "Keep doing that,", he said, "and eventually it will come all right." Of course he was quite correct. A new cap made one look like a bus conductor - quite the wrong image. An early photograph showed me like that and I hope I have got rid of all the copies.

On the following day Mr Pearce gave me his routine 'pep talk' for new middies. The amiable 'Danny' Pearce had a rather soft businessman look about him although he had been a ship's officer prior to suffering an injury. I was exhorted to work to the highest standards for the greater glory of Alfred Holt and Company.

After leaving the office Donald and I walked to the Birkenhead docks. Dockland had a dreary appearance with its high walls and grimy warehouses. At the dock-gate, policemen examined our passes. Inside the docks it was all bustle and activity with ships loading and unloading. Our ship lay at the Outer Basin and we went on board. The *Empire Lancer* was one of a wartime series built to a standard design, operated by Holts on behalf of the MOWT and assigned to their Glen Line. Brief details are:- triple-expansion steam engine, coal-fired, speed 11 knots, 450 feet long, 7000 tons gross, number of crew about 50, launched by Lithgow's of Port Glasgow in November, 1942.

On deck, everything seemed to be in confusion. Shore staff were carrying out last--minute repairs. Wrens were proving their sex equality, splicing heavy wire ropes that were part of the ship's anti-torpedo defence. One of the ship's lifeboats was being lowered into the dock to see if it was watertight. It wasn't. The boat filled with water quite rapidly and there was some agitation among the observers lining the ship's rail. There seemed a hit of a panic about getting a replacement before the day of sailing.

I was introduced to the officers. The mournful-faced 2nd Mate told me he didn't like midshipmen and he didn't like Scotsmen. I didn't like him either when I got to know him. The Chief Officer, from Dunblane, was more pleasant and made some cheerful comment. The friendly 3rd Mate smiled in welcome; he was uncertificated and was due to sit for his 2nd Mate's 'ticket' at the end of the trip. The genial 4th Mate had been promoted from the lower deck. The Master, Captain Jollivet, came from Mauritius. He was a stickler for high standards of appearance despite war conditions. We had little direct contact with him, but I liked him well enough. He could be quite excitable. When another vessel came far too close for his liking, he gripped the rail and jumped up and down shouting, "Bloody swine! Bloody swine!"

Later I got to know the Scottish Chief Engineer, Angus Wilkieson, who was a good friend to a raw first-tripper. He came from the small village of

Easterhouse - before it became part of a huge housing estate - not far from Glasgow. Others who became good friends included the young ship's carpenter, a Welshman from Aberdovey, and the junior radio officer, a Yorkshireman, who was about my own age.

July 6th. The ship should have sailed this day, but the replacement lifeboat hadn't arrived. Donald and I went for breakfast. in the saloon in uniform then changed into our working gear. For me, this was dungaree trousers - nowadays called jeans - and a khaki shirt given to me by an uncle. Routine day-of-departure tasks were carried out. Contents of lifeboat lockers were checked and life buoys with lamps were lashed to life rafts. Telephones were checked to see if they were in order but on the bridge we also laid out. a megaphone -. a simple cone-shaped device - as the Master still preferred to shout his orders.

The layout of the ship was not too difficult to learn, but where to find equipment took a lot longer. I stuck closely to the senior middy and paid attention. Our duties were normally given to us directly by the Chief Officer. Often we were sent to help the bo's'n, but usually we worked independently. The tasks could be pretty mundane and boring. Nevertheless we carried them out with a will and a lot of enthusiasm. There was no such thing as paid overtime for us and we turned out. to work at any time of day or night, seven days a week. The initials of the company, AH, were said to mean 'All Hours'.

On that first working day, our job was to shift material out of an A.R.P. (Air Raid Precautions) locker in a for'd mast house so that some welding could be done. It was probably unconnected but the steel plating of the fore deck was buckled and undulated like waves between the frames. That may have been caused by heavy weather and poor design. Number 2 and number 3 hatches opened into the same extra-large hold that some said was a design weakness. Anyway, we placed the mast locker gear temporarily in the ship's hospital. The so-called hospital was usually used for storing spare gear. It contained two metal-framed cots with sides on them to stop anyone falling out. But there was no doctor on board and medical first aid was a duty of the Chief Steward. I still have a scar on my side where he used a pair of tweezers to remove the root of a large boil.

At 5, we 'knocked off' during a violent rain shower.

July 7th. After breakfast at 7.30, I continued with the squaring-up of the bridge, wheelhouse and chart room. The new lifeboat arrived on the back of a lorry. It didn't fit our davits so it was lifted over the side and placed on No.3 hatch. The police came to inspect our identity cards; merchant seamen did not have passports. There was a delay for a few minutes while the welders finished their last job.

At 2 o'clock, the ship moved out to an anchorage in the River Mersey opposite New Brighton. My post was with the 2nd Mate aft on the poop, standing by the telephone, relaying messages to and from the bridge. The Master and the 3rd Mate were on the bridge and the Chief Officer was on the fo'c'sle head. A group of four or five seamen looked after the stern ropes and a similar group handled the bow ropes.

Donald went on anchor watch while I tidied out our room, as we preferred to call our cabin. Middies' quarters were also known as the half-deck, a term from the days of sailing ships. When my steel sea-chest was emptied of clothing and navigation books, it was stored for'd in the fore peak. Back on deck work, I had to hoist the convoy lights to the top of the signal mast. Before turning in, I started work on the exercises given out by the Midshipmen's Department.

July 8th. Donald was again on anchor watch. I rose at 6.30 and put on oilskins and sea boots. The black oilskins were made from cloth treated with linseed oil. The sleeves often stuck to the body and the material crackled with each movement. In rough weather we tied rope yarn round the bottom of the sleeves and round the waist. This was known as 'body and soul' lashings. The sou'wester was a broad-brimmed oilskin hat that tied under the chin. The sea boots were black rubber, three-quarter length, that is, mid-thigh. In ordinary conditions the top part was doubled down below the knee. My job on deck that morning was to scrub the pilot ladder with soogee. The wooden steps of the pilot ladder were painted white for better visibility in the dark. The bad weather continued; thunder and lightning was terrific. There was a blue flash in the cabin and a fire-axe on the chart room bulkhead had a faint glow that reminded me of the St. Elmo's fire of sailing ship stories.

It had cost my father a fair sum of money to get the articles specified in the Company's clothing list. My No.1 uniform was of excellent quality and I tried to keep it in good condition by wearing my No. 2 as much as possible. The latter was a navy blue railwayman's uniform given to me when I had a. holiday job as an assistant purser on the Loch Lomond steamers. Although it was commonplace serge material I thought it might be acceptable when the Alfred Holt Company's brass buttons were sewn on to it - replacing those of Dumbarton and Balloch Joint Line Committee. However, I became the object of some gentle mockery from some of the officers - serge was not at all 'correct'. They didn't appreciate that not everyone had comfortable financial resources.

I washed and put on the serge uniform for breakfast, then changed back into working gear. The wearing of uniform was compulsory at mealtimes and this could be irksome as many of our duties left us with oil, grease or paint on hands and arms. This was usually removed using kerosene or turpentine and finally rinsed with soap and water. Then it was on with the white shirt, complete with collar studs, followed by the white (hopefully) collar and black tie. Next went on the uniform trousers with braces, the double-breasted brass-buttoned jacket, the black socks and black shoes.

In the officers' saloon, middies had their seats at the foot of a long table that had the Captain and senior officers presiding at the top. After half-an-hour we would be changing back into dungarees. Attempts to sneak into the saloon wearing polo-neck sweaters or patrol jackets or the like, were doomed to failure. The culprit was sharply reminded by the Captain of the need to be properly dressed and it didn't happen again. An engineer noticed that the Company's Regulations did not actually specify a white shirt so he turned up in a kaki one. He was given the benefit of a formal interview with the Master and, thereafter, wore a white shirt like everyone else. I tried to get by with a blue shirt on watch, but that didn't work either.

Eventually the items we'd placed in the ship's hospital were taken back to the A.R.P. locker and tallied. After lunch, it was Donald's watch below and I carried on alone. The ship was being made ready for sea; loose oil drums were lashed down; lumber and other dunnage from the previous voyage wore thrown over the side, no doubt to the delight of beachcombers. The bridle of the companion ladder and two cane fenders were taken for'd to the fore cabin; the cover of the new No 3 boat was rolled up and placed in the boat; paravane booms (part of mine-sweeping gear) were squared up and fire buckets filled. The derricks were lowered, housed and clamped down; mooring ropes stowed in lockers or lashed down on gratings - all the routine chores for a ship going deep-sea.

When the span of the lifeboat carried on No.3 hatch was to be slackened, I was shown how to operate a steam winch for the first time. The cylinder valves were opened first and then a valve on the deck pipeline was opened to 'put steam on the winch'. The small cylinder valves allowed any water to drain out. Then pure steam came through they were closed. The controls were simple; a valve for controlling the steam pressure and a lever with three positions, forward, neutral and reverse. Reverse had to be used with great caution as a load of any weight would come 4own fast enough in neutral, overcoming the winch, another lever engaged or disengaged a dog-clutch that connected with the driving mechanism on the central drum.

The Fleming hand-propelled screw lifeboat on No.3 hatch was a replacement for the unusable No.2. It was rigged so that it could be slung over the side by a derrick, a doubtful arrangement for any likely emergency. (In 1941 when the ship was torpedoed in the Indian Ocean it sank within eight minutes.) The Fleming patent was a design that enabled unskilled people to get the lifeboat moving. Levers at each thwart were pushed back and forward; this motion operated a boat-long shaft that was connected to a small propeller.

Royal Navy personnel came on board and directed the crew through the drill for rigging the torpedo nets (officially known as the Admiralty Net Defence or AND). The anti-torpedo nets when streamed were like a curtain held out on a *wire stretched between booms. The nets would be about twenty feet out from the ship's side over about half her length. The drag of the nets brought down the ship's speed from 11 knots to about 7 knots. They did work; on another voyage in the Med. an aerial torpedo was caught by the nets of a ship in the next column to us. *Known as the Blondin wire after the great tightrope walker.

A tug came to swing the ship for the compass adjuster. The ship was fitted with an anti-magnetic mine loop and the compass was calibrated twice, loop in use and loop not in use. In the Mersey were several wrecks of ships, their positions marked by green painted buoys. It was said that one of these ships had anchored over a magnetic mine dropped from a German aircraft. Then the anti-magnetic loop was switched off the ship was blown up by the mine.

During the calibration checks Donald reported that the vessel had dragged her anchor a bit, nothing serious. One of the duties on anchor watch is to take bearings of conspicuous objects on the land to verify the ship's position. The weather was now clearer with a sky of high altitude cirro-stratus aloud.

The 'galley wireless' - the name for the source of rumours, well-founded or not -.said our convoy of about ninety ships would be the biggest so far to cross the Atlantic. Convoy speed nine-and-a-half knots. Bed about 10.30.

July 9th. Donald woke me at 6.30 with a cup of tea - a very pleasant start to the day. My first task was sorting out lifeboat gear. This checking was a pretty regular task. By this stage in the war at sea the lifeboats were jammed full of additional items thought to be essential. There was a small distillation plant for producing fresh water from sea water. Along with two cases of coal briquettes as fuel, the whole lot took up a fair amount of boat space. In case someone might have been tempted to distil some illicit spirit, the Excisemen made a regular check on these stills!

A mast, complete with its rigging, lay alongside oars on the thwarts - standard equipment. Because of many deaths due to exposure protection was provided, by a canvas cover with side screens and support rods. Everything was lashed down and fastened so that none of it would be lost if the boat turned upside down. A capsize was very possible during lowering. The lifeboats were carried outboard with the covers left off, ready for quick lowering.

A lot of ship duties are a form of seagoing housework, lashing soda in water, known as soogee, was used for washing down paintwork. Thankfully most of the brass-work had been painted Admiralty grey. Where brass existed, we used the well-known Brasso and lots of 'elbow grease'. As rags we used cotton waste or old flags, even old ensigns. War-time built ships did not have wood-covered decks so there was no 'holystoning' to do. The bridge and wheelhouse had wooden gratings. During my first few days at sea, I had to scrub the gratings with soogee in place of the usual caustic soda which was not available. The wheelhouse deck was also to be cleaned and, without thinking, I applied the soogee to it as well. The Chief Officer was not amused. Enough said! Later I went back and washed off the white deposit with fresh water.

Our own room was cleaned daily by us and we made our own beds. We did our own dhobi (washing clothes), sewed on buttons and darned our socks - woollen socks needed regular darning. One of the first things to acquire was a spare bucket to keep for dirty clothes. Ironing was not permitted - the Chief Engineer pointed out that over twenty electric lamps could be lit with the current used by one electric iron. In our room there was a convenient washhand basin, but, in the best British fashion, it had a tap but no waste pipe. Underneath the sink was a can which had to be emptied over the side when we remembered.

We had no cargo for the voyage to the States. Without cargo, a vessel sits high with her propeller partly out of the water - not desirable for an ocean voyage. Some tanks are filled with sea water to bring the vessel to a safer draught. Extra weight is added by loading low cost material which can be dumped at the destination. In Birkenhead, the ballast we loaded was several hundreds of tons of stones and building rubble from bomb sites. Our convoy number was 131 i.e. the first/leading ship in the thirteenth column. The *Bellerophon* was also in the convoy.

After lunch, I went to the bridge to log telegraph and steering orders and signals. We weighed anchor about 1.30. and were passing Rock Light about 2.10. The ships kept in line ahead through the swept channel, kept clear by regular mine-sweeping. Progress was slow and it took about two hours to the bar where the pilot was dropped.

For the passage through the Irish Sea the ships formed smartly into two lines. By 1943, the merchant ship masters were well experienced in carrying out the manoeuvres expected by the Navy. We went on to double watches, four hours on and four hours off. Double watches worked out at more than twelve hours a day. They were regular practice on 19th century sailing ships. No wonder the old-time sailors were called 'iron men on wooden ships' and the modern sailors were 'wooden men on iron ships'.

Anglesey was sighted on the port bow. We were passing the Isle of Man and Chicken Light House in the afternoon and evening. On the bridge my duty was to look out for flag signals about speed and course. There was great competition among merchant ships to be first in acknowledging the Commodore's signals. For instance, if he hoisted the code flags K9 (convoy speed 9 knots) all ships repeated the signal. In less than a minute, every ship would be flying the same hoist on its signal halyards. When the Commodore lowered his signal, the command was executed and all ships lowered their hoists too. On this voyage the Commodore ship was a Norwegian vessel, the *Laurits Svenson* (convoy number 81/first ship in the eighth column). The Commodore was usually an older Royal Navy man brought back from retirement. With him he brought some additional staff to cope with the many signals.

July 10th. Sighted Ailsa Craig about 0630. Kintyre, Islay, Skerryvore. Passed Barra Head about 2200, heading north-westerly. That was the last of the land to be seen. The convoy had, by now, formed into 14 columns of about 7 ships in each column. The columns were 1000 yards apart and the ships in each column 400 yards apart. The array of vessels was about 6 miles wide. So many ships in convoy was a stirring sight. A benefit of standing watch on the bridge was the opportunity to use the signal telescope or the binoculars to study ships in detail. Many years later I learned that our ocean escorts were the Canadian vessels *Saskatchewan, Burnham, Skeena, Mayflower, La Malbaie, Bittersweet* and *Pictou.*

In the chartroom was a diagram showing the names, positions and convoy numbers of the ships. Also given for each ship was the height of its masthead above the waterline. Station-keeping at the correct distance was maintained by checking the angle of elevation of the mast of the vessel ahead. For instance, if the vessel ahead had a mast height of 80 feet, then, at the correct distance, the angle would be 3 degrees 49 minutes. If the angle found was more or less than calculated, then the engine room was informed to change speed... "Down two" or "Up two" propeller revolutions as required. Some deck officers had been known to order speed corrections of only one revolution. The engineers regarded this as impossible to achieve and ignored such commands. On one of my visits to the engine room, I was shown a grimy looking rivet on the bulkhead near the control platform. The engineer told me that whenever he received such a daft order, he obeyed it by pressing his thumb on the rivet. Talking about rivets reminds me that a favourite ploy among the engineers was to tell first--trippers about the 'golden rivet'. This was solemnly declared to be the last rivet hammered into place when the ship was built. The credulous beginner could be led a merry dance going round looking for it. Other tricks were to send the greenhorn for a bucket of steam or a left-banded screwdriver. Some first-trippers had heard of these tricks, but still pretended to be taken in. One apprentice gave me his opinion that it was more fun running round the ship than washing down paintwork.

Messages from the bridge could be sent by telephone but we also had the older fashioned voice pipe. It was a copper pipe, about two inches in diameter, with a removable whistle-plug at each end. You simply removed the plug and blew down the pipe thus blowing the whistle at the other end. When the engineer removed his plug you could converse with ease.

Sometimes the middy was sent to deliver a message by hand. From the main deck you opened a heavy steel door to be met with a strong draft of warm air, smelling distinctively of steam. Steep steel ladders led down several levels of cat walks. Imitating the 'black gang', I would slide down each section with hands on the rails and feet held up clear of the steps. The triple-expansion steam engine turned at 76 revolutions per minute at full speed. The large cranks and piston rods rotated and reciprocated in a fascinating rhythm. The engineers kept up the old rivalry between deck and engine room. When I appeared they would shout, "Here comes the spy from the bridge!" Some traditional banter would follow; all good fun.

To go from the engine room to the stokehold was to pass into a different world. The firemen were stripped to the waist; sweat glistening on their skin. Each wore a sweat-rag round his neck for wiping the sweat out of his eyes.

Every few moments one of them would use the end of his shovel to hook open one of the furnace doors that were about chest height. Behind him was the bulkhead of the main coal bunker. Hundreds of tons were behind that steel wall, at the bottom of which were small openings to allow some coal through. The fireman took a shovelful off the deck and then pitched it neatly to a chosen spot in the nine-foot long bed of glowing coals. To quench their constant thirst there were teapot-shaped containers filled with oatmeal water. The firemen drank this straight out of the spout. A stone-like ash called clinker was raked out after each watch. This was placed in the bucket of a chain-operated hoist. By hand, it was hauled up, clanking, to deck level then taken across the deck to be dumped over the side. (I don't remember any engine power being used for the hoist on that ship but many had that facility.) This operation was carried out after dark apparently because some clinker floated and left a detectable track. For the same reason any gash or garbage was dumped over the side after dark. Submarines had been known to track convoys from a trail of floating rubbish. With the best Welsh steam coal, the work of the firemen may have been tolerable, but, with poor coal, it was an unrelenting treadmill. No wonder that 18 was set as the minimum age for firemen. The stokehold was a terrible place in which to work.

July 11th. I was now on watch with the Chief Officer and the 3rd Officer. The Captain popped up now and then. His dayroom and bedroom were on the bridge deck. I found it curious that the Captain, 1st Mate and 2nd Mate all wore tammies (berets) on watch. Certainly they were less liable than a cap to blow over the side.

The convoy, steered NW and it was very cold. I felt the cold most in my legs, the small of my back and the back of my neck. The Captain did not like us to wear polo-necked sweaters and I did not have a scarf. Wearing my pyjama trousers under my uniform trousers helped a lot as regards the legs. For the feet it was a problem. My warmest stockings could only be worn with sea boots and the Captain did not permit them except in wet weather.

An important duty of the watch-keeper was to keep a close eye on the Commodore vessel for any signals made by flag or Morse lamp. Signals were decoded from Mersigs, the wartime codebook. Signals by lamp were sent down each line from vessel to vessel. The Aldis lamp was in standard use. When in use, the light stayed on all the time and behind it was a parabolic mirror on pivots. The beam of light was directed on the receiving vessel and a trigger was pulled. The speed of transmission was probably less than ten words a minute.

July 12th. Started on single watches, four hours on and eight hours off (continuously night and day of course). I now kept watch with the 2nd Mate, Haines, on the 12 to 4. This was the least preferred watch because of the broken sleeping time. The 2nd Mate had peculiar habits. During the night, about 1a.m., he would defecate into a wooden fire bucket that he then emptied over the side. Later he would send me down to the galley to scrounge sandwiches. This was perilous because the key to the galley was kept in a wall case in the Chief Steward's room. His doorway was closed by only a curtain; fortunately he always slept soundly.

The weather continued very cold and the thick woollen bridge coat proved its worth. Our watch was kept in the open wings of the bridge, never inside in the wheelhouse. That would have been considered soft and decadent. Mid-watch, at 2 a.m., the stand-by man brought a cup of tea. You could feel the warm liquid running all the way down the gullet into the stomach.

You must not stamp your feet to keep your toes warm. First-trippers always do daft things and for one night only I stomped up and down like a soldier on sentry duty. The next night, the Chief Radio Officer appeared in his pyjamas and told me firmly to stop it; his cabin was only a few feet away.

The ship tended to roll a bit, being in ballast, but nothing like the Liberty ships I sailed in later. Then the wind got up to gale force – a usual expectation in the North Atlantic - narrow lines of foam formed across the water in the direction of the wind.

Going west means that the clocks are put back one hour for every 15 degrees of longitude. The one hour is split in three and each watch of four hours has 20 minutes added. The length of day becomes 25 hours. Eastbound, the opposite rule applies. We worked to various time scales: Greenwich Mean Time, Mean Time Ship, Convoy Time.

July 16th. A week at sea. We put on our working togs and painted the pilot ladder white. At 11 o'clock, we knocked off for a break of 15 minutes known as 'Smoke-o'. Cigarettes were quite cheap, one shilling and six pence for a tin of fifty. Some seamen rolled their own from the 'makings', a tin of loose cigarette tobacco and a packet of cigarette papers. Bull Durham was a commercial brand of 'makings' with the material contained in a small cotton bag closed by a drawstring.

The work on deck was additional to our bridge watch so we were working a ten-hour day. Sunday was usually free from day work. The ratings qualified for overtime for Sunday work, but not if it was a day of departure or arrival. In Dana's book, Two Years before the Mast, the seamen allege that the owners deliberately arranged arrivals and departures for Sunday - some attitudes never change! As middies, we didn't qualify for overtime payment under any circumstances so those particular moans didn't concern us.

One daily duty was to take out the boat plugs and allow the rainwater to drain out. It was quite difficult to get into the lifeboats when they were swung out and Chippy, the ship's carpenter, had fitted each one with a plank from the deck up to the edge of the gunwale. One day, unknown to me, the wedge holding the plank in place had slackened. I walked up the plank as usual and just near the top the plank gave way. I fell and the plank below my feet tumbled straight into the North Atlantic. By good fortune, my arms lay in across the boat's gunwale and I quickly scrambled to a safer position. Our naval signalman said he was ready to send out a 'Man overboard' signal – he had seen the accident from the bridge. I was relieved that I hadn't provided some practice for the rescue ship. It isn't easy to spot someone's head in the surging seas of the Western Ocean.

As we approached North America, visibility grew less with a sort of Scotch mist filling the atmosphere. Finally it became a thick fog. We couldn't see the other ships and we started to sound our convoy number on the steam whistle in Morse code every five minutes; .---- ...-- .---- (one short and four longs, three short and two longs, one short and four longs; 131). The steam whistle was on top of a pipe on the for'd side of the funnel. From a valve below the whistle, two lanyards stretched to each side of the bridge. To operate the whistle you just reached up and pulled on the lanyard. Ships now streamed their fog buoys. These had a piece of metal fixed on top that caught the surface and threw up a small plume of water that could be seen by the next ship in the column.

We moved into the ice region, 39 degrees North and 48 degrees West. Very cold. A scarf and a storm cap would hare helped a lot. Boat drill at 1630. Like fire drill, regular practice was mandatory, but if the weather were bad, it was just a log-book entry, 'Boat drill carried out as per Board of Trade regulations.'

Every member of crew had a steel hat to be worn at the guns on action stations and a lifejacket which we wore or carried with us at all times. The wartime lifejacket was a padded kapok-filled waistcoat fitted with a red light and a whistle. In our cabins, each of us had a small 'panic bag' with personal items we valued. Members of the crew who had been on torpedoed ships warned us to waste no time getting out on deck.

July 17th. Still on the 12 to 4 watch with the 2nd Mate. The stand by man calls the men at half-past and the middy calls the officers at quarter to (known, somewhat confusingly, as one bell.). Some men get up right away when called and make a cheery remark; others will grumble and curse and may even strike out. It is best not to touch the sleeper at all. Switch on the bed light, bang a couple of times on the side of his bunk and call out the time. When he wakes up, tell him the weather so that he knows what clothing to put on. With experience you learn which men need a second call. When it is your own turn to go on watch, you try to be there a couple of minutes early. Two minutes late invites a strongly worded comment. A cup of tea is ready at the change of the watch; the next one is two hours later. A scrap log and wireless slate are made up at 3:15. The wireless slate contains our position in case it is needed for an SOS. The 2nd Mate and I went off watch at 4 a.m.

At 7.30 a.m., I rose and had breakfast at 8. Stewed pears and shredded wheat, bacon, liver and potatoes, marmalade, bread, butter and tea - a peacetime English breakfast! It was obvious that the ship got its stores from the American side of the Atlantic. On Sunday, our dessert was an apple or another fresh fruit. On Thursday and Sunday we got 'tabnabs' which were fruit buns. The middy on watch was relieved at meal times by the middy on watch below.

On the *Lancer*, the seamen's quarters were right aft and the galley was amidships. A fifteen--year old deck boy carried the food along in large pots known as dixies. He was known as the Mess-room Peggy and did not stand watches - a day man, like the Bo's'n, the Carpenter and the Donkeyman. (Maybe 'Lamps', the Lamptrimmer, was a day-man too, but I'm not sure.)

More than once our seamen complained that the Peggy didn't rise early enough to carryout his duties. By the time he had brought the dixie of porridge (burgoo) along for breakfast it was cold. Many warnings and threats were given, but he ignored them. One morning, the seamen had enough and they emptied the contents of the dixie over his head. I saw him running along the deck with his head and shoulders covered in cold porridge. After this affair, it might have been thought that he would improve. He didn't. So the seamen had another go at him and this time they clipped his hair off right down to the 'bone'. This had the desired effect and he finally realised the wisdom of early rising!

The fog lifted a little after breakfast time, but settled in again. In another day, we expected to be off Cape Race, Newfoundland.

As already mentioned, the middies were called upon at any time for all sorts of duties. On this day the Chief Officer hauled Donald and me out of our watch below to help him throw a greasy old torpedo net over the stern. I had on my best trousers, but no time was given to change – chief officers like to be seen as men of instant action! Afterwards, it took quite some time to clean the thick black grease from my trousers. I tried to save my No.1 gear by using my No. 2 suit and wearing a blue shirt instead of one of my two white ones. Leech had a lot of shirts and never had to wash one. He threw the old ones up on top of the locker. For me the problem of smoothing washed collars was partially solved by pressing them on the mirror when wet. When they dried and fell off they had a slight gloss which was the nearest possible to an ironed finish without an iron.

Later, we changed into our working togs and checked the food in the replacement No.2 lifeboat, the Fleming hand-propelled screw type carried on the hatch between the bridge and the centre island.

At midday, I was on watch again. At 12.30, Donald came up to the bridge and relieved me for chow. Because of the thick fog, we were still sounding our number on the whistle every 5 minutes. Over our meal, the engineers complained about the loss of fresh water each time it blew – "A whole bucketful of fresh water!"

The 4th Officer was pleased if I took the azimuths for him. He yarned a lot about his time out in Australia. At this position, the compass error was found to be 35 degrees West. After tea, I was yarning with the 3rd Engineer, a fine pleasant chap. Eventually, we all knew each other's life story by heart.

The Steward kept some stores and I bought six bars of chocolate and a 1lb tin of sweets to take home. Cash was not required for these transactions, just a chit to be signed. It was all deducted from the signing-off pay.

A note from my diary, "I am lying on my bunk writing this. I can hear all the ships sounding their whistles - so many different notes. From the wireless cabin above, I can hear the radio giving out Morse and crashing noises of static. The sea washes against the ship's side. Footsteps ring on the steel deck. Both lights are on in the room, but the sun is breaking through the fog and shining brightly through the porthole."

Sometimes the Chief Officer sent us to the 'barrel' some sixty feet up on the foremast. From this lookout position we could see that the fog was in a layer across the surface of the water. At times, the tops of ships' masts were visible, ghosting along above the fog bank. The sun was visible, but not the convoy. As the ship rolled in the swell, the hull seemed to swing below you like the bob of a pendulum.

July 18th. Sunday. On watch 12 to 4. The fog had lifted until 1.45 a.m. Full moon. Away from the moon, the sea looked black and the ships shone white like icebergs. Nearest the direction of the moon, the seas shone and the ships were darkly silhouetted. After my watch I felt very wide awake and read a bit before turning in.

Rose at 7.35, breakfasted at 8 and relieved Donald at 8.30. Together, we stayed on the bridge until 1015 waiting for an expected Morse signal which did not come. The *Kafiristan*, number 141, passed across our bows in the fog. She was so close that the fog buoy she was towing went right under our hull. We were now somewhere off Cape Race, an area notorious for shipwrecks. The fog lifted now and then.

The Steward handed out fresh linen today, sheet, pillowslip, towel. Apples for dessert today. When you get fruit it must be Sunday. I did some more exercises from the seamanship book.

July 19th. Patches of fog. The seamen's watches were changed, but not the officers'. There were three seamen in each watch. One went on lookout in the bows, another took the wheel and third was on stand-by. The latter was called by blowing a whistle. The men's duties were rotated so that they were not on lookout or steering for more than two hours at a stretch. The officers' watches corresponded to their rank; the Chief Officer took the 4 to 8, the 2nd Officer took the 12 to 4 and the 3rd Officer took the 8 to 12. At noon it is usual for all the deck officers to be on the bridge to take a sun sight for a latitude by meridian altitude. This is an easy calculation compared to any observation away from the meridian.

July 20th. Fog. Wind SW and sea water temperature 79 degrees Fahrenheit.

July 21st. Wednesday. Getting to be quite warm. Went on watch wearing my white shirt, mindful of the Captain's rebuke regarding the blue shirt. Stars showing through some cloud. Fine and clear visibility. Slight sea and swell. Temperature of sea water 63 degrees. In the middle of the night, the 2nd Mate was still performing into the wooden fire bucket.

Too warm in our room, even with both ports open. The fan had not yet been repaired. Rose at 7.25 and got washed before the 2nd Mate appeared. Took an azimuth, error 16 degrees west. Went over lifeboat gear again and lashed down gear as required. The motion of the ship at sea often loosens lashings and there has to be constant checking.

Part of the convoy on the starboard had a firing practice today at a smoke float; quite good shooting. It may have been on this day that the Holman projector was tried out. A hand grenade was dropped down a pipe. A lever was pulled allowing high pressure steam to throw the grenade at an attacking U-boat! In the trial, I remember the missile dropped about 25 yards from the ship. There wasn't a lot of confidence in this device. On the bridge, we had another gadget, a rocket which, when fired, carried a long length of piano wire into the sky. It was intended to catch on the wings of low-flying aircraft!

Our defensive armament also included 0.5inch Colt Browning machine guns in twin mountings. While one was being cleaned by a DEMS rating, he pulled the trigger and a shell went right through the steel plate of the gun pit. He'd removed the belt, but said he didn't know there was still one up the spout. The accidental demonstration showed that the ship's plating was not bullet proof.

On watch it was very hot and we were in shirt sleeves. Changed course to 270 degrees at 2.30. The 3rd Mate and the Junior Radio Officer came in for a yarn with some lemonade and chocolate. A junior engineer had repaired the fan and we found it had 3 speeds which for some silly reason pleased us no end.

On watch at 12. There was nearly a collision with another ship, said to be Dutch, which appeared out of the fog without warning. (About this date a few ships left the convoy for Halifax, N.S. and Saint John, N.B. The greater part of the convoy was going to New York.) The night was fine and clear. Sea water temperature 75 degrees - very warm due to the Gulf Stream.

July 22nd. Thursday. Rose at 7.40. The convoy was breaking up and it was every ship for herself. The Commodore sent a signal saying that if we could do eleven and a half knots we could go on independently to New York. We got 12 knots out of the *Lancer* and tried to beat other ships, but several overtook us instead. The weather didn't look too good, but we hoped to reach New York that evening. It rained heavily about 11.

Changed togs and turned to with Donald to do the brasses and tidy up the wheelhouse and chartroom. Catalina flying boats and U.S. Navy blimps flew overhead as escort; excellent for submarine spotting if you have control of the air. About 3 o'clock, land was sighted. There was an air of excitement. Every moment that could be spared from duty was spent at the ship's rail looking ahead at the changing scene.

As we went up the swept channel, a smoke trail could be seen trailing away in a long curve to the horizon. We came at last to Ambrose Light Vessel and took the pilot on board. What a difference from the chap in a shabby raincoat in Liverpool! The American wore a smart uniform with gold braid. When he wanted to go faster he said, "Hook her up a bit." Nearer the land were hundreds of ships and small craft and many coloured lights. Soon we could see the lights of cars and buildings on the land, Staten Island to port and Long Island to starboard. On the bridge, the Captain stood alongside the pilot. Although the pilot was giving orders, strictly speaking, the Captain was still in charge. The log book usually showed the courses and speeds as 'Various' followed by an entry, 'Captain's orders to pilot's advice.'

For the land approach, the Chief Officer took his place on the fo'c'sle head ready for any order to drop the anchor. Earlier, the engine room had been told to put steam on deck to the anchor windlass. After two weeks of being sprayed with sea water, it had to be checked and turned over out of gear. The Bo's'n and his men removed various lashings from the chain and then the anchors were slowly lowered until they were clear of the hawse pipes. The strong brake on the windlass was put on and the gear disengaged. Each anchor was now held back only by a brake. Chippy stood by with a 'munday' hammer ready to knock the brake open when the order was passed by the bridge. Off Brooklyn, the ship slowed down, then the engines were put astern. When the turmoil of water disturbed by the screw reached a position abreast of the bridge, the ship was beginning to move astern. The order was given to drop the anchor. Chippy released the brake and the chain ran out for a length of about 50 or so fathoms. The tide then swung the vessel to lie heading into the stream. We had arrived in the 'States'.

The crew was taken off sea watches and port routine was started. This meant that most of the crew went on day shift and only a few were needed for night duty.
The Americans were supposed to have some sort of blackout ashore which they called a 'brownout', but it didn't look anything like that to us. On board our vessel, we were very strict about blackout. After dusk, Donald had the duty of going right round the ship to check that there was no light showing –

not the slightest chink. Now we opened the ports for fresh air and left the lights on, shining across the water.

July 23rd. Up at 5.30. We went straight into our working gear and cleaned out our room. The Immigration authorities came on board and examined identity cards. The U.S. Coastguard photographed and fingerprinted us all for entry passes. The 'Old Man', as we called our Captain, treated his guests to drinks in his dayroom. There seemed to be no end of visitors who wanted to see the Captain! From the for'd side of the bridge, I could see the Statue of Liberty. Against the Manhattan Island skyline the statue was not as prominent as I had anticipated. Across the East River was a distinctively-shaped bridge and the harbour was a fascinating, ever-changing, parade of fast-moving ferries, towboats with barges, many of the latter carrying strange names such as Lackawanna Railroad. The latitude here is about 41 degrees north of the equator; roughly the same parallel as Madrid.

When it was time to weigh anchor, we all took up our stations. The windlass turned slowly bringing up the anchor cable. As each section of 15 fathoms, known as a shackle length, came on board, the number left was called out to the bridge. The bo's'n and his men played a hose on the chain to remove the mud. With the anchor up and clear, we got under way and moved over to a pier in Brooklyn where we tied up, bow ropes, stern ropes and back springs. The pier was not far from the Brooklyn Navy Yard, opposite the beautifully-kept Governor's Island. From this position, there was an even better view of the skyscrapers of downtown Manhattan Island.

The ship was made ready to discharge the ballast and to receive cargo. The wireless antennas stretched between the masts were lowered and coiled up out of the way. The derricks were unlashed and rigged, then winched up to their working positions. Iron straps across the hatches were removed then Chippy knocked out the wooden wedges holding the tarpaulin hatch covers in place. There would be two, perhaps three, covers to roll up and stow out of the way. Then the hatch boards were taken off and stacked nearby. This left only the hatch girders which were lifted off with the aid of the derrick and laid. The ship was made ready to discharge the ballast and to receive cargo. The wireless antennas stretched between the masts were lowered and coiled up out of the way. The derricks were unlashed and rigged, then winched up to their working positions. Iron straps across the hatches were removed then Chippy knocked out the wooden wedges holding the tarpaulin hatch covers in place. There would be two, perhaps three, covers to roll up and stow out of the way. Then the hatch boards were taken off and stacked nearby. This left only the hatch girders which were lifted off with the aid of the derrick and laid alongside the open hold. It was a time to keep alert when on deck with the winches turning, wire ropes straining arid loads swinging overhead.

In the morning, the first stevedores came on board and I was amazed to hear them speaking Italian; 'Buon giorno.' 'Come sta.' 'Va bene.' They were brawny and capable men, but from the sound of their imperfect English they were first-generation immigrants. In American films, the man from Brooklyn is cast as an amusing rough diamond who speaks in a funny way - just like the Scots?

Brooklyn in July was very warm compared to Edinburgh. The heat seemed to create an outdoor society which would not be possible in our cooler clime. People sat out on steps at the front of their houses. A school playground with basketball stands had a shower in one corner. Some shops had tables of fruit and vegetables out on the 'sidewalk'. The painting by Edward Hopper, "Early Sunday Morning", captures the mood of the quieter streets of Brooklyn; undistinguished buildings with stuccoed fronts and sun-canopied shops.

SECOND TRIP ON THE EMPIRE LANCER

I had a short leave before rejoining the *Empire Lancer* in Liverpool at the end of August, 1943. Two more midshipmen, David and Henry, came as first trippers. The half-deck had space for only two so the ship's hospital was cleared of stores to make room for two more. The crew turned up in dribs and drabs. Navy-blue suits and brown shoes seemed to be the favoured rig.

Composed of fifty-six ships, convoy ON 200 left the Mersey on the second of September. The weather was bad in the Atlantic and we struggled to keep our position in the convoy. The poor quality of the coal made it hard to maintain a full head of steam. The firemen and trimmers worked like Trojans. Even the engineers went into the stokehold to give a hand, but it was all to no avail and we became a straggler. When it became clear that we could not catch up with the other ships, we switched to an alternative course for 'independently routed ships'.

A day or two before our expected arrival time in New York, we had a minor collision during the Second Mate's midnight to 4am watch when I was with him on the bridge. The patchy cloud occasionally allowed some moonlight to trickle through so that, although the sea was moderate, the visibility was generally poor. Strict blackout was being observed – no lights of any kind.

About 2.20am, the dark shape of another vessel was sighted about a couple of miles away on the port bow. She was on a converging course and our navigation lights were lit. She did the same. According to the rules for the prevention of collision at sea, we had nothing to do except maintain our course and speed. For crossing vessels, it was the other vessel's duty to keep clear of us. But *were* we crossing vessels? In the darkness, the other vessel seemed to see the scene as one where two vessels were 'meeting end-on' and, in that case, we were both to alter course to starboard.

The Second Mate ordered hard-a-starboard; giving one short blast on the whistle. Then he decided to ring for full astern and sounded three short blasts on the whistle. The other vessels gave two short blasts and turned to port. From then on, it was like watching a slow-motion film. Nothing more could be done and we watched as the two vessels came swinging closer and closer. The other vessel, smaller than we were, nearly cleared, but, at the last moment, her bow overhang and starboard anchor struck us at No.3 hold; tearing a large hole above the waterline. The engines were stopped and the two vessels lay alongside for some seconds before drifting slightly apart.

On our vessel, only four of us, the Second Mate, a seaman lookout, the helmsman and me, had been eye-witnesses, but, in an astonishingly short time, the engine room gang appeared on deck complete with life-jackets. They thought we had 'got the hammer' i.e. that we had been torpedoed.

We had collided with the s.s. *Wistaria*, a United States coaster, and, after exchanging names we went our separate ways. Our crew were quite happy. It was the equivalent of a First World War 'blighty' – there was enough damage to take us out of the war for a short time, but not enough to cause us lasting harm.

At Brooklyn Navy Yard, the ship went into dry dock. Damaged plating and bent frames were removed. Work went on twenty-four hours a day and, after only five days, we were ready to sail again.

There was an enquiry into the circumstances of the collision and evidence was given by the Second Mate, the lookout and the helmsman. The former had 'forgotten' that I was also present, but, when this fact was disclosed by the helmsman, I was ordered to appear. Before I did, however, the Mate and Second Mate went over every detail with me in order that my evidence would corroborate that of the Second Mate. Although I largely agreed with him, the sequence of putting on lights and giving signals was not entirely the way I remembered it.

At a lawyer's office in downtown New York, I attended a meeting between the two sets of lawyers. Two model ships were on the table and I was asked to place them in the relative positions as I saw them at each stage of the incident. As in so many of these cases, I heard no more about the sequel. Perhaps the blame was equally divided.

Back again at our loading berth in Brooklyn, the holds were gradually filled with foodstuffs and war supplies for Britain. Among the firemen and trimmers there was great discontent, the cause of which was supposed to have a connection with our failure to keep up with the convoy. One evening, a group of them went ashore for a booze-up and some hours later returned, staggering about on the quay beside the ship, shouting and bawling.

A young DEMS rating – one of our own crew – stood on guard at the head of the gangway with a Lee-Enfield rifle slung over his shoulder. The *black gang* came on board and, in a destructive mood, they grabbed loose items on the deck and threw them overboard – the large ventilators, easily lifted off their bases, being the next target. The young rating, about eighteen years old, on this own and in a bit of a panic, fired his rifle into the air. This had the desired effect; the drunken demonstration stopped in an instant and the men disappeared like rabbits in a field going to ground.

This is likely to have been the end of it, but the shot had been heard ashore and, within a short time, the U.S. Navy turned up in force; sharp faced sailors armed with Tommy guns and Colt automatics. Attempts to converse with them were either ignored or acknowledged by mere grunts. Clearly the whole crew was under suspicion of trying to sabotage the war effort. But, a day or two later when the culprits were identified, the Americans left and six armed seamen of the Royal Navy replaced them as the enforcers of order.

At ten minutes to midnight on Monday the 4th of October, the ship sailed with two of the armed guard patrolling the entrances to the engine room. We sailed up the East River, passing, in succession, under the Brooklyn, Manhattan, Williamsburgh and Queensboro bridges. As we approached each one, it seemed as if the masts were going to strike the structure; a kind of optical illusion. Continuing through Hell's Gate, we entered Long Island Sound, a sheltered passage of nearly one hundred miles, and anchored for the night at the entrance to Cape Cod Canal as our destination was Boston.

On the Wednesday morning, we sailed through the Canal, on the banks of which the autumn tints of the trees were striking, and, on arriving in Boston harbour, a police launch came out and two members of the crew were taken ashore on the alleged charge of mutiny.

Without any knowledge of the fate of the mutineers, we sailed for Halifax, N.S. the following day. With the convoy commodore on board, we were Commodore Ship and, as we moved northwards along the rocky coast of Nova Scotia, it struck me as being similar to that of the Western Isles of Scotland. After two days in Halifax harbour, without shore leave being granted, we again had the honour of being Commodore Ship when we sailed for the UK on Monday, 11 October.

Although the slow convoy received no attention from U-boats during its crossing of the Atlantic, it was so delayed by bad weather that the passage took seventeen days. We arrived in Avonmouth on 28 October with one of our lifeboats stove in and iron stanchions bent over by the weight of water coming on board.

1943
JULY
8th   Thursday. Left Birkenhead for New York in Convoy ON192 (Escort Group C3).
22nd   Thursday. Arrived Brooklyn.
AUGUST
23rd   Monday. Arrived at Gladstone Dock, Liverpool.
29th   Sunday.   Returned from leave. Stayed at Midshipmen's Hostel in Riversdale Road, Liverpool.
31st   Tuesday.   Rejoined *Empire Lancer*.
SEPTEMBER
2nd   Thursday. Left Mersey. Convoy ON200; 56 ships in all. (Escort Group B7 under Cdr. Gretton with the destroyers *Duncan* and *Vidette*, and the corvettes *Loosestrife, Pink* and *Sunflower* – all RN.)
17th   Friday. Arrived New York
OCTOBER
4th   Monday. Left New York at 2350. Armed guard on board.
5th   Tuesday. East River, Hell's Gate and Long Island Sound to anchor at south entrance Cape Cod Canal.
6th   Wednesday. Through Canal to Boston. Anchored. Two members of crew taken ashore for alleged mutiny.
7th   Thursday. Left Boston in morning. Commodore ship.
9th   Saturday. Arrived Halifax, Nova Scotia, in afternoon. Anchored.
11th   Monday. Departed Halifax; Commodore ship of Convoy HX.260. Escorted by Escort Group C4 with the destroyers *Hotspur* (RN) and *Churchill* (RN) and the corvettes *Nasturtium* (RN), *Trillium* (RN), *Orillia*, (RCN) and *Woodstock* (RCN).
28th   Thursday. Arrived Avonmouth in Bristol Channel.

Almost all the crew were then sent to other ships and Douglas' next ship was the Liberty Ship *Samharle*, the story of which is recounted in my Kindle book, Dangerous Voyaging.

This was fortunate for them as, when sailing unescorted on 16 August 1944, the *Empire Lancer* was torpedoed and sunk by U.862 (Korvettenkapitän Heinrich Timm) when on passage from Durban to Majunga (Mahajanga), on the northwest coast of Madagascar. Captain Jollivet, all the Deck and Radio Officers, the four midshipmen, 5 DEMS gunners, and 21 members of the Chinese crew, were among the 37 who died. Ten days later, a lifeboat, with

Chief Engineer Angus Wilkieson in charge, landed at Lumbo in Portuguese East Africa/Mozambique.

S. S. OCEAN TRADER

Ocean Trader, Bombay, January, 1946

When the war in Europe ended in May, 1945, I was attending an outward-bound course at Aberdovey, in Wales, where Alfred Holt and Company had sent me to 'provide a stiffening of leadership'. Their next orders took me to the Mercantile Marine office in Birkenhead where, on Tuesday 19 June 1945, the crew signed the articles of the S.S. *Ocean Trader* and the particulars of Dauncey, the other middy, and I were written on them.

The American-built ship was lying in the docks at Port Sunlight and my first impression was her neglected appearance. The vessel seemed to have an air of gloom which was not dispelled on closer acquaintance. The Captain, T. A. Kent, who had been through some harrowing wartime experiences, was sick with shingles and seemed scarcely fit to speak. When Singapore was attacked by the Japanese in February 1942 he escaped with his crew, but without his ship, the bomb-damaged *Talthybius*. Also, he had served in the Malta convoys, which had been so strongly opposed by enemy aircraft and submarines, and, in December 1943, he was a survivor of the torpedoing of the *Phemius* in the Gulf of Guinea. The Captain's poor health meant that he was, in effect, not able to be much .more than a figurehead and many of his executive duties were delegated to the 1st Mate.

The latter turned out to be a humourless, surly and ill-tempered individual. It is possible that his war service had been sorely trying, but we never knew the real reason for his continual griping. At our very first meeting he expressed his low opinion of all midshipmen and for the next eight months of the voyage he kept up an aggressive manner towards the other apprentice and me.

His sour manner was copied by the 2nd Mate, a Geordie, who was a bully if given half a chance. In contrast, the 3rd Mate was a passive, almost timid, inoffensive soul.

Dauncey came from Johannesburg in South Africa, but his parents were English. Among the rest of the crew were some ABs who had sailed on my last ship, the *Samharle*, and it was good to meet them again. The Donkeyman, the most senior of the engine room ratings, was a memorable character, a real tough guy with hard fists, but who had a likeable direct and forthright manner.

The ship sailed from the Mersey on Friday, 22 June, loaded with war materials. We passed Cape St Vincent on the 26th, Gibraltar on the 27th, Cape Bon in North Africa on the 30th and arrived at Port Said on the 3rd July. At our speed of about 11 knots, fairly typical for cargo vessels of that era, it took approximately five days to Gib and another five through the Med. The weather was pleasant and, at last, there were no U-Boats to trouble us.

A strange incident took place one night in the Med. I went down to the galley on the main deck to make tea. The 1st Radio Officer and an AB were there. The Sparks made some remark to the AB who replied with his fists, knocking the Radio Officer to the deck. The AB then went off without glancing behind him. I helped the R/O to his feet, but he said there was nothing wrong and asked me not to say anything about the incident to anyone. Next day, when one of his friends, the 3rd Mate, took me to see him, he was in his bunk with a black eye and a bruised face. Round the ship, however, the word was that the R/O was off duty with the flu and this fiction prevailed. I do not think I need spell out the explanation for the foregoing where a seaman attacked an officer and the matter was kept quiet with no repercussions.

Moving at only 7 or 8 knots, so as not to damage its banks by our wash, it took 8½ hours to clear the Suez Canal and anchor in Suez Bay. The ship was a coal burner, burning about 35 tons a day, and we loaded several hundred tons of bunker coal from barges.

The loading was done, quite speedily, by hand. Two barges lay along each side of the ship and wooden platforms, or stages, were put in position with a series of short ladders joining the stages. Bags of coal were passed up the side from platform to platform by a chain of men, then carried across the deck to be tipped down the bunker hatchway. Coal dust covered the deck, deck houses, boats - everywhere. The famous Jock Ferguson (perhaps there was more than one person using that name) came on board to sell his wares of camel-leather wallets and purses and other local items. He claimed to come from Glasgow, but was visibly Egyptian although his Scots accent was realistic and I believe he was equally good with other accents and tongues.

The ship left Suez on 6th July, arrived at Aden on Wednesday 11th July, and departed at 1330 the same day. The title of a well-known pipe tune, 'The Barren Rocks of Aden' is a fair description of the place as there was only reddish rock and not a blade of grass to be seen. Bombay was reached on Tuesday 17th July, 25 days out from the Mersey.

The ship berthed the following day and our cargo of crated landing-craft and foodstuffs was unloaded. Some of the heavy crates had been badly stowed on top of cardboard cartons of condensed milk and, as the crates were being dragged out by wire runners, milk from burst tins squirted right and left. Also loaded at the Mersey, had been thousands of green-painted wooden boxes called Pacific compo rations — enough for six soldiers for one day. The English dockers had opened many of them with their cargo hooks looking for the tin of cigarettes each box contained and, near the end of unloading, the bottom of one hold was littered with hundreds of broached boxes. These supplies were intended for our troops fighting the Japanese in the Burma jungle and the tins, and even the toilet paper, were painted green.

About this time, I suffered an accident which should not have happened. On the highest part of the bridge there was a small mast, about 25 feet high. On it, suspended from a wire halyard, was a group of six heavy bronze lamps, known as the convoy lights. The wire rope was old and rusty with broken strands, a sure sign that it needed to be replaced, and although we had reported this to the Mate, he had taken no action. On arrival in port, the lights had been lowered to the deck and, the Mate ordered Dauncey and me to hoist them up again. We were heaving them up, and they were nearly at the top, when the wire rope broke. The lamps fell, missing Dauncey, but, struck me on the head with such force as to cut a hole through my cap that I saw 'stars' and hung semi-conscious over the rail. After being helped down to my bunk, the Mate came in and brusquely enquired if I needed a doctor, but when, playing the part of the brave young lad, I answered in the negative, he quickly departed as his temporary concern was more for his own sake than mine. As it would have exposed his negligence, no official accident report was made and the lump on my skull is there to this day.

Much of the work we were given to do was boring and stultifying. There was a dreary monotony in chipping rust from acres of steel deck and applying red lead paint by the gallon. So many people ashore have a glamorous image of seafaring that it seems a shame to voice a sour note. However, I can truly say that no attempt was made 'to teach the said Apprentice … the business of a seaman, and …of a ship's officer' as was stated in our indentures. Dauncey and I could never be faulted on any of our work, a fact which I noted was of some annoyance to the 2nd Mate who was always trying to find something to nark about. The ungentlemanly Mate was also given to bawling and snarling, jerking his thumb to point to our next menial task. All in all, the only way to survive was to adopt a philosophical stance.

As we had voyaged independently, I missed the intense involvement of convoy procedures. On watch on the bridge in convoy, you felt you were part of something much bigger so that what you did had some importance. You were also close to the watch-keeping officer and learned something of the trade from him. About this time, Captain Kent returned to England. My memory of him is a rather sad figure, leaning back, somewhat hunched, in a corner of the bridge, saying nothing and taking no part in the activity around him. Later I heard that he recovered and took a post as a marine superintendent.

On 31st July, we went out to an anchorage in the roads and, on Tuesday 14 August, moved to another anchorage. During this time, Dauncey and I ran a motor lifeboat back and forward to the shore as required. Lifeboats are designed to carry a large number of people and when they are light they sit high out of the water. To keep the propeller under the surface, it is usual to put some ballast, such as old fire bars from the stokehold, in the boat, but we had none. The first time we took the Mate ashore, he asked why we didn't go faster. I replied that the boat was unable to and, without a word, he reached over and pushed the throttle to its full extent. The propeller then raced and vibrated so dangerously that, after a couple of minutes, he reached out and throttled back. His face was a study. He didn't like being wrong and, as he seemed to be incompetent in every aspect of navigation and seamanship, Dauncey and I had no respect for him.

Wednesday 15th August 1945 was V-J Day, Victory over Japan. Out in the anchorage it was difficult to celebrate adequately the occasion which we had all forgotten would come sooner or later - peace! The subdued reaction on board our vessel created a feeling of anti-climax. But many of the ships around us fired rockets and even Oerlikon 20mm cannon and, in dark of the evening, the tracer made a colourful, but dangerous, display. The following day, some ships started cleaning off the Admiralty grey paint from their funnels and one ship started painting their company colours.

On Thursday 23rd August, we berthed to load supplies for the previously planned invasion of Malaya - Operation Zipper. Even though the Japanese had surrendered, the assembled fleet was ordered to sail with substantially the same orders. The fleet comprised about a dozen landing ships, 25 warships and 200 other vessels. During our preparations, the ship had been fitted with extra anti-aircraft guns and a large identification code, S3, had been painted on each side of the hull. Other ships were similarly coded to identify their function.

Sunday, 2 September - Returned to anchorage.
Wednesday, 5 September - Compass trials and bunkered.
Thursday, 6 September - Left Bombay after 51 days in port. Full away at 1400.
Monday, 10 September - Passed Cape de Galle, Ceylon at 2200.
Sunday, 16 September - Entered Malacca Strait.
Monday, 17 September - Convoy formed line ahead. In my diary is the note, 'What a mess!'.
Tuesday, 18 September - Arrived at Sugar Charlie, the code name for a nodal point on our route.
Thursday, 20 September - Near the Malayan coast a group of ships was at anchor. The Mate, in charge on the bridge, took our ship in beside them, looking for a place to anchor.

The H.Q. ship called us up on the signalling lamp and asked, "What are you doing here?" It was then realised that we were in the wrong place. We were at Port Swettenham and still had 10 more miles to go before we reached the correct point at Port Dickson. (Now that the country is independent these place names have been changed back to the original Malay.)

The Mate looked at the group of us on the bridge and said, "Not a word of this to the engine room." Obviously, the engineers would have a field day ragging the deck officers if they got to know and, although we thought the Mate a 'rotten sod', we didn't tell on him. Without stopping, we sailed round and then further south to Port Dickson where we anchored in an attractive bay fringed with palm trees and a sandy beach.

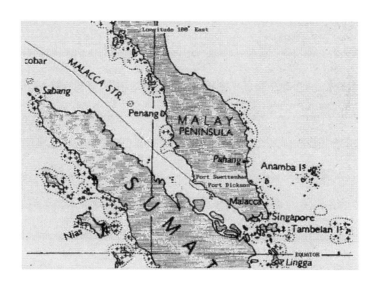

Our stay on the Malayan coast lasted about four weeks during which Dauncey and I were set on anchor watch, sharing out the whole day between us. There was little danger of the ship dragging her anchor and constant position-checking not required, there wasn't much to do and I devised my own training programme of navigation exercises. As the ship's position was hardly an unknown quantity, they were a little artificial, but I practised taking sights of the sun with the sextant at various times of the day. One of my exercises is dated 5th October in my notebook and the calculation of our position put us in Latitude 2 degrees 25 minutes North and Longitude 101 degrees 49 minutes East. On that occasion, I used the method known as Longitude by chronometer. Later, when I became a watch keeper, I preferred to use the Marcq St Hilaire or Position Line method.

When the sun rose about 6 a.m., the hills to the east had pleasant graded tones of black for a short time before the sun cleared the land horizon. During the day, the heat was tempered by a light onshore breeze and, towards sunset, the hills darkened to lovely shades of purple -. a very pleasant climate for a place so near to the Equator.

The ship was unloaded by soldiers of the Indian army, using amphibious wheeled vehicles, known as DUKWs, to take the material to the beach. About fifty yards from the shore, they ran across a coral reef, then back into deeper water, before coming into the shallows. This hazard which could have been a problem in an opposed landing, yet it was rumoured that the army did not know about its existence.

The tyre pressures of the DUKW could be adjusted from a point near the driver's seat - lowered for crossing the soft sand then increased for the harder

166

surfaces beyond – but their load capacity seemed quite small for the size of the vehicle. One afternoon, I obtained permission, with difficulty, to go ashore. From the beach, I walked up to the coast road and thumbed a lift from a jeep. It took me to the nearest village, where not one local person was to be seen and, although I thought of travelling onwards, I was under pressure to return and got a lift back. During the two months of September and October these two hours were my only shore leave.

The days passed placidly, or boringly, according to one's point of view. We had no signalling duties because the Navy had put two signalmen on board to operate a small V.H.F. portable radio, linking us with the H.Q. ship. Among other ships which came to the anchorage were the escort carrier HMS *Trumpeter* and the naval tug *Assiduous*. Chinese-style junks, with their sails made of six separate slats to allow quick changes of the sail area according to the strength of wind, were numerous.

One day, when some ducks were paddling in the sea between our ship and the shore, the 2nd Engineer fired some shots at them with his point 22 calibre rifle. Not to be outdone, the daft 2nd Mate opened fire with the 0.303 rifle kept on the bridge. The ducks survived, however, as, in a very short time, the H.Q. ship signalled an angry message telling them to stop immediately because the bullets were ricocheting over the beach.

At 0800 on Monday, 15th October, we departed from the anchorage at Port Dickson, anchored in Pinto Gedong at 1300 and sailed for Madras at 0700 the next day. After we left soundings and were in deep water, the ammunition, consisting of brass cartridge cases of all sizes from 20mm to 4inch, was dumped overboard.

On Tuesday, 23rd October, we arrived in Madras where fishermen paddled out to sea in canoes; throwing their fine-meshed nets ahead on to small shoals of sardine-sized fish. Others worked in groups from the shore, hauling in much larger nets for catches of the same kind of fish.

After three days in port, we were about to leave when two firemen appeared on the quay, dragged along between two policemen, and, as soon as they were on board, the ship left. One of the firemen staggered along the deck shouting in the direction of the bridge, "Stop the ship!" as his false teeth were lying ashore in the gutter where he had vomited. As the ship didn't stop and he swayed about, mouthing drunken obscenities, the 2nd Mate, quite unnecessarily, went over and knocked him down with a blow to the jaw.

On Thursday, 1st November, 1945, the *Ocean Trader* anchored in Bombay and, a week later, berthed in Princes Dock. The crew were paid off to be repatriated to the UK and the rest of us retained while the ship was refitted as a troop transport.

Two additional lifeboats were placed on the gun deck aft, the British crew's accommodation re-arranged to accommodate a larger lascar crew and, in the 'tween decks, where troops were to be carried, blower fans and ventilation ducts were fitted. The Indians who made the ducts arrived on board with the flat sheets of metal, hammers, metal snips and metal blocks and, with this simple equipment, they bent and efficiently shaped the metal.

For a couple of weeks, I carried out the duties of the ship's carpenter, part of which was to sound the ship daily and, to do this, I collected two sounding rods, one for oil and one for water. At the end of a cord, the jointed metal rod, marked in inches and 3 feet 6 inches long, was chalked, lowered down the sounding pipe and the measurements noted on a board.

Ballast and peak tanks were cleaned out by a gang of young Indians prior to being cement-washed so that they could take fresh water. The double bottom was about one metre deep and I had to go down to see if the work had been carried out correctly and that nothing had been left which would clog the pumps. Crawling from section to section was, to say the least, claustrophobic and I much preferred the more congenial task of making lists of deck and carpenter's stores.

In our leisure time, we went a lot to the Excelsior, Strand, Regal and Eros cinemas and, sometimes, would pass long queues of Indians waiting to see Ek Din ka Sultan, presented in their own language and meaning, as far as I can remember, One Day as King.

As he liked a gamble, the renowned race-track attracted Dauncey. He usually went on his own while I went ashore with the 4th Engineer, a Liverpudlian of amiable disposition. In the streets, there was an astonishing variety of races. In Europe, the day has long since passed when you could tell a person's religion from his or her dress, but not so in India. Among the Hindus, there was the added differentiation of the castes and it all added up to an endless stream of fascinating variety. As we knew only enough of the language to say the simplest words and phrases, we didn't get to know any of the locals and this has always been a source of regret to me. However, Malim Sahib's Hindustani, sent to me by my father, was based on bazaar 'bat' and fairly helpful for anything to do with handling the ship.

I walked for miles through the city. In the smarter end, there were fine, Indian-owned, houses which would not have looked out of place in the most fashionable part of Paris or London. Ayahs (nurse maids) pushed their charges in high prams and an air of prosperity was all around. But near the docks it was quite different and, on areas of open ground, makeshift tents sheltered the poorer women and their children while husbands and older sons were among the thousands who, lying on cane rattans, slept on the pavements at night. Beggars were numerous and I recall a typical incident, near the dock gates, when a Hindu woman with a child in her arms and a small boy at her side, pleaded "Ek anna, sahib. Ek anna," as she held out her cupped palm towards me. Touching his bare tummy, the little boy joined in, saying "Buka, sahib". It would take a hard heart to refuse, but, it was impossible to give alms to them all. (Ek =1. Buka = hungry.)

On the 10th January, 1946, we played cricket against a team from the *Samingoy,* a Liberty ship managed by the New Zealand Shipping Company. The ground was mostly reddish hard-baked earth with little grass and, in the heat of the afternoon, when the shade temperature was about 90 degrees Fahrenheit, I was pleased to be sitting in the shade of a tent, drinking cool lemonade while keeping the score.

The lascar crew, who signed on, were Hindus, apart from the Goanese stewards and cooks who were Roman Catholics and had no taboos about handling beef or pork. The first morning the new lot was on duty, they woke everyone at 7.30 a.m. and gave each of us a cup of tea. On learning that the middies had been included, the Mate, whose name I have thankfully forgotten, went into a rage and told the Chief Steward that this must not apply to us and, in the same vulgar language, told us that we were to go to the galley for our morning cup. The reason for his bile was never clear to me as we carried out our duties to his apparent satisfaction. However, the immediate effect was to lower our status in the eyes of the Goanese and Dauncey and I had to assert ourselves in the galley to re-establish a proper relationship. As we were both nearing the end of our apprenticeships, we refused to be browbeaten by the stewards and our defence against the Mate was to stay silent in the face of his incomprehensible emotional fury.

Also, as the 2nd Mate sometimes appeared clenching his fists in the hope that an unwise riposte would give him the excuse for handing out a 'mouthful of fives', I learned to live 'inside my head' which, I believe, is the usual response from those who suffer from petty persecution which cannot be directly countered. I quote a relevant motto, which I have somewhat anglicised, sculpted on the old Abbot House in Dunfermline –

'When word is thrall and thocht is free,
Keep well thy tongue I counsel thee.'

When the refitting of the ship was complete, we sailed to Rangoon to collect a detachment of Indian troops for repatriation and where, all day long, records of Indian music (gilly-gilly) were played over our public address system. Nowadays, Indian music, played on the radio, seems to have overtones of Western origin, but they had unusual, wild and captivating rhythms.

Although the topaz acted as dhobi-wallah, he was not allowed to use an electric iron - a restriction imposed on all by the Chief Engineer. When he used a non-electric iron, it was somewhat startling to see smoke rising and this came from lumps of hot charcoal inside a compartment in the iron. The topaz was also known as the 'shit-house wallah' because he also cleaned out the toilets, a task which the Hindu seamen considered to be beneath them.

At the mouth of the Rangoon river, there is a bar - a sandbank with changing depths of water over it – and, although we had an echo-sounder, the pilot requested that hand soundings be taken. I asked permission to carry out the task and, as our vessel did not have 'chains', it was necessary to hang over the side to 'swing the lead'. One of the lascars stood by to coil the line for me as I hauled it in and it was quite a thrill to give the depths in the old traditional manner, "By the mark, five!" and "A half, five!" As the silt-laden river flowed strongly, mooring at Rangoon was a bit tricky. In the distance the golden roof of the Shwe Dagon pagoda shone brightly, but no one was allowed ashore as it was said that dacoits were operating in the town area.

Some of the officers, of the hundreds of Indian troops who embarked, were British and they told me that they had been offered promotion if they would agree to staying on another year in Burma. I was rather envious of them as, although not much older than Dauncey and me, they had a status far above us and were puzzled that middies had to carry out so many trivial, stultifying duties. Similar to ourselves, who could not do much about it, they found it hard to believe that this was the training offered by Alfred Holt and Company to their future deck officers.

With the Indian soldiers on board, the ship sailed down river to the Bay of Bengal then westerly to the River Hoogli and Calcutta which, in my recollection, is about 100 miles upriver and virtually an inland port. The climate is not as good as Bombay and, at night, the mosquitoes were a nuisance. Because of the strong river current, mooring required care and special hawsers were used to hold the vessel in her berth.

The Indian troops looked very smart, in clean, jungle-green, uniforms as they marched down the gangway to the tune of 'You Are My Sunshine, My Only Sunshine'; played over our Tannoy loudspeakers. Once ashore, they formed up in orderly rows and a General, standing on a small, temporary, platform, gave a speech of welcome.

As Dauncey and I had nearly completed the sea-time necessary before sitting the 2nd Mate's examination, we had applied, sometime earlier, for permission to leave the ship. Permission was granted and, when we left, on 23rd February, 1946, our feelings can only be compared with those of prisoners obtaining release from jail! Dr Johnson said, "... being in a ship is being in a jail, with the chance of being drowned..." and, although I could not completely agree with that declaration, I know how happy we were to be free.

For the next couple of weeks, the Marine Club in Kidderpore was our home. For the first time I slept under the protection of a mosquito net, but, no matter how careful I was, a mosquito always managed to come inside the net when I retired for the night. The insect seemed to make a 'zing' as it approached the bare skin. That was the moment to pounce and bring its dangerous existence to an end.

Each day, we trekked into the town centre to see the Company's Agent and, each time, were told that there were no berths to the U.K. Now that the war was over, thousands were returning home. Sometimes we travelled in a taxi, when the driver was usually a Sikh, and, at other times, we thumbed a lift from Army vehicles which always stopped for us. One day, I got a lift on an American truck, the driver of which had just received news that he was to be in the next batch of soldiers to return to the States. No doubt because of this, he drove like a madman, shouting and singing wildly, swerving from side to side in streets packed with people so that they had to jump for their lives. I, too, was alarmed and, as soon as I saw the Maiden parade ground and the main thoroughfare of Chowringee, I asked him to stop and jumped out. According to Naval historians, there was a mutiny in the Indian Navy in February, 1946, but we saw no sign of anything untoward.

At last, Dauncey fixed up a berth in a ship going to Mombasa and he thought it would be easy enough to get home to Johannesburg from there. I had a stroke of luck too. The Dutch Blue Funnel (Nederlandsche Stoomvaart Maatschappij Oceaan) motor ship *Alcinous* came into port; from Singapore and on her way back to the Netherlands. Her passenger accommodation was filled to capacity with men, women and children who had been prisoners of the Japanese, but, Tommy Butler, her 3rd Radio Officer, was an old friend of mine from the *Empire Lancer* and there was a spare bunk in his double berth cabin. With Tommy's approval, I approached the Captain for permission to join the ship, this was readily agreed to and I signed on as supernumerary at a shilling a month. The Captain and officers of the *Alcinous* were first-class; true gentlemen in the best sense of the word and they greatly restored my morale. I collected my gear from the Marine Club; my sea-chest, an Indian carpet I had purchased for my parents and a couple of canvas sea bags. At the parting of the ways, Dauncey and I, who had shared and suffered the same unhappy experience, were sorry to separate. With the benefit of hindsight, it has to be admitted that we were too obedient and docile under deliberate harassment, but I think that response was typical of our generation.

Earlier on her voyage, the *Alcinous* had been in a part of Indonesia occupied by US forces who, as soon as peace was declared, had started getting rid of equipment and stores considered not worth taking back to the States. The crew had collected, or maybe bartered for unused items such as camp beds, boots, shirts, vests and trousers. Their lockers were full of the stuff and I was given enough khaki shirts to last me for years.

We sailed on 26th March and, although the civilians who had been prisoners in Japanese hands did not talk much about their experiences, I gleaned a few things from them. They had been forced to bow from the waist on meeting a Japanese soldier. If they looked up at the sky when an allied plane flew overhead they were knocked to the ground. They had been taken out of the camp to clean out roadside sewers with Malay villagers deliberately lined up so as to increase the 'loss of face'. When freed, they had been warned about the dangers of over-eating although one of them, Pieter, who had some connection with the radio station at Hilversum, was very overweight. He and I used to meet on the aft gun deck each morning for some physical exercises such as skipping and press-ups and, another of my divertissements was playing Monopoly with Dutch children, after first learning the numbers in Dutch.

The food on board was Indonesian in style and I liked Nasi Goreng and Pilau of chicken. Old-fashioned manners prevailed. On entering the saloon one said, "Smakelijk eten" (Enjoy your meal) and, on leaving, "Wel bekomen" (May you benefit from the meal).

On the 8th April, we arrived at Karachi, a town which has not remained in my memory as having any outstanding features. The area seemed to be very dry and camels were in use for transport. At the spacious harbour, a Sunderland flying boat touched down, creating graceful bow waves as she taxied along.

On 2nd May 1946, just over five weeks after leaving Calcutta, we reached Antwerp where there was a lot of war damage. The main railway station was in a terrible state, the roof having collapsed into a heap of twisted ironwork and broken concrete. Some of us went ashore in a group and, as we didn't have any small change for the tram, the conductor was delighted to accept a cigarette from each of us. Not being a smoker, I carried no cigarettes, but someone gave him one for my fare.

On 6th May, a short run took the ship to Rotterdam where the bomb-devastated centre was clear of any buildings, apart from a line of wooden huts, and this street was later rebuilt as the Lijnbaan. At a nearby funfair, there were merry-go-rounds and cheerful music coming from loudspeakers fixed on lampposts. Bicycles, without rubber tyres and running across cobbles, could be heard a long way off. Some cyclists had only the bare metal rims while others had fastened small blocks of wood to the circumference of the wheels.

When friends and relatives of the Dutch crew came on board, we heard stories of the German occupation such as that of the Captain's teenage son who had spent months hiding in the loft of his home to avoid being taken away to work in Germany.

The British section of the crew bundled up their gear and set off in a bus for the ferry at Hoek van Holland. We landed in Harwich on 8th May 1946 and the voyage was over at last.

MINED COASTS

Ian M. Malcolm

FOREWORD

Although up to a million mines were laid during WWII, and were a constant menace to vessels sailing in coastal waters, the general public has never been aware of the massive toll they took on both ships and lives.

From British Vessels Lost at Sea 1939-45, published by HMSO in 1947, the author has extracted those that were mined and added as much additional information as he could find about each incident, including those where the ship was damaged, but not sunk.

Regrettably, in all too many cases, the information is scanty indeed, and, as that from sources sometimes differs, it is inevitable that inaccuracies will occur. Please, too, be aware that DEMS gunners, both Maritime Regiment and Royal Navy, served on British merchant ships, as did lascars, Chinese, and other foreign seamen. Although DEMS gunners signed ships' articles as deckhands, their names are not recorded on the Tower Hill Memorial, as they were military and not Merchant Navy personnel.

A Fishing Vessel section is included.

Thanks go to Mr Brian Watson/Benjidog for granting permission to use information contained in his Tower Hill Memorial website.

MERCHANT SHIPS SUNK AND DAMAGED BY MINES DURING WWII

1939

September 1939

GOODWOOD. Steamship. 10th. Sunk one mile SE of Flamborough Head, by a mine laid by U.15 (Kptlt. Heinz Buchholz). One man died. Captain H.S. Hewson and 22 crew members picked up by a fishing boat and landed at Bridlington.

MAGDAPUR. Steamship.10th. At 5.25pm, struck a mine laid by U.13 (Kptlt. Karl Daublebsky von Eichhain) and sank within minutes in position 52°11′N 1°43′E, off Orford Ness. Six died. Captain A.G. Dixon and 74 crew members rescued by the Aldeburgh Lifeboat and a coaster.

CITY OF PARIS. Steamship. 10th. In position 52°14′N 1°43′E, 3.5 miles ENE of Aldeburgh, when damaged by a mine laid by U.13 two days previously. One died and 138 survived. Towed to Tilbury and returned to service a month later.

BRAMDEN. Steamship. 16th. Sunk on a British minefield, in position 51°22′N 02°31′E. Three died.

October 1939

MARWARRI. Steamship. 5th. In the Bristol Channel, heading for Newport, Mon., when damaged by a mine laid by U.32 (Kptlt. Paul Büchel) on 17 September. Two died - Second Engineer R. Birlison and Quartermaster F. Lofthouse - and 29 survived. Beached in Mumbles Bay, repaired in Newport and returned to service in February 1941.

LOCHGOIL. Motor Vessel. 6th. In position 51°24′N 04°00′W in the Bristol Channel, bound for Newport, Mon. from Vancouver, when damaged by a mine laid by U.32 (see *Marwarri*). No information on casualties. Beached in Mumbles Bay, rebuilt as the CAM ship *Empire Rowan* and returned to service in 1940.

ORSA. Steamship. 21st. Shortly after 4am, struck a mine laid on 5 September by U.15 and sank in position 53°54′N 0°07′E, about 15 miles 150° from Flamborough Head. Sixteen died. Several survivors and four bodies, including that of Captain A. Simpson, were picked up by HMS *Woolston* and landed at Rosyth.

WHITEMANTLE. Steamship. 22nd. Sunk by a mine when 5 to 6 miles east of Withernsea Light, Yorkshire. All 14 crew died.

November 1939

CARMARTHEN COAST. Steamship. 9th. At 7.20am, in position 54°51′N 1°16′W, off Seaham Harbour, County Durham, when sunk by a mine laid by U.24 (Kptlt. Harald Jeppener-Haltenhoff). Two died, 6 injured, and the Master and 14 crew rescued by the Seaham Lifeboat.

PONZANO. Motor Vessel. 13th. Off North Foreland when sunk by a mine in position 51°29′N 1°25′E. All crew rescued by 2 Norwegian fishing boats.

MATRA. Steamship. 13th. In Convoy HXF.7, and bound for London from Baltimore, when struck by a mine one mile east of the Tongue Light Vessel. Beached at Shingles Patch, but declared a total loss. Sixteen died. (The *Matra* and *Ponzano* were struck by magnetic mines laid in the Thames Estuary by four German destroyers.)

SIRDHANA. Steamship. 13th. Leaving Singapore, and about three miles off the port, when she hit a mine which had broken loose from the naval defence field, and sank. Among her many passengers, were 137 Chinese deportees who had to be released from a forward hold, but were later recaptured. Twenty Asiatic deck passengers died.

WOODTOWN. Steamship. 15th. Off Margate, and ¼ mile NE of NE Spit Buoy when she struck a mine and sank within a minute. Eight died and 5 rescued.

BLACKHILL. Steamship. 18th. Sunk 145° 7½ cables from the Longsand Head buoy, in the Thames Estuary. One died and survivors rescued by the destroyer HMS *Gipsy*. (Three days later, HMS *Gipsy* was herself sunk by a mine off Harwich. Thirty died and 116 rescued.)

JAMES J. MAGUIRE. Motor Vessel/Tanker. 18th. Bound for North America in Convoy OA.37 when damaged by a mine off Gravesend, in position 51°46′N 01°40′E, and towed to Tilbury for repair. No information on casualties. Later renamed *Stanvac Nairobi* and broken up in Japan in 1962.

TORCHBEARER. Steamship. 19th. Sunk 25° 2 nautical miles NNE of the Shipwash Light Vessel, off Harwich. Four died and 8 rescued by HMS *Greyhound*.

GERALDUS. Steamship. 21st. Sunk 3 nautical miles WNW from the Sunk Light Vessel in the Thames Estuary. Survivors rescued by HMS *Wivern*.

LOWLAND. Steamship. 22nd. Sunk 2 miles ENE of NE Gunfleet Buoy, off Clacton-on-Sea, Essex. Nine died and remaining 3 rescued by HMT *Myrtle*.

HOOKWOOD. Steamship. 23rd. Sunk 3½ nautical miles ENE of the Tongue Light Vessel, near Margate. John Duthie, Fireman, and James Shearer, Donkeyman, died and remaining 15 rescued by HMS *Bittern*.

DAVISIAN. Steamship. 23rd. Damaged off the Nore Light Vessel.

MANGALORE. Steamship. 24th. Left Hull the previous day and at anchor in the Hawke Roads, Spurn, when struck by a drifting mine at 7.30am, broke in two, abandoned, and sank. A pilot boat took off the lascar crew while the remainder were rescued by the Spurn Lifeboat and landed at Grimsby. All 77 survived.

SUSSEX. Motor Vessel. 25th. Outward bound in ballast when damaged by a mine off Southend. Returned to London for repairs.

RUBISLAW. Steamship. 28th. Sunk 1 to 1½ miles nautical miles ENE of the Tongue Light Vessel. Thirteen died.

IONIAN. Steamship. 29th. In Convoy FN.43 (Thames to Firth of Forth), when, at 1.30am, struck by a mine laid by U.20 (Kptlt. Karl-Heinz Moehle) on the 21st. Abandoned, and all 37, including Captain W. Smith, picked up by HMS *Hastings* which landed them at South Shields. Sank in approximate position 52°45′N 01°56′E.

SHEAF CREST. Steamship. 30th. Sunk in position 51°32′N 01°26′E, off Margate. Captain H.L. Banks died and remaining 29 rescued; 12 by the Polish destroyer ORP *Blyskawica*.

December 1939

DALRYAN. Steamship. 1st. Sunk 2 to 2½ nautical miles SW of the Tongue Light Vessel, in approximate position 51°31′N 1°19′E.

SAN CALISTO. Motor Vessel/Tanker 2nd. Bound for Houston, and on passage from Hull to Southend to join a convoy, when struck by two mines as she altered course to pass the Tongue Light Vessel shortly after noon, and sank. Six died and 36, including 8 seriously injured, landed at Margate. Captain A.R. Hicks was one of the injured.

MEREL. Steamship. 8th. Sunk west of the Gull Light Vessel, off Ramsgate. Sixteen died and 2 survived.

COREA. Steamship. 8th. Sunk 2½ miles NE ½ mile N of Cromer Light. Eight died and the remaining 7 rescued by the Cromer Lifeboat, *H.F. Bailey III*.

WILLOWPOOL. Steamship. 10th. Bound for Middlesbrough, from Bône, Algeria, with a cargo of iron ore, when she struck a mine laid by U.20 (Kptlt. Karl-Heinz) on 21 November, and sank in position 52°53′N 1°51′E, about 3 miles E of Newarp Light Vessel. All 36 picked up by the Gorleston Lifeboat.

MARWICK HEAD. Steamship. 12th. At 8.15am, struck a mine laid a week earlier by U.59 (Oblt. Harald Jürst), and sank ½ mile south of North Caister Buoy, Caister-on-Sea, Norfolk. Five died and 5, including Captain J.J. Thain, landed at Great Yarmouth.

KING EGBERT. Motor Vessel. 12th. Sailed in Convoy FS.53 which left the Tyne on the 11th. Struck a mine and sank 4 miles of Happisburgh Light Vessel, Norfolk. One died and 32 survived.

INVERLANE. Motor Vessel/Tanker. 14th. Bound for Invergordon from Abadan when mined in the North Sea in position 55°05′N 01°07′W. Drifted ashore at Seaburn in Northumbria where she burned for 5 days. Four crew died and many injured. In 1944, her fore section was filled with 3000 tons of rubble and stone before it was towed to Burra Sound in Orkney and sunk as a blockship.

ATHELTEMPLAR. Motor Vessel/Tanker. 14th. In Convoy FN.53 (Thames to Firth of Forth), and off the River Tyne, when damaged by a mine laid by German destroyers. Two died – Patrick Connelly, AB, and George Alfred Getty, Sailor. Escorted by destroyers *HMS Kelly* and HMS *Mohawk*, towed to the Tyne by tugs *Joffre*, *Langton*, *Great Emperor* and *George V*. Repaired and returned to service in April 1940. *HMS *Kelly* also struck a mine and was towed to the Tyne for repairs.

AMBLE. Steamship. 16th. Damaged off Sunderland, Co. Durham, and crew rescued by HMS *Wallace*. Came ashore between Sunderland and Whitburn and refloated on the 25th. Declared a total loss and scrapped.

CITY OF KOBE. Steamship. 19th. In Convoy FS.56 (Firth of Forth to Thames) when, at 3.35am, she struck a mine, laid by U.60 (Kptlt.Georg Schewe) on the 15th, and sank off the coast of Suffolk, in position 52°35′N 01°59′E. One died. Thirty picked up by the MS trawler HMS *Tumby* (Skipper J.W. Greengrass) and the coasters *Corinia* and *Faxfleet*.

DOSINIA. Motor Vessel/Tanker. 21st. In Convoy FN.57 when damaged by a mine, near Haisborough Light, off Cromer in Norfolk. Escorted by sloop HMS *Weston*, towed to Hull for repair. (See under October 1940.)

GRYFEVALE. Steamship. 22nd. Bound for Leith, from Alexandra, and off Newcastle at 1.40pm when damaged by a mine laid by U.61 (Oblt. Jürgen Oesten). Towed to the Tyne and beached. No casualties.

STANHOLME. Steamship. 25th. On passage from Cardiff to London when she struck a mine laid by U.33 (Kptlt. Hans-Wilhelm von Dresky) on 9 November, and sank in position 51°20′N 3°39′W – off Foreland Point in the Bristol Channel. Thirteen died while the remaining 12 were picked up the *Liv* (Nor.) and landed at Cardiff.

ADELLEN. Motor Vessel/Tanker..26th. Requisitioned into the Royal Fleet Auxiliary. Damaged when in position 51°30′N 01°43′E, northeast of North Foreland. Arrived Gravesend the next day and repaired.

SAN DELFINO. Motor Vessel/Tanker. 28th. Damaged when off Holme Ridge Buoy in the Humber Estuary. Beached, but later refloated and repaired.

BOX HILL. Steamship. 31st. Bound for Hull from Saint John, New Brunswick, when she struck a mine, broke in two and sank within minutes, 9 nautical miles from the Humber Light Vessel, in position 53°32′N 00°24′E. Twenty died and 12 survived.

1940

January 1940

CITY OF MARSEILLES. Steamship. 6th. From Calcutta and in the Tay estuary with a pilot on board to take her into Dundee, when she struck a mine laid by U.13 (Oberleutnant zur See Wolfgang Lüth) on 12th December 1939. One lascar died, and the remaining 163 crew, including an injured lascar, picked up by the pilot cutter, an RAF launch, the Broughty Ferry lifeboat *Mona*, and landed at Broughty Ferry. Towed into Dundee the next day and, after temporary repairs were made, taken to the Clyde for repair. Returned to service in April.

CEDRINGTON COURT. Steamship. 7th. Sailed from Buenos Aires on 22 November, 1939 and in Convoy SL.13 which left Freetown on 18 December. Detached from Convoy when she struck a mine, laid by a German destroyer, on 7 January, 1940 and sank in position 51°23′N 1°35′E, 2 miles north-east of North Goodwin Light Vessel. All 34 survived.

TOWNELEY. Steamship. 7th. Sunk 1 mile ENE of NE Spit Buoy, near Margate. All rescued by the Margate Lifeboat.

DUNBAR CASTLE. Motor Vessel. 9th. Bound for Beira, Mozambique, left Southend in Convoy OA.69. Struck a magnetic mine when off Ramsgate and sank in about 30 minutes, in position 51°23′N 01°34′E. As the Master was mortally wounded, Mr H.H. Robinson took charge and organised the abandonment of the ship. One passenger and 8 crew died, including Captain H.A. Causton. One hundred and forty-two crew and 47 passengers picked up from the lifeboats by the trawler *Calvi* and other small vessels.

EL OSO. Steamship/Tanker. 11th. In Convoy HX.14 which left Halifax, Nova Scotia on 29 December 1939. At 11am, struck a mine laid on the 6th by U.30 (Kptlt. Fritz-Julius Lemp) and sank 6 miles 280° from the Bar Light Vessel, Liverpool, in position 53°32′N 3°25′W. Four died, including 1 of the 8 wounded and hospitalised. Thirty-three, including the wounded, picked up by HMS *Walker* (LtCdr. A.A. Tait, RN).

GRANTA. Steamship. 12th. On passage from London to Blyth when sunk off the Wash, in position 53°13′N 1°21′E. Ten died.

KILDALE. Steamship. 15th. Damaged when 2 miles East of South of the Shiphead Buoy, off the Naze. 1st Mate David Horn died.

INVERDARGLE. Motor Vessel/Tanker. 16th. Bound for Avonmouth and laden with aviation spirit from Trinidad, when, at 4.19pm, she struck a mine laid by U.33 (Kptlt. Hans-Wilhelm von Dresky) on 9 November 1939 and sank in the Bristol Channel, in position 51°16′N 03°43′W. All 44 died.

GRACIA. Steamship. 16th. In Convoy OB.72 which sailed that day from Liverpool. When about five miles WSW of the Bar Light Vessel, struck a mine laid by U.30 (Kptlt. Fritz-Julius Lemp). Beached, salvaged and repaired. Returned to service in February, 1941. No casualties.

CAIRNROSS. Steamship. 17th. Bound for Saint John, New Brunswick, when struck by a mine laid on the 6th by U.30 (Kptlt. Fritz-Julius Lemp), and sank 7 miles 276° from the Bar Light Vessel, Liverpool, in position 53°32′N 3°27′W. All 48 rescued by HMS *Mackay* (Cdr. G.H. Stokes) and landed at Liverpool.

CARONI RIVER. Motor Vessel/Tanker. 20th. Carrying out paravane trials and armament tests in Falmouth Bay when struck by a mine laid by U.34 (Kptlt. Wilhelm Rollmann) the previous day, and sank in position 50°06′N 5°01′W. All 55 picked up by the Falmouth Lifeboat and a naval cutter, and landed at Falmouth.

FERRYHILL. Steamship. 21st. At 2pm, enroute from Blyth to Aberdeen when sunk 5° 1½ miles from St Mary's Light Vessel, off Blyth. Nine died and the only 2 survivors – 1st Mate J.M. Ovenston and the 2nd Engineer – were landed at North Shields and taken to Preston Hospital.

PROTESILAUS. Steamship. 21st. At about 9.30am, struck a mine when in position 51°31′N 4°04′W, off the Mumbles Lighthouse in the Bristol Channel. Taken in tow, but grounded and became a total loss. Crew taken to Swansea. No casualties.

ESTON. Steamship. 28th. On passage from Hull to Blyth, and a straggler from Convoy FN.81, when she struck a mine laid on 20 December 1939 by U.22 (Kptlt. Karl-Heinrich Jenisch) and sank off Blyth, in position 55°03′N 1°24′W. All 18 died.

February 1940

MUNSTER. Motor Vessel. 7th. At about 6am, struck a mine laid on 6 January by U.30 (Kptlt. Fritz-Julius Lemp) and sank in the Queens Channel,

Liverpool, in position 53°36′N 3°24′W. All 235 picked up the coaster *Ringwall*, and landed a Liverpool where 20 injured were taken to hospital.

CHAGRES. Steamship. 9th. At 1.05am, struck a mine laid on 6 January by U.30 and sank 5½ miles 270° from the Bar Light Vessel, Liverpool. Two died, Fireman/Trimmer Hugh Gribbin and Bosun Arthur Reilly, and the remaining 62 picked up by the ASW trawler HMS *Loch Monteith* (LtCdr. F.R. Pope), and landed at Liverpool.

AGNES ELLEN. Steamship. 9th. Left Holyhead for Workington, but not seen again. All 7 died. No further details.

BRITISH TRIUMPH. Motor Vessel/Tanker. 13th. Bound for Aruba, from Hull, and in Convoy FS.93, when she struck a mine off Cromer. After the *British Officer* attempted to tow her, the tug *Irishman* was sent for, but she sank in position 53°06′N 1°25′E before the tug arrived. Four died and the remaining 43 rescued by the *British Officer* and HMS *Stork*.

BARON AILSA. Steamship. 17th. Left Algiers on 31 January, bound for the Tyne with a cargo of iron ore. Sailed in a convoy to Gibraltar where she joined Convoy HG.18F, bound for the UK. Subsequently joined Convoy FN.96 which left Southend-on-Sea on the 16th. At 6.25am the following day, sank in about 6 minutes in shallow water, in position 53°17′4″N 01°11′30″E. Fireman A. Abdi and Captain G.R. Logan died, the latter from a heart attack when he jumped from the ship. Thirty-six picked by the ASW trawler HMS *Beech* (Skipper W. McRuvie, RNR) which landed them at Grimsby at 3.15pm.

ROYAL ARCHER. Steamship. 24th. Enroute from London to Leith, and dispersed from Convoy FN.100, when she struck a mine laid by U.21 (Kptlt. Fritz Frauenheim) on 4 November 1939 and sank about 15 miles west of May Island, in the Firth of Forth, in position 56°06′N 2°55′W. All 28 picked up by HMS *Weston* (LtCdr. S.C. Tuke, RN) and landed at Rosyth.

CLAN MORRISON. Steamship. 24th. Bound for Blyth from Southampton, and in Convoy FN.102, when sunk off Cromer, in position 53°07′N 01°22′E. One died and 31 picked up by the minesweeping trawler HMS *Nogi*.

JEVINGTON COURT. Steamship. 24th. In Convoy FS.103 which left the Tyne on 23 February, 1940, bound for Southend. Struck a mine the next day when 8¼ miles 161° from *Cromer Knoll Light Vessel*, in position 53°08′N 01°22′E. All picked up by the minesweeper HMS *Dunoon* (LtCdr. H.A. Barclay) which was herself mined on 30th April while sweeping off Great

Yarmouth and sank in position 52°45′N 2°23′E. Twenty-six died and 47 rescued.

March 1940

ALBANO. Steamship. 2nd. Bound for Bergen from Hull when sunk off Coquet Island, Northumbria, in position 55°15′17″N 01°22′21″W. Nine died. Survivors rescued by the armed trawler *Stella Carino* and HMS *Wallace*.

CATO. Steamship. 3rd. Bound for Bristol from Dublin, when struck by a mine laid by U.29 (Kptlt. (Otto Schuhart) the previous day. Sank 2½ miles west of Nash Point in the Bristol Channel, in position 51°24′N 3°33′W. Thirteen died, including Captain R. Martin, and the remaining 2 picked up by the MS trawler HMS *Akita* (Chief Skipper W.A. Watson, DSC, RNR.

CHARLES F MEYER. Motor Vessel/Tanker. 4th. Damaged when off Dungeness in position 50°28′N 00°16′E. Towed to Southampton by the destroyer HMS *Boadicea*, escorted by the destroyer HMS *Keith*. Repaired, but no further details.

COUNSELLOR. Steamship. 8th. Bound for Liverpool from New Orleans, Commodore ship of Convoy HX.22 which sailed from Halifax on 22 February. Struck a mine laid by U.30 (Kptlt. Fritz-Julius Lemp) on 6 January and sank the next day 6 miles 280° from the Liverpool Bar Light Vessel, in position 53°38′N 3°23′W. All 78 picked up by HMS *Walpole* (LtCdr. H.G. Bowerman, RN) and landed at Liverpool.

CHEVYCHASE. Steamship. 9th. Bound for London from Blyth when sunk off Great Yarmouth in position 53°18′N 1°13′E. All 21 picked up by the MS trawler HMS *Monimia* (Skipper J. Watt, RNR).

GARDENIA. Steamship. 12th. Bound for Middlesbrough from Casablanca when sunk off Cromer in position 53°04′N 1°33′E. All 33 picked up by the ASW Trawler HMS *Viviana* (Skipper G.L. Olsen, RNR).

MELROSE. Steamship. 15th. Sunk off the Belgian coast in position 51°21′N 2°13′E. Five died and remaining 18 rescued.

April 1940

HAWNBY. Steamship. 20th. On passage from the Tyne to Gibraltar when sunk off the coast of Kent, in position 51°32′N 01°13′E. All 39 rescued by *MTB 4*.

MERSEY. Steamship. 20th. Sank in about 3 minutes off the coast of Kent, in position 51°17′N 1°28′E. Fourteen died and as J.A. Vickers, her 2nd Mate, died in hospital, only 5 survived.

LOLWORTH. Steamship. 23rd. Bound for the Tyne from Portsmouth, sunk off Ramsgate in position 51°22′N 1°26E. Chief Engineer J.O. Huntley and 2nd Mate R. Wickman died, and the remaining 22, including 8 injured, rescued.

STOKESLEY. Steamship. 24th. Bound for London from Antwerp, sunk in the Thames Estuary in position 51°32′N 1°16′E. Fifteen died.

RYDAL FORCE. Steamship. 24th. Sunk 400 yards south of the Gull Light Vessel, in the Thames Estuary. Eleven died and the remaining 2 rescued by the minesweeping trawler, *Sarah Hyde*.

MARGAM ABBEY. Steamship. 25th. Sunk due north, 9 cables from East Knob Buoy in the Thames Estuary. None died.

SEMINOLE. Motor Vessel/Tanker. 25th. Damaged in the Bristol Channel, in position 51°29′N 04°07′W.

CREE. Steamship. 26th. In Convoy FS.154 which sailed from the Tyne on the 24th, bound for Southend and escorted by the destroyers HMS *Westminster* and HMS *Wolsey*. Damaged in position 53°53′N 02°19′E by a mine laid by a German mine sweeper.

May 1940

SAN TIBURCIO. Steamship. 4th. Bound for Invergordon from Scapa Flow when she struck a mine at 8.10pm, in position 57°46′N 03°45′W. Broke in two and sank. All 40 picked up by the ASW trawler HMS *Leicester City* (T/Lt. A.R. Cornish) and landed at Invergordon.

BRIGHTON. Steamship. 6th. Approaching Dunkirk from Immingham when sunk in position 51°03′N 02°09′E. All 34 rescued.

HENRY WOODALL. Steamship. 10th. Bound for Seaham from Yarmouth when sunk 3 nautical miles east of Withernsea. Seven died and the remaining 7 rescued by the Estonian ship *Viiu*.

ROEK. Steamship. 12th. Sunk in the Nieuwe Waterweg, Rotterdam, in position 51°54′N 4°21′E. All 51 rescued.
FIRTH FISHER. Steamship. 21st. Bound for Boulogne from Fowey when sunk ½ mile east of Boulogne Pier. Seven died and the remaining 4 rescued by the *Sparta*.

CARARE. Steamship. 28th. Sunk by a magnetic mine in the Bristol Channel, in position 51°18′N 03°44′W. Seven crew and 3 passengers died. Eighty-six rescued by the armed yacht *Rhodora* and 2 by the ASW trawler *Cambridgeshire*.

MONA'S QUEEN. Steamship. 29th. Engaged in the Dunkirk Evacuation, sank in about 2 minutes outside Dunkirk harbour at 5.30am. Twenty-four died, including 14 in the engine room. Captain A. Holkham and 31 others were picked up by destroyers.

June 1940

DORIS. Sailing Barge. 1st. Sunk 3 miles off Dunkirk. No further details.

DUCHESS and LADY ROSEBERY. Sailing Barges. 1st. Sunk 3 miles off Dunkirk when alongside a tug which was blown up by a mine. All crew of the *Duchess* were rescued, but John Edward Atkins, aged 15, an Ordinary Seaman on the *Lady Rosebery*, died.

SWEEP II. Sludge Vessel. 5th. Sunk 1.4 miles 138° from Landguard Point, Felixstowe. G.E. French, her Mate, died.

CAPABLE. Motor Vessel. 5th. Sunk 2.8 miles 131° from Horse Sand Fort in the Solent. All 7 died.

HARCALO. Steamship. 6th. Sunk near the Goodwin Knoll, in position 51°19′N 01°32′E. Three firemen died.

HARDINGHAM. Steamship. 8th. Bound for Villa Constitucion, from Blyth, when sunk in the English Channel, in position 51°34′N 01°37′E. Firemen S.C. Sutherland and W. Sutherland died.

EMPIRE COMMERCE. Steamship. 9th. Off Margate when severely damaged. Towed to Mucking Sands and beached. Cargo of wood pulp discharged, but declared a total loss. Canadian Firemen J.P. Butler and G. O'Neill died.

SAINT RONAIG. Motor Vessel. 11th. Sunk 132° 1 mile from West Breakwater Light, Newhaven. Four died and 4 rescued.

BARON SALTOUN. Steamship. 12th. Bound for Cherbourg from Hull when sunk in Cherbourg Roads. 3rd Engineer J. Bradley died.

BRITISH INVENTOR. Steamship/Tanker. 13th. Bound for Abadan, when struck by a mine off St Alban's Head, Dorset. Broke in two when beached and the after section subsequently towed to Portland.

NIAGARA. Steamship. 19th. Shortly after leaving Auckland, New Zealand, on her regular run to Suva and Vancouver, off Bream Head, Whangarei, when sunk, in position 35°53′S 174°54′E, by a mine laid by the German auxiliary cruiser *Orion*. All 203 crew and 146 passengers were picked up from the ship's 18 lifeboats by the coastal vessel, *Kapiti*, and another ship, and returned to Auckland in the evening.

July 1940

COQUET MOUTH. Dredger. 4th. Sunk just off the Pan Bush Rocks by a parachute mine dropped by a German bomber, when leaving Amble in Northumberland. Three died.

BELLEROCK. Steamship. 15th. Bound for Corunna, from Barry, sunk in the Bristol Channel, in position 51°20′N 03°47′W. All 17 died.

TROUTPOOL. Steamship. 20th. Bound for Glasgow from Rosaria, struck by 2 mines when leaving Belfast Lough. Eleven died and the wreck blown up, in position 54°40′N 05°40′W, because it was a hazard to shipping.

THE LADY MOSTYN. Motor Vessel. 23rd. Sunk when 1½ miles 79° from the Formby Light Vessel in the estuary of the River Mersey. All 7 died.

HAYTOR. Steamship. 26th. On passage from London to Blyth when sunk in position 51°47′N 01°48′E, off Frinton-on-Sea, Essex. Second Engineer C.D.Simpson died.

DURDHAM. Sand Dredger. 27th. Sunk 1.54 miles 140.5° from Lavernock Point, in the Bristol Channel, in position 51°23'18"N 3°08'48". Seven died.

SALVESTRIA. Steamship/Tanker. 27th. Sunk 2.8 miles 42° from the Inchkeith Light House, in the Firth of Forth. Ten died.

OUSEBRIDGE. Steamship. 29th. Bound for Manchester from Pepel, sunk in the Queen's Channel, River Mersey, 800 feet from Q5 Red Buoy on a bearing of 005°. W. Keating, AB, and G.T. Simpson, Sailor, died.

MOIDART. Steamship. 29th. On passage from London to Newcastle when sunk off Harwich, in position 51°59'N 01°49'E. Eleven died.

CLAN MONROE. Steamship. 29th. Bound for the Tees from Cochin, Kerala, India, when she struck a mine off Harwich, in position 51°52'N 01°48'E. Beached in Hollesley Bay and declared a total loss. Thirteen died.

August 1940

CITY OF CANBERRA. Steamship. 1st. Damaged when in position 52°06'N 01°52'E and, assisted by the sloop HMS *Sheldrake*, towed to Hollesley Bay, Suffolk. It may be as a result of this that Captain R.F. Henry died in 1947.

WYCHWOOD. Steamship/Collier. 3rd. On passage from Blyth to London when sunk NE of Felixstowe in position 52°00'N 1°48'E. All 22 rescued by HMS *Mallard*.

BRIXTON. Steamship. 15th. Sunk off Orford Ness in position 52°06'N 1°49'E. All rescued.

CITY OF BIRMINGHAM. Steamship. 16th. Approaching Hull when sunk off Spurn Head in position 53°32'26"N 0°15'30"E. All 80 rescued.

MEATH. Steamship. 16th. Sunk by an acoustic mine 6 to 7 cables NE of Breakwater Light. Holyhead, Anglesey. All 20 crew and 8 cattle drovers, including 3 wounded, rescued.

September 1940

GOTHIC. Steamship/Tanker. 12th. Sunk 130° 7500 yards from Spurn Point. Twelve died and 12 rescued.

SHELBRIT I. Motor Vessel/Tanker. 19th. Sunk in the Moray Firth, in position 57°39′N 3°56′W. All 21 died.

October 1940

LADY OF THE ISLES. Cable ship. 3rd. Sunk about 3 miles east of St Anthony Point, near Falmouth. Sixteen died.
ADAPTITY. Steamship. 5th. Struck a mine laid by a German torpedo boat on 30 September and sank off Clacton-on-Sea, in position 51°′44′N 01°17′E. Four died.

JERSEY QUEEN. Steamship. 6th. On passage from Blyth to Plymouth when sunk 160° 1½ miles off St Anthony Point, Falmouth. 1st Mate David Carson and Ordinary Seaman Tom Daw died.

TILL. Motor Vessel. 10th. Damaged off the Kent coast, in position 51°36′N 01°12′E.
THYRA II. Steamship. 11th. Damaged off East Barrow Light Vessel, Thames Estuary.

CARGO FLEET NO.2. Hopper Barge.13th. Damaged 1 cable W of the Datum Buoy, off the mouth of the River Tees and declared a total loss.

RECULVER. 14th. Trinity House Vessel. Sunk 195° 1.2 miles from Spurn Point. All 31 rescued.

ACTIVITY. Motor Vessel. 16th. Damaged in position 51°31′N 00°55′E.

ETHYLENE. Steamship. 17th. Damaged ¼ mile NNE of East Oaze Light Buoy.

GEORGE BALFOUR. Steamship. 17th. Damaged 12900 yards 230° from Aldeburgh Light Vessel.

FRANKRIG. Steamship. 17th. Sunk south of Aldeburgh, in position 52°03′N 1°48′E. Nineteen rescued by HMS *Holderness*.

ARIDITY. Motor Vessel. 19th. Sunk 40 yards NE of the Oaze Light Vessel, in the Thames Estuary.

HOUSTON CITY. Steamship. 21st. Arriving from Rosario with a cargo of grain when she struck a mine northeast of the East Oaze Light Vessel, in the

Thames Estuary. Beached and declared a total loss when salvage attempts failed.

DOSINIA. Motor Vessel/Tanker. 26th. Sunk near Q1 Black Buoy, Queens Channel, River Mersey. All rescued.

SUAVITY. Motor Vessel. 27th. Sunk off Hartlepool in position 54°44′N 1°05′W. All rescued.

DEVONIA. Steamship. 28th. Sunk in the Bristol Channel, off Newport, Mon., in position 51°23′N 3°15′W. Three died. One rescued.

SHEAF FIELD. Steamship. 28th. Sunk 2 miles SW of the Sunk Light Vessel, Thames Estuary. All 26 rescued.

SAGACITY. Steamship. 28th. Sunk 148° 4000 yards from Spurn Main Light. All rescued.

WYTHBURN Steamship. 28th. Sunk in the Bristol Channel, off Newport, Mon., in position 51°22′N 3°15′W. Five died.

G.W. HUMPHREYS. Sludge Carrier. 29th. Sunk in the East Oaze Deep, in the Thames Estuary near Leysdown-on-Sea. Seven died.

November 1940

LEA and DEANBROOK. Tugs. 2nd. Both sunk when tied up at Tilbury. Six died on the *Lea* and all died on the *Deanbrook*. Both tugs were subsequently raised and scrapped.

CAIRGORM. Motor Vessel. 3rd. Damaged in the Bristol Channel.

HAIG ROSE. Steamship. 5th. Sunk in the Bristol Channel when bound for Plymouth from Barry. All 13 died.

BEAL. Motor Vessel. 9th. Damaged off the River Tees, and towed to Middlesbrough.

HERLAND. Steamship. 7th. Sunk 2 cables 146° from the Nore Light Vessel. Eighteen died.

CAMBRIDGE. Steamship. 7th. Bound for Sydney and Brisbane, from Melbourne, when, at 11pm, she struck a mine and sank 2½ miles SE of

Wilson's Promontory. The only casualty was the carpenter, Mr J. Kinnear, who returned to his cabin to retrieve money. The other 55 were picked up from lifeboats by HMAS *Orara* and landed at Port Welshpool.

BALTRADER. Steamship. 9th. Sunk in the North Sea, in position 51°41′N 01°18′E. Two died, F.H. Rickus, AB and G.H.Smith, AB.

SKARV. Steamship. 11th. Sunk in the Bristol Channel. Five died.

GRIT. Motor Vessel. 11th. Damaged off Margate, Kent.

ARGUS. Trinity House Vessel. 12th. Sunk 3 cables 199°.from South Oaze Buoy. Thirty-four died. Sole survivor was eighteen-year-old Quartermaster Archie Smith.

BRITISH PRESTIGE. Motor Vessel/Tanker. 13th. Damaged when off the Humber boom. It may be as a result of this that Chief Engineer T. Helme died in 1946.

LEON MARTIN. Steamship. 13th. On passage from Swansea to Hamble when sunk 202° 5.2 cables from St Antony Point, near Falmouth. Sixteen died.

FAIRY. Motor Vessel. 14th. Damaged near the Chequer Buoy, off the mouth of the River Humber.

BUOYANT. Barge. 14th. Last sighted off Skegness Middle Buoy. All 6 died.

AMENITY. 15th. Motor Vessel. Sunk in position 53°33′N 00°09′E. All 7 rescued.

DAGENHAM. Steamship. 16th. Damaged when two and a half cables ENE of the Mouse Light Vessel in the Thames Estuary.

ABILITY. Motor Barge. 18th. In position 51°45′N 1°11′E when sunk by a mine laid by a German schnellboot. All 7 rescued.

DAKOTIAN. Steamship 21st. Sunk when dropping anchor in Dale Roads, Milford Haven. All rescued.

PIKEPOOL. Steamship. 22nd. Bound for Barry from Glasgow when sunk 23 miles ESE of the Smalls Light, Pembrokeshire. Seventeen died.

HERCULES. Tug. 22nd. Sunk while towing a Hopper Barge, about ¾ of a mile east of the entrance to the Tyne, in position 55°00′33″N 01°22′45″W. Five died.

PRESERVER. Salvage Vessel. 24th. Sunk 54° 1 cable from No.1 Buoy, Milford Haven. Three died.

RYAL. Motor Vessel. 24th. Sunk in the North Sea, in position 51°32′N 01°04′E. Nine died.
BEHAR. Steamship. 24th. Leaving Milford Haven when damaged in position 51°42′N 5°07′W. Beached, but declared a total loss.

THOMAS M. Motor Vessel. 24th. Sunk 135° 1½ miles from Great Yarmouth harbour entrance. Junior Engineer L. Carter and AB F.W. King died.

ALICE MARIA. Steamship. 24th. Sunk 255° 8 cables from the Knob Light Vessel, Barrow Deep, in the Thames Estuary. All rescued.

CAMROUX IV. Motor Vessel. 24th. Damaged when one mile 45° from the East Oaze Light Vessel in the Thames Estuary.

ALMA DAWSON. Steamship. 24th. In Convoy SC.11, and bound for Ipswich, from Montreal, when sunk on a British minefield in position 55°32′N 06°44′W, off Northern Ireland. All rescued by the Norwegian ship *Spurt*.

T.C.C. HOPPER NO.3. Hopper Barge. 25th. Sunk off Stockton-on-Tees, in position 54°40′N 01°07′W. All rescued

GALACUM. Steamship. 27th. Damaged when in position 51°34′N 01°09′E, off the north coast of Kent.

December 1940

BRITISH OFFICER. Steamship/Tanker. 1st. Struck about ½ a mile E of North Pier Light when arriving at the mouth of the Tyne, from Sheerness. The stern section sank and the bow section towed to port. Four engine room staff died.

JOLLY GIRLS. Motor Vessel. 2nd. On passage from London to Rosyth, when damaged. With her 10 crew on board, the *No.2 Examination Cutter* took her in tow, but she sank off Newcastle-on-Tyne, in position 55°00′29″N 01°23′08″W.

ROBRIX. Motor Vessel. 3rd. Damaged when two miles 110° from the Spurn Light House, Humber Estuary.

NIMBIN. Motor Vessel. 5th. On passage from Coffs Harbour to Sydney, New South Wales, Australia, when sunk off Norah Head, in position 33°15′S 151°47′E. Seven died and the remaining 13 survived by clinging to bundles of plywood until spotted by an RAAF plane and subsequently picked up by the *Bonalbo*.

SUPREMITY. Motor Vessel. 6th. On passage from Blyth to London when sunk WSW 3 cables from the East Oaze Light Vessel, in the Thames Estuary, north of Whitstable.

HERTFORD. Steamship. 7th. Damaged when in position 35°30′S 135°25′E, west of Kangaroo Island, near Adelaide, Australia.

ACTUALITY. Motor Vessel. 8th. Sunk 3 miles SW of the Mouse Light Vessel. All 6 died.

ROYAL SOVEREIGN. Motor Vessel. 9th. Sunk in position 51°24′N 03°08′W. One died – Mr H.V. Clarke, 1st Mate.

The following 5 ships were sunk when 2 coastal convoys ran into a minefield off Southend in the Thames Estuary on the 17th.

INVER. Steamship. Blyth to London. 15 died.

MALRIX. Steamship. Hull to London. Seven died.

BENEFICIENT. Steamship. Sunderland to London. Six died.

ACQUIETY. Motor Vessel. London to Sunderland. Five died.

BELVEDERE. Steamship. London to the Tyne. Four died and 2 survived.

ARINIA. Motor Vessel/Tanker. 19th. Laden with oil from Aruba, dropped anchor 8 miles ESE of Southend Pier to await the opening of the dock gates at the Isle of Grain. The engines were then shut down, but, as this also switched off the anti-magnetic (degaussing) system, a nearby mine was drawn into her and exploded. Fifty-six, including the pilot, Mr. W.H. Hopkins, died, and only 2 survived. All the ratings were Hong Kong Chinese.

INNISFALLEN. Motor Vessel/Ferry. 21st. Sunk at entrance to Canada Dock, River Mersey. Four crew died, but all passengers rescued.

T.I.C. 12. Barge. 21st. Sunk in the Thames Estuary, in position 51°28′N 00°46′E. All rescued.

SUN IX. Tug. 21st. Sunk between buoys Yantlet Channel, Thames Estuary. Three died.

RIVER THAMES. Tug. 21st. Sunk in the Thames Estuary, in position 51°28′N 0°46′E. Three died.

POOLGARTH. Tug. 22nd. Sunk off the South Canada Dock entrance, Liverpool. All 7, including 16- year-old Trimmer Michael Stevenson, died.

ELAX. Motor Vessel/Tanker. 22nd. Damaged when off No.10 Buoy, Liverpool.

LLANDILO. Steamship. 22nd. Damaged when between No.2 and No.3 Yantlet Buoys in the Thames Estuary.

LADY CONNAUGHT. Steamship. 27th. Damaged in Liverpool Bay, in position 53°37′N 03°43′W.

VICTORIA. 27th. Steamship. Damaged when eight miles 290° from the Bar Light Vessel, River Mersey.

KINNAIRD HEAD. Steamship. 27th. Sunk 7 cables north of No.2 Buoy, Southend. Six died.

ARABY. 27th. Motor Vessel. Sunk approximately 1800 yards from the Nore Light Vessel on a bearing of 093°. Six died.

LOCHEE. 28th. Motor Vessel. Damaged when four miles NE by N of the Bar Light Vessel, River Mersey.

CATRINE. Motor Vessel. 29th and 30th. Damaged by a mine in Liverpool Bay and by a second one the next day near Q.1 Buoy, in the Queen's Channel, Liverpool.

DORCASIA. Motor Vessel/Tanker. 30th. Damaged when three miles 250° from the Bar Light Vessel, River Mersey.

CALCIUM. Steamship. 30th. Struck a mine then collided with the *Sodium*, and later sank in Liverpool Bay, in position 53°25′N 3°45′W. One died.

1941

January 1941

ATTENDANT. Steamship. 1st. Damaged when one cable E of No.9 buoy, Sheerness.

PINEWOOD. Steamship. 3rd. Sunk in the Thames Estuary in position 51°29′N 00°44′E. Six died and 12 rescued.

LION. Tug. 6th. Sunk 2½ cables from No.5 Medway Buoy on a bearing of 320°. Five died.

H.H. PETERSEN. Steamship. 7th. Sunk in the North Sea, in position 55°22′N 2°05′E. All rescued.

STRATHEARN. Motor Vessel/Trinity House Lighthouse Tender. 8th. Sunk in the North Sea, in position 51°45′N 1°10′E. Fifteen died.

DORSET COAST. Motor Vessel. 9th. Damaged in Bristol Channel, in position 51°24′N 03°08′W.

MIDDLESEX. Steamship. 10th. Sunk 198 0.8 mile from Flat Holm in the Bristol Channel. All rescued.

BRITISH FIDELITY. Motor Vessel/Tanker. 11th. Damaged in the Bristol Channel, in position 51°22′N 03°05′W.

MANCUNIAN. Sludge Vessel. 15th. Sunk 2 nautical miles NE of the Bar Light Vessel in Liverpool Bay. All rescued.

MAYWOOD. Steamship. 15th. Damaged in the Irish Sea, in position 51°21′N 3°16′W. Beached at Whitemore Bay, Barry, Glamorgan.

KARRI. Motor Vessel. 15th. Damaged 2 miles N of the Bar Light Vessel, River Mersey. AB James Brennan died.

ROMSEY. Steamship. 16th. Damaged in position 51°41'N 5°09'W and beached at Dale, Pembrokeshire.

ATHELDUKE. Motor Vessel/Tanker, 17th. Damaged in the Bristol Channel, in position 51°21'N 03°20'W, and beached in Whitmore Bay, Barry, Glamorgan. None died.

JAMAICA PLANTER. Motor Vessel. 22nd. Damaged in the Bristol Channel, 2500 yards 196° from Neil's Point, and beached at Barry.

CORHEATH. Steamship. 24th. On passage from Portsmouth to Blyth when sunk 1 mile 270° from the Botany Buoy in the Thames Estuary. Three died.

TASMANIA. Motor Vessel. 24th. Damaged in the North Sea, 11.5 miles from Rattray Head, Aberdeenshire.

CATFORD. Steamship. 26th. Damaged off Oaze Bank, in the Thames Estuary. Beached and later refloated. (See May 1943)

SANDHILL. Motor Vessel. 26th. Damaged in Irish Sea, in position 53°43'N 3°15'W.

RINGWALL. Steamship. 27th. Sunk south of the Isle of Man. Seven died.

TAFELBERG. (South Africa) Steamship/Oil Refinery. 28th. Damaged in the Bristol Channel, in position 51°21'N 3°16'W. Returned to service as the *Empire Heron*.

WESTMORELAND. Steamship. 29th. Damaged in the Irish Sea, 3 miles 270° from the Bar Light Vessel. Abandoned, reboarded and towed to Liverpool.

BOTUSK. Steamship. 31st. Bound for Cardiff, sailed in the Halifax Section of Convoy HX.103 which departed the port of the 15th. Sunk 6 nautical miles NE of the island of North Rona, 44 miles NNE of the Butt of Lewis. Three died and survivors rescued by HMS *Verbena*.

February 1941

DERWENTHALL. Motor Vessel. 3rd. Damaged in the Suez Canal. No casualties. Subsequently towed to Calcutta for repair.

CALYX. Motor Vessel. 3rd. Damaged 8 miles NE of the Bar Light Vessel, Liverpool.

GWYNWOOD. Steamship. 4th. At the Hawke Road Anchorage in the Humber Estuary when a parachute mine landed on her deck. Eleven died, including 15-year-old Mess Room Boy Tom McAthey.

RANEE. Steamship. 5th. Sunk in the Suez Canal. Nine died.
SCOTTISH CO-OPERATOR. Motor Vessel. 7th. Damaged 2 miles SW of Workington Pier, Solway Firth.

CRISTA. Motor Vessel. 9th. Damaged in Tobruk harbour.

FULHAM II. Steamship. 19th. Damaged off Tyne Piers and went ashore at Frenchman's Point. Later refloated and towed to Jarrow. One died.

BEN REIN. Steamship. 17th. Sunk off Falmouth. Two died by drowning, E. Parker, Sailor, and 17-year-old J.T. Williams, Fireman.

FORT MÉDINE. Steamship. 20th. Bound for Swansea from Wabana, Newfoundland, when she was sunk in the Bristol Channel, in position 51°35′N 3°56′W. Captain Louis Rebour was the only casualty.

CAPE CLEAR. Motor Vessel. 27th. Bound for Garston, sailed in Convoy HX.108 which left Halifax, NS, on the 9th. Damaged when about 35 miles from the mouth of the Mersey, in position 53°27′N 04°01′W. Anchored off the Bar Light Vessel and docked in Liverpool on 1st March.

CABENDA. Motor Vessel. 28th. Bound for Briton Ferry from Shoreham-by-Sea, when sunk in the Bristol Channel, in position 51°34′N 3°54′W. Chief Engineer James Winning was the only casualty.

March 1941

ANONITY. Motor Vessel. Sunk 1½ miles SE of Skegness Pier. Four died and 2 rescued.

RUTH II. Motor Vessel. 4th. Damaged 2 cables NNE of Bar Light Vessel.

ANGLIAN COAST. Motor Vessel. 4th. Damaged 2 cables 75° from Bar Light Vessel.

LYNDIS KIRKWOOD. Pilot Cutter. 4th. Damaged off Skegness.

SILVERSTONE. Tug. 5th. Towing four barges when sunk 3 nautical miles upstream of Rochester Bridge in the River Medway. Two of the barges were also sunk.

SUN VII. Tug. 6th. Sunk 60° 1 to 2 miles from the North Knob Buoy in the Thames Estuary. Five died.

EILIAN HILL. Steamship. 6th. Damaged 2 cables 75° from Bar Light Vessel.

CORINIA. Steamship. 10th. Sunk in the North Sea, in position 50°55′N 0°35′E. Fourteen died.

SPARTA. Steamship. 10th. Sunk in the North Sea, in position 50°55′N 0°35′E. Nine died.

WATERLAND. Steamship. 10th. Sunk in the North Sea, in position 50°55′N 0°35′E. Seven died.

CAMROUX I. Motor Vessel. 12th. Damaged 3 miles east of Blyth and towed to Blyth.

NGATIRA. Motor Vessel. 13th. Damaged in position 51°21′N 3°17′W. Beached, refloated and towed to Barry.

TACOMA CITY. Steamship. 13th. In Convoy HX.110 which left Halifax on 19 February and arrived in Liverpool on 11 March. Sunk by a parachute mine which exploded beneath her in the Formby Channel of the River Mersey. Four died. Forty-one picked up by a motorboat from the training ship HMS *Conway* and transferred to other larger boats for landing.

MYRMIDON. Motor Vessel. 13th. Being towed to safety after a mine had exploded at Henderson's Wharf, Birkenhead, when she struck an acoustic mine and sank to the bottom. Subsequently raised and repaired.

ULLAPOOL. Steamship. 13th. In Convoy SC.23 which left Halifax on 18 February and arrived in Liverpool on 9 March. Struck by a parachute mine when approximately 215° 1500 feet from the North End of the Princes Stage and broke in two. Fifteen died and 23 survived.

BULLGER. Tug. 13th. Towing the *Empire Breeze* when sunk in Druridge Bay, 16 miles north of the Tyne.

HERPORT. Steamship.14th. Sunk in position 53°15′N 1°05′E. Four died.

EMPIRE SIMBA. Steamship. 14th. Damaged by bombing in the Irish Sea on the 1st, abandoned and towed to Liverpool. On the 12th, a parachute mine was found on board after an air raid and, on the 14th, it exploded and damaged her amidships.

WARRIOR. Tug. 15th. Towing the *Ferncourt* (Nor.) when damaged at entrance to the River Cart, Glasgow.
TOTTENHAM. Steamship. 19th. Damaged when a nearby mine exploded and towed to Gravesend the next day.

LINDENHALL. Steamship. 19th/20th. Damaged in Victoria Dock, London.

HALO. Steamship. 21st. Sunk off Beckton No.1 Pier. Raised and taken to Royal Arsenal, Woolwich. Four died.

GRANAA. Steamship. 29th. Damaged at Rotherhithe. Temporarily repaired on the beach at North Woolwich before being dry-docked. Seven died and 12 rescued.

EMMA. Barge. 29th. Damaged at the same time as the *Granaa*. With her stern blown off, she was grounded and declared a total loss. No casualties.

April 1941

MELROSE ABBEY. Steamship. 2nd. Sunk in the River Ythan, Aberdeenshire. Raised on 26 July and towed to Aberdeen.

ELIZABETH. Steamship. 7th. Sunk in the English Channel 5 nautical miles ENE of Portscatho, near St Mawes, Cornwall. 10 died.

AHAMO. Steamship/Tanker. 8th. Sunk in the North Sea, in position 53°22′N 0°59′E. Fourteen died.

LUNULA. Steamship/Tanker. 9th. In Convoy HX.114 which sailed from Halifax, Nova Scotia, on 11th March. Arrived at Thames Haven on 9th April, and proceeding to berth with the assistance of the tug *Persia*, when struck by a parachute mine dropped the previous night. Twenty-seven died and the *Lunula* burned for 2 days.
.
PERSIA. Tug. 9th. Badly damaged in the above incident, but repaired in Ramsgate, renamed *Muria* and returned to service. Seven died.

CLAN CUMMING. Steamship. 14th. Although in a heavily escorted convoy, torpedoed and damaged by the Italian submarine *Neghelli* on 18 January, in position 37°15′N 24°04′E. Returned to Piraeus, where she had discharged her outward cargo, to undergo repairs in dry-dock. The first German air raid took place on the 6 April and, when the *Clan Fraser*, blew up while discharging ammunition, the *Clan Cumming* rolled on to her beam ends, a steel plate measuring 23 feet X 3 feet landed on her bridge top, and half of a windlass crashed through No 4 hatch and started a fire. With repairs completed, she sailed from Piraeus but, after shooting down a German plane, sunk by a mine in the Gulf of Athens on the 14th. Survivors were picked up by a Greek destroyer, but no further details.

REGENCY. Tug. 21st. Sunk at Dagenham in the Thames Estuary when towing barges. One crewman
and 1 lighterman died. Later raised, repaired and returned to service.

CORONATION OF LEEDS. Steam Barge 22nd. Sunk off Thameshaven. All 3 died.

PROWESS. Motor Vessel. 29th. Damaged off the Projector Buoy in the Humber.

May 1941

SEA FISHER. Steamship. 1st. Damaged in the North Sea, in position 55°34′N 1°28′W. Beached, refloated and taken to Middlesbrough.

CORBET. Steamship. 4th. Sunk 248° 400 yards from entrance to Herculaneum Dock, Liverpool. Eight died and 1 survived.

KILEENAN. Steam Barge. 7th. Sunk at Liverpool. All 5 died.

IRISHMAN. Tug. 8th. Together with dredger F.W. No.20, sunk in Langstone Harbour, Portsmouth. Five died on the tug and 3 on the dredger.
EMPIRE SONG. Steamship. 9th. Bound for Alexandria and loaded with 10 Hurricanes and 57 tanks, sailed in Convoy WS.58 which left the Clyde on 28 April, 1941. The Convoy consisted of only four other ships – *Clan Chattan*, *Clan Lamont*, *Clan Campbell* and *New Zealand Star*.

About 45 miles west of Pantelleria when struck by two mines, only minutes apart, shortly after midnight on 8 May. The Master gave the order to abandon ship, but asked for volunteers to remain on board in an attempt to save the ship. Seven, including L/Cpl. G.R. Myers of the Royal Tank Regiment, answered the call, but two hours later, the situation had deteriorated to such an extent that they had to slip into the sea from the badly listing and burning ship.

The destroyers HMS *Fortune* (LtCdr. E.N. Sinclair, RN) and HMS *Foresight* (Cdr. J.S.C. Salter, RN) were standing by, and a whaler from the latter containing both RN and MN volunteers whose intention was to save the ship and her badly needed cargo, was approaching her when she blew up and sank, in position 37°9′N 11°01′E. Bits of the ship, tanks and other debris were thrown into the air, and the whaler was sunk with the loss of one man. Ordinary Seaman Albert Howarth, D/JX. 229949, who had been in the whaler, was subsequently awarded the Albert Medal as, although his right foot had been blown off, he kept a shipmate afloat for ten minutes until a lifebelt was thrown to him. Nineteen-year-old B.S. Evenden, her 4th Mate, and 17 Indian seamen died. One hundred and twenty-eight were rescued by HMS *Foresight* and taken to Malta.

F. Hopper Barge. 13th. Sunk 350 yards south of Dingle Oil Jetty, County Kerry. Five died and 6 survived.

DIXCOVE. Motor Vessel. 19th. Damaged in position 51°36′N 1°11′E and towed to Gravesend.

WINKFIELD. Steamship. 19th. Sunk in the Thames Estuary, in position 51°35′N 1°10′E, 1 mile SW of Buoy B4. Ten died.

OCTANE. Motor Vessel/Tanker. 24th. Damaged in the English Channel and beached at Antony in Cornwall. Refloated, repaired and returned to service.

WESTAVON. Steamship. 30th. Sunk in the North Sea, in position 51°36′N 1°11′E. All rescued.

June1941

ROBERT HUGHES. Dredger. 4th. Sunk in the entrance to Lagos Harbour, Nigeria, by a mine laid by U.69 (Kptlt. Jost Metzler) on 29 May. Fourteen died and 17 rescued.

MYRMIDON. Motor Vessel. 5th. Having been repaired from mine damage, sailed from Birkenhead and again struck a mine in the Mersey. Repaired and returned to service in December.

ROYAL SCOT. Steamship. 10th. Sunk off the mouth of the Humber, in position 53°30′N 0°53E′. Eleven died.

ILSE. Steamship. 20th. Off Hartlepool when had her back broken in position 54°41′′N 1°20W. Towed to Middlesbrough where a new bow section was fitted and she returned to service. One man, AB George Inglis, died.

GASFIRE. Steamship. 21st. Sunk 10 nautical miles east of Southwold, Suffolk, in position 52°19′N 1°59′E. Ten died.

KENNETH HAWKSFIELD. Steamship. 21st. Sunk 10 nautical miles east of Southwold, Suffolk, in position 52°18′N 1°59′E. One died.

CAMROUX II. Motor Vessel. 23rd. Damaged 1 mile SE of No.17 Buoy, Flamborough Head. Towed to Immingham and repaired.

HULL TRADER. Steamship. 23rd. On passage from London to Hull when sunk about 1 mile 270° from 57C Buoy, Cromer. Eleven died and 3 survived.

July 1941

ROSME. Spritsail Barge. 3rd. Sunk in the Thames Estuary, in position 51°34′12"N 1°03′00"E

LUNAN. Steamship. 4th. Sunk in the Bristol Channel, in position 51°26′48"N 03°10′24"W. Six died and Mr O'Leary, with lacerated hands and suffering from shock, was the sole survivor.

GOLDFINCH. Motor Vessel. 4th. Damaged 10 miles 273° from St Bees Head, Solway Firth, and towed to Whitehaven.

BENCRUACHAN. Steamship. 5th. Sailed from Barry, bound for Alexandria via the Cape and the Suez Canal. Entering the port with four other ships in single file when she struck an acoustic mine. Sank bow-first in shallow water so that cargo shifted and her back was broken. Scrapped in 1950. Three men died and 21 injured.

BLUE MERMAID. Sailing Barge. 9th. Sunk 8 miles 185° from Clacton, in position 51°39'01"N 01°08'05"E. Two died, P.J. Bird, Master, and G.W. Lucas, Mate.

RIVER TRENT. Motor Vessel. 11th. Damaged west of Comer, in position 53°00'N 01°15'E, and towed to Great Yarmouth.

COLLINGDOC. Canadian Steamship. 13th. Struck when 4 cables 200° from Southend Pier. Chief Engineer William Wilson and Second Engineer William Stutchbury died. Scuttled at Scapa Flow in March 1942.

ADAMANT. Sailing Vessel. 23rd. Sunk in Alexandra Dock, Hull, but later salvaged.

SOAVITA. Sailing Vessel. 23rd. Sunk in Alexandra Dock, Hull, but later salvaged.

OMFLEET. Steam Barge. 23rd. Sunk in Alexandra Dock, Hull. No casualties.

August 1941

GOLDEN GRAIN. (Motor Barge) 19th. Sunk in the River Thames, in position 51°35'18"N 01°03'18"E. Three died.

DURHAM. Motor Vessel. 22nd. Enroute to Gibraltar from Malta, and west of Pantellaria, when damaged, but reached Gibraltar on the 24th. (See under September.)

SKAGERAK. Steamship. 24th. Sunk in the River Orwell, at Harwich, in position 51°58'08"N 1°16'06"E. Eighteen died and 6 rescued.

September 1941

TAI KOO. Tug 12th. Sunk in the Red Sea, in approximate position 16°45'N 40°05'E. Four died.

COLLINGDOC. Steamship. 13th. Sunk 4 cables 200° from Southend Pier. Two died, 1st Engineer W.M. Wilson and 2nd Engineer W.E. Stutchbury. Scuttled at Scapa Flow in March 1942.

PONTFIELD. Motor Vessel/Tanker. 15th. Struck in position 52°03N 1°20′30"E and ruined in two. The forepart sank, but the after part was towed to Salt End and a new forepart subsequently fitted at the Tyne.

ATLANTIC COCK. Tug. 15th. Damaged off the Dalmuir Basin, Glasgow. Beached and refloated on 11 October.

FLYING KITE. Tug. 15th. Sunk off the Dalmuir Basin. Five died and 3 survived.
BIRTLEY. Steamship. 15th. Damaged and 3 died. Sank the next day in position 53°06′N 1°18′E

BRADGLEN. Steamship. 19th. Sunk in position 51°31′N 01°03′W. Nine died.
PORTSDOWN. Paddle Steamer/Ferry. 20th. Bound for Ryde, Isle of Wight, when broken in two and sank in position 50°46′N 01°06′W, 10 minutes after leaving Portsmouth. Eight seamen and approximately 15 passengers died.

DURHAM. Motor Vessel. 20th. Anchored in Gibraltar Bay, and already damaged by a floating mine, when further damaged by limpet mines placed by Italian frogmen operating from their base ship, *Olterra*, in Algeciras, Spain. Beached at La Linea and refloated on 16 December. Subsequently towed to Falmouth by the RFA tug *Bustler*, arriving on 3 September 1942. Repaired and returned to service in July 1943.

VANCOUVER. Steamship/Tanker. 21st. Sunk about 2 miles 263° from the Sunk Light Vessel, Thames Estuary, in position 51°51′N 01°31′E.

DALTONHALL. Motor Vessel. 24th. Damaged in position 51°45′06"N 51°63′0"W. Reached Holyhead unaided and subsequently proceeded to Liverpool for repair.

ORIOLE. 26th. Motor Vessel. Damaged off the South Bishops, Cardigan Bay. Towed to Milford Haven the following day.

October 1941

TYNEFIELD. Motor Vessel/Tanker. 5th. Sunk in the Suez Canal. Seven died.

ICEMAID. Steamship. 11th. Damaged off Orfordness, near Shipwash Light Vessel. Towed to Harwich the following day.

MAHSEER. Steamship. 18th. Sunk in Barrow Deep, 4 to 5 cables from B7 Buoy in the Thames Estuary, in position 51°41′N 1°19′E. All rescued.

EMPIRE GHYLL. Steamship. 18th. Sunk at the same time and in the same position as the *Mahseer*. Seven died.

CORDELIA. Motor Vessel/Tanker. 20th. Damaged off Great Castle Head, but arrived in Milford Haven.

November 1941

FOREMOST 45. Hopper Barge. 2nd. Sunk in Barry Roads, in position 51°21′N 03°17′W. One died and 8 rescued, including 1 injured.

BRITISHER. Steamship. 4th. Sunk north of West Mouse Buoy, Maplin Sands, Essex. Both crewmen died.

MAURITA. Steamship. 12th. Sunk at Hibre Swash in the estuary of the River Dee, Liverpool Bay. Five died.

December 1941

BRITISH CAPTAIN. Steamship/Tanker. 2nd. Sunk 15 miles east of Aldeburgh, Suffolk, in position 52°13′N 01°55′E. Second Engineer Herbert Brown and Fireman Charlie Green died.

MACLAREN. Steamship. 3rd. Sunk in the Bristol Channel, in position 51°21′21″N 3°17′17″W. Three died.

GREENLAND. Steamship. 6th. Sunk in position 52°14′N 02°06′E. Eight died.

WELSH PRINCE. Steamship. 7th. Bound for New York from London, sailed in Convoy FN.71 which left Southend at 8.55am gmt on the 6th. Struck a mine when off Spurn Head, broke in two, and sank in position 53°23′N 00°58′E. All survived.

SEVERN TRANSPORT. Motor Vessel. 7th. Sunk in the Bristol Channel, in position 51°27′N 3°04′W. All 4 rescued.

FIREGLOW. Steamship. 8th. Sunk 3 miles south of Dudgeon Buoy, Norfolk, in position 53°19′N 01°05′E. Donkeyman Richard Nelson was the sole casualty.

DROMORE CASTLE. Steamship 12th. Sunk 20 nautical miles SSE of the mouth of the Humber, in position 53°29′08″N 05°20′0″E. All rescued.

BENMACDHUI. Steamship. 21st. Bound for Hong Kong, sailed from Immingham on 17th. Left the convoy anchorage at 4pm on the 21st to proceed to the Humber light float to join a convoy, but, as it could not be located in the poor visibility, Captain Campbell decided to return to the wreck buoy at the mouth of the river. When at 9.35pm, a smell of burning rubber was detected, the Chief Officer and 1st Mate were sent to locate the source. And, ten minutes later, when they were reporting their failure to do so and the ship was again turning to head for the light float, there was a violent explosion and she sank in 20 minutes, in position 53°40′N 00°30′W. Storekeeper Fung Shing and AB Edward McDonald died and the rest were picked up from two lifeboats and a raft by the *Peronne*. One source states that it may have been sabotage.

PHENIX. Steamship/Tanker. 24th. Sunk at Haifa, Palestine. Four died.

STANMOUNT. Steamship/Tanker. 24th. Sunk off Great Yarmouth in position 52°39′22″N 2°00′31″E. All rescued.

MERCHANT. Steamship. 24th. Sunk off Great Yarmouth in position 52°40′N 2°04′E. Donkeyman John O'Brien died.

EASTWOOD. Steamship. 24th. Damaged 2½ miles 270° from Aldeburgh Light Vessel. Three died.

CORMEAD. Steamship. 25th. Struck when 350 3 miles from No.5 Buoy, Lowestoft. All rescued and the ship sank the next day in position 52°25′N 02°13′E.

1942

January 1942

KENTWOOD. Steamship. 1st. Damaged off Happisburgh, Norfolk and sank 2 cables NE of 56 Buoy off Yarmouth while being towed by a Royal Navy ship. All rescued.

CORFEN. Steamship. 3rd. Damaged in the Thames Estuary. Taken in tow, but sank in position 51°50′N 01°27′E.

ROBERT. Steamship. 3rd. Damaged off Lowestoft. Taken in tow, but sank the next day in position 52°17′30″N 02°00′00″E.

SCOTTISH MUSICIAN. Motor Vessel/Tanker. 5th. In Convoy FN.97 when damaged off Southwold, Suffolk, in position 52°16′N 01°59′E, and subsequently dry-docked at Tilbury.

LARGO. Steamship. 5th. In Convoy FN.97 when damaged off Southwold. With assistance, reached Harwich on the 6th.

NORWICH TRADER. Steamship. 6th. Sunk in position 51°55′07″N 1°32′05″E. All 6 died.

BORDERDENE. Steamship. 10th. Sunk 3 or 4 miles SW off Brean Down, Somerset, in position 51°18′N 03°03′W. Four died.

QUICKSTEP. Steamship. 12th. Sunk in position 51°46′N 1°26′E. Eight died.

MERCIA. Tug. 14th. Sunk in the Bristol Channel, in position 51°31′21″N 2°46′44″W. Four died.

H.K.D. Sailing Barge. 19th. Sunk in position 51°28′12″N 0°52′42″E. Both men rescued.

SWYNFLEET. Steamship. 25th. Sunk off Landguard Point, Suffolk, in position 51°55′N 01°19′E. All rescued.

February 1942

ENSEIGNE MARIE ST GERMAIN. Steamship 22nd. Damaged off Yarmouth. Subsequently towed to the Tyne for repair and returned to service on 3rd June.

March 1942

AUDACITY. Steamship/Tanker. 1st. On passage from Selby to Purfleet when sunk in position 53°34′N 00°23′E, south of the Humber Light Vessel. Eight died.

POLGARTH. Steamship. 1st. Bound for Southampton from Blyth when sunk 2 miles SSW of Aldeburgh Light Float.

FRUMENTON. Steamship. 4th. Bound for London from Saint John, New Brunswick, when sunk off
Orford Ness, Suffolk, in position 52°21′N 01°58′E. (I deduce that she had crossed the Atlantic in either Convoy SC.70 or Convoy HX.176 which sailed from Halifax on the 16th and 19th February respectively.)

CRESSDENE. Steamship. 16th. Bound for Methil and Rosario from London when she struck a mine in position 52°08′N 01°52′E. Sank the following day when under tow.

April 1942

ROBERT W. POMEROY. Canadian-registered. 1st. In Convoy FN.70 when sunk off Cromer, in position 53°10′N 01°10′E. One killed and 2 injured.

PLAWSWORTH. Steamship. 20th. On passage from Sunderland to London when sunk off Aldeburgh in position 52°09′20"N 01°42′50"E.

JERSEY. Motor Vessel. 23rd. Sunk when about to anchor in Suez Bay.

CHATWOOD. Steamship. 23rd. Sunk off Cromer, in position 53°19′N 01°00′′E. All rescued.

ALLIANCE. Tug. 29th. At 7.45pm, sunk off Famagusta, Cyprus, in position 35°09′N 33°56′E by a mine laid by U.562 (Kptlt. Horst Hamm) on the 13th. Captain A. Vassiliu and Firemen N.H. Antoni and G. Zeibekis died. Seven survived.

May 1942

DALFRAM. Steamship. 2nd. Enroute to Alexandria from New York, and had just left Cape Town,
when she struck a mine laid by the German ship *Doggerbank* (ex- *Speybank*, captured by the Raider *Atlantis*) . Returned to Cape Town under her own power and repaired.

UNIQUE. Schooner. 2nd. Sunk in position 51°38′N 01°00′E, but no further details.

SOUDAN. Steamship. 15th. In Convoy WS.18 which sailed from the Clyde on 15th April and arrived off Cape Town on 15th May. Sunk in position 36°10′S 20°22′E, off Cape Agulhas, by a mine probably laid by the

Doggerbank. The crew got away in 3 lifeboats. The occupants of 2 of them were picked up within 40 hours, but it was 6 days later when the 31 in the remaining boat, commanded by the 2nd Mate, were picked up by the *Clan Murray*.

ARDUITY. Motor Vessel. 16th. Sunk 5 miles off Mablethorpe, in position 53°22′N 00°30′E, while on passage from Keadby, North Lincolnshire, to Cantley, Norfolk.
June 1942

ORARI. Motor Vessel. 16th. In the convoy named Operation Harpoon when damaged ½ a mile off Malta, but made it to Valetta. Temporarily repaired and returned to the UK. Of the original 6 ships in the Convoy, only the *Orari* and the *Troilus* reached the port.

DALRIADA. Steamship. 19th. Sunk 2 cables NE of the North Shingles Buoy in the Edinburgh Channel, Thames Estuary. Donkeyman James Thomas, died.

AFON DULAIS. Steamship. 20th. Sunk SE of the Isle of Wight, in position 50°04′N 00°23′W, when on passage from Seaham to Poole.

July 1942

SHUNA, EMPIRE SNIPE and BARON DOUGLAS. Steamships. 14th. At anchor in Gibraltar Bay when damaged by limpet mines placed by Italian frogmen operating from their base ship, *Olterra*, in Algeciras, Spain.

August 1942

KYLOE. Steamship. 25th. Damaged north Harwich by a mine laid by a schnellboot, but no further details.

September 1942

RAVENS POINT. Steamship. 15th. At anchor in Gibraltar Bay when sunk in shallow water by limpet mines placed by Italian frogmen operating from their base ship, *Olterra*, in Algeciras, Spain. Raised, repaired and resumed service on 27th December.

October 1942

IGHTHAM. Steamship. 7th. Sunk in position 55°33′N 00°26′E. All 24 rescued.

November 1942

LINWOOD. Steamship. 15th. On passage from Sunderland to London when sunk ¼ mile east of the Longsand Buoy in the Thames Estuary. Three engine room staff died.

BANKSIDE. Sailing Vessel with auxiliary motor. 19th. Sunk at 7.30am near Maplin Spit in the Thames Estuary. Captain G.R.N. Dent died.

GERTRUDE MAY. Sailing Barge. 27th. Sunk in position 51°45′N 01°19′E. The Mate, Mr J.E. Eriksson, died.

December 1942

Nothing found.

1943

January 1943

AILSA. Sailing Barge. 13th. Sunk near Whitaker Spit in the Thames Estuary. All rescued.

RESOLUTE. Sailing Barge 28th. Sunk in the estuary of the River Crouch, Essex, in position 51°47′N 01°14′E. Mr A.H. Collins, the Mate, died.

February 1943

BALTONIA. Steamship. 7th. In Convoy MKS.7 (Mediterranean to UK Slow) and bound for Belfast Lough from Seville, when it ran into mines laid by U.118 (KrvKpt. Werner Czygan), west of Gibraltar, on 1st and 2nd February. Sank in position 35°58′N 05°59′W and 11 died. Fifty-one picked up by the *Kingsland* were subsequently transferred to HMCS *Alberni* (T/Lt. A.W. Ford) and landed at Londonderry.

MARY SLESSOR. Motor Vessel. 7th. In Convoy MKS.7, and bound for Liverpool from Algiers, when it ran into mines laid by U.118 and sank in position 35°58′N 05°59′W. Thirty-two, including 2 military passengers died, and 48 picked up by HMS *Landguard* (LtCdr. T.S.L. Fox-Pitt, RN), and landed at Liverpool.

EMPIRE MORDRED. Steamship. 7th. In Convoy MKS.7, and bound for the UK from Bône (Annaba), Algeria, when it ran into mines laid by U.118 in position 35°58′N 05°59′W and sank. Fifteen died, and 55 picked up by HMS *Scarborough* (LtCdr. E.B. Carnduff), and landed at Londonderry.

March 1943

GLENDALOUGH. Steamship. 19th. Sunk off Blakeney Point, Norfolk, in position 53°16′N 01°30′E. Five died and 11 rescued.

BECKENHAM. Steamship. 26th. Damaged by a mine laid by a schnellboot when off Tripoli, Libya, in position 32°56′N 13°19′E. Towed to Malta for repair.

April 1943

JOSEFINA THORDEN. Motor Vessel/Tanker. 6th. On passage from Curacao to Shellhaven when sunk 4 miles 232° from the Sunk Head Buoy in the Thames Estuary. Fifteen died and many injured.

DYNAMO. Steamship. 17th. In a coastal convoy and on passage from London to Hull when sunk 1 mile 040° from B8 Buoy, Barrow Deep, in the Thames Estuary. Seven died and 12 rescued.

EMPIRE MORN. Steamship/CAM Ship (Catapult Aircraft Merchant Ship). 26th. Bound for Casablanca, sailed from Milford Haven on the 14th in Convoy OS.46/KMS.13. Arrived in Casablanca on he 25th and sailed the next morning for Gibraltar. At 9.45pm on the 26th, when off Rabat in position 33°52′N 7°50′W, damaged by a mine laid by U.117 (KvtKpt. Hans-Werner Neumann) on the 10th. Towed back to Casablanca and subsequently to Gibraltar by the tugs *Lorient* and *Schelde*, arriving on 1 September. Not repaired and used as a store ship in Gibraltar. Forty-six died and 25 survived. Among those who died was Galley Boy Raymond Steed who was 14 years and 207 days old and the second youngest British serviceman to died in WWII. (The youngest was Galley Boy Reginald Earnshaw who was 14 years and 151 days old when killed on the SS *North Devon* off the coast of Norfolk on 6 July 1941.)

May 1943

MAHSUD and CAMERATA. Steamships. Both at anchor in Gibraltar Bay when Italian frogmen, operating from their base ship, the *Olterra*, at Algeciras, Spain, attached limpet mines to their hulls. The *Mahsud*, with the bottom blown out of her engine room, sank in shallow water and 2 years later she was raised, strengthened, and towed home for repair. The *Camerata* sank in deeper water and was lost. None died on the *Mahsud*. (The US Liberty Ship *Pat Harrison* was damaged at the same time and became a total loss. Two men died.)

CORMULL. Steamship. 15th. Damaged 14 miles NE of Yarmouth, but reached the port.

CATFORD. Steamship. 31st. Sunk off the Humber, in position 53°37′N 00°42′E. Four died.

June 1943

Nothing found.
July 1943

J.B.W. Sailing Barge. 15th. Sunk NNE of Maplin Buoy, Burnham-on-Crouch, Essex. J.W. Ward, the Master, and T.J. Hill, the Mate, died.

KAITUNA. Motor Vessel. 19th. On passage from Mersin, Turkey, to Haifa, Palestine, and in position 35°15′N 35°35′E, when damaged by a limpet mine attached by Italian frogmen in Mersin on the 9th. Arrived in Haifa on the same day. Temporarily repaired in Alexandria. No casualties.

August 1943

Nothing found.

September 1943

FORT DREW. Steamship. 6th. On passage from Syracuse, Sicily, to Malta, when damaged in position 35°52′N 14°47′E. Arrived in Valetta the same day and subsequently towed to Taranto for repair.

SELLINGE. Steamship. 6th. Sunk off Hurd bank, Malta. No details.

ALMENARA. Steamship. 20th. Sunk in the Gulf of Taranto, in position 40°15′1"N 17°16′3"E. Forty-one died and 43 rescued.

October 1943

LAURELWOOD. Motor Vessel/Tanker. 7th. Damaged off Taranto. No details.

OCEAN VIKING. Steamship. 11th. Damaged off Taranto in approximate position 40°19′N 16°59′E. Towed to Bari and scuttled to act as a breakwater. Salvaged after the war, repaired, and returned to service.

PENOLVER. Steamship. 19th. In Convoy WB65, and about 15 miles from St John's, Newfoundland, in position 47°19′N 52°27′W, when sunk a mine laid by U.220 (Oblt. Bruno Barber) on the 9th. When the US steamship *Delisle*, also in the Convoy, was stopped and picking up survivors, she, too, was sunk by a mine. Twenty-six died on the *Penolver* and 14 survived. All 42 from the *Delisle*, plus the survivors of the *Penolver*, were taken on board the MS Trawler HMCS *Miscou* (Lt. C.R. Clark, RNR) and landed at St John's.

November/December 1943

Nothing found.

1944

January 1944

LARGS BAY. Steamship. 2nd. Damaged while entering Naples Harbour, but damage appears to have been slight as she sailed about 2 weeks later.

February 1944

CORFIRTH. Steamship. 12th. Damaged 1 mile 170° from Ajaccio, Corsica.

NOLISEMENT. Steamship. 20th. Damaged 3½ miles off Monopoli Lighthouse (Puglia, SE Italy), in position 40°54′N 17°32′E. Proceeded to Brindisi and Catania, and later dry-docked in Lisbon.

March/April/May 1944

Nothing found.

June 1944

ST. JULIEN. Steamship/Hospital Carrier. 7th. Damaged while assisting in the D-Day Landings in Normandy. Towed to England, and back in service within 2 weeks.

DINARD. Steamship/Hospital Carrier. 7th. Damaged off Juno Beach while assisting in the D-Day Landings. Towed to Southampton, repaired, and returned to service 10 days later.

BRITISH ENGINEER. Steamship/Tanker. 12th. Damaged in position 50°10′N 00°59′W.

VICEROY. Steamship. 13th. Damaged while assisting in the Normandy Landings.

ALERT. Steamship/Trinity House Vessel. 16th. Sunk in position 49°25N′ 00°40′W when returning home after assisting in the Normandy Landings. All rescued.

WESTDALE. Steamship. 20th. In Convoy ETC.12 which left Southend on the 17th and arrived in Seine Bay, Normandy, the next day. Sunk while at anchor in the Bay, in position 49°24N′ 00°38′W.

FORT NORFOLK. Steamship. 24th. Left Juno Beach anchorage at 8.03am to join a convoy returning to the UK. Struck a mine 14 minutes later and sank. Several abandoned the ship in No.2 lifeboat, but most had to jump into the water. Survivors were picked up by motor launches then transferred to the Norwegian destroyer, HNoMS *Stord*, which landed them at Portsmouth in the evening. Eight died and 6 injured.

DERRYCUNIHY. Motor Vessel. 24th. Embarked A and C Squadrons of the 43rd (Wessex) Reconnaissance Regiment (43 Recce) at West India Docks, London, on the 18th, and joined a convoy off Southend-on-Sea. Arrived at Sword Beach on the evening of the 20th, but owing to three days of high seas and heavy shelling, it was decided to move to Juno Beach to disembark the troops. However, when the engines were started at 7.40am on the 24th, a mine exploded under the ship's keel, splitting her in two. The after part, packed with sleeping troops, sank rapidly and a 3-ton ammunition lorry caught fire so that oil, floating on the surface of the water, was set alight. Landing craft and HMS *Locust* picked up survivors, most of whom were transferred to the depot ship *Cap Touraine*. One hundred and eighty-three men of the regiment died and approximately 120 were wounded. Twenty-five of the ship's crew also died in what was the largest single loss of life off the invasion beaches.

July 1944

EMPIRE BROADSWORD. Steamship. 2nd. After disembarking troops, sunk by 2 mines when off Arromanches, Normandy, in position 49°25′N 00°54′W. T.B. Boyle, an Engineer, and J. Russell, a Sailor, died and 70 rescued by the US Patrol Craft USS *PC-1225*.

EMPIRE HALBERD. Steamship. 6th. Off Landsend, in position 50°08′N 5°44′W, when her stern was damaged by a mine laid by U.218 (Kptlt. Richard Becker) on the 2nd. Temporarily repaired in Falmouth before proceeding to Glasgow. Returned to service as HMS *Silvio*.

EMPIRE BRUTUS. Steamship. 8th. Damaged when off Arromanches, in position 49°27′N 00°29′W. Beached on Juno Beach, but refloated and towed to Middlesbrough for repair.

ORANMORE. Steamship. 17th. Damaged when about 10 miles off the coast of Normandy, but succeeded in discharging her cargo.

NO.36. Hopper Barge. 20th. Sunk off Cherbourg.

August 1944

T.C.C. HOPPER NO.1. Hopper Barge. 4th. Sunk at Cherbourg. Raised on 8 September and broken up.

AMSTERDAM. Steamship/Hospital Carrier. 7th. Sunk in position 49°25′N 00°35′W, shortly after leaving Juno Beach, Normandy. Fifty-five patients, 10 RAMC staff, 31 crew (9 assistant stewards and 22 engine room staff) and 11 German prisoners of war died.

FORT YALE. Steamship. 8th. In Convoy ETC.72 when damaged by a mine in position 49°26′N 00°33′W. Being towed from Juno Beach to Portsmouth on the 23rd when torpedoed and sunk by U.480 (Oblt. Hans-Joachim Förster) 17 miles SE off St Catherine's Point, Isle of Wight. One naval signalman died when she was torpedoed.

HARPAGUS. Motor Vessel. 19th. Damaged off Arromanches, Normandy. Fore part sank, after part towed to Southampton and then to the Tyne. New fore part fitted and, renamed *Treworlas*, returned to service in May 1946.

EMPIRE ROSEBERY. Steamship/Tanker. 24th. Sunk off Arromanches, in position 49°22′N 00°36′W. Eleven died.

September 1944

MORIALTA. Motor Vessel. 21st. Took part in the landings in the south of France and damaged when on passage to Marseilles from Oran. Towed to Alexandria for repair and returned to service in June 1945.

October 1944

COTTON VALLEY. Motor Vessel/Tanker. 4th. Damaged when 6 miles south of Port de Bouc, south-east France. Abandoned, broke in two and bow sank. Stern towed to Marseille, temporary bow fitted in Toulon in 1945, and served in the port as a water carrier.

GUERNSEY QUEEN. Motor Vessel. 21st. Damaged at entrance to Boulogne harbour. Hull cut in two to clear the lock, and the stern subsequently towed to Grangemouth where a new bow section was joined to it. J. Santos, 1st Mate, and J. Divver, AB, died.

ROUSEVILLE. Motor Vessel/Tanker. 26th. Sunk in the River Seine, in position 49°26′N 00°36E.
November 1944

FORT LA BAYE. Steamship. 10th. Damaged off Port Said, Egypt, in position 31°25′N 32°23′E. None died.

FAIRPLAY I. Salvage Tug. 12th. Damaged in Ostend Harbour. Towed to Grimsby for repair by the Tug *Empire Jester*.

December 1944

EMPIRE DACE. Steamship/Ferry. 1st. Sunk off Missolonghi, Greece. Forty-five, including 20 crew, died.

SAMSIP. Steamship. 7th. Damaged off Blankenberg, Scheldt Estuary, in position 51°23′N 03°03′E, and the wreck sunk by gunfire. Five died.

FORT MAISONNEUVE. Steamship. 15th. Bound for Antwerp when sunk about 8½ miles from NF14 Buoy in the Scheldt Estuary on a bearing of 105°. Four died.

EMPIRE OSBORNE. Steamship. 20th. Damaged in the River Seine. Carpenter F. Davis died.

TID 70. Tug. 23rd. Damaged in the English Channel and sank about 12 nautical miles SE of Ventnor, Isle of Wight, in position 50°28′N 0°58′W, while being towed by the US Tug *LT533*. None died.

EMPIRE PATH. Steamship. 24th. Blown in half in the Scheldt Estuary, in position 51°22′N 02°52E. Five engine room staff died. Fifty-four survivors taken to Ostende and eventually carried to London on an over-crowded LST.

1945

January 1945

D. Hopper Barge. 15th. At 11.30pm, left her anchorage in the River Mersey, and sunk when on her way to the West Bank Dock, Widnes. Regrettably, the names of the 5 who died, including that of Eric Booth, a Boy Rating aged 16, are not recorded on the Tower Hill Memorial, London. (The barge may have been sunk by an internal explosion, and not a mine.)

DALEMOOR. Steamship. 15th. Sunk off the Humber, in position 53°22′N 00°50′E. None died.

SAMVERN. Steamship. 18th. Sailed from Antwerp, bound for London, and the last in a line of five ships making their way through the Scheldt Estuary when she struck a mine in position 51°22′N 03°02′E. Two lifeboats left the ship, but a full gale was blowing and one of them turned over. Some of its occupants succeeded in swimming to the other boat, but, when the upturned boat drifted away, those clinging to it were lost. Sixteen, including both the Antwerp and London pilots, died. Forty-seven survived.

February 1945

CITY OF LINCOLN. Steamship. 19th. Damaged 300° 8 cables from 14 Buoy, off the Humber, by a mine laid by a schnellboot.

AURETTA. Steamship. 26th. Bound for Antwerp, sailed from Southend in unescorted Convoy TAM.91 on the 25th. Sunk off the Scheldt Estuary, in position 51°24′N 02°49′E. Firemen Trimmers H. Everitt and E. Williams died.

SAMPA. Steamship. 27th. In a convoy bound from Antwerp to the UK when she struck a mine at 5.12pm, and sank within 15 minutes in position 51°23′N 02°53′E. Nine crew and 3 passengers died. Fifty, including 4 who died later, rescued by the destroyer HMS *Middleton* and landed at Sheerness.

CYDONIA. Steamship. 28th. Damaged in position 53°17′N 00°57′E by a mine laid by a schnellboot. .

March 1945

SAMSELBU. Steamship. 19th. Sunk of the coast of Belgium in position 51°23′N 03°06′E. None died.
EMPIRE BLESSING. Steamship. 19th. Sunk off Knocke, Belgium, in position 51°24′N 3°17′E.

April 1945

CONAKRIAN. Steamship. 15th. In Convoy ATM.125 which sailed from Antwerp that day, bound for Southend. Damaged in the English Channel and towed to Tilbury to discharge her cargo, and for temporary repair. Towed to the Tyne in June for repair. None died.

SAMCLYDE. Steamship. 30th. Damaged in the Aegean Sea, in position 40°22′N 22°51′E

GOLD SHELL. Motor Vessel/Tanker. 16th. Approaching the Scheldt when sunk in position 51°21′N 02°55′E. A lifeboat from the *Portia*, manned by her 2nd Mate, D. Davidson, and four other volunteers, braved the burning sea and picked up five DEMS gunners who had been blown clear. The gunners were subsequently landed at Antwerp. Thirty-five died. Twenty-nine, including the gunners, survived. Among the survivors was her newly-promoted Chief Engineer, W.W. Burns, who was permanently disfigured and blinded.

May 1945

Nothing found.

FISHING VESSELS SUNK AND DAMAGED BY MINES DURING WWII

1939

September/October/November 1939

Nothing found.

December 1939

RESERCHO. Steam Trawler. Sunk when about 6 miles SE by E of Flamborough Head by a mine laid by U.15 (Kptlt. Heinz Buchholz) on 5 September. All 7 rescued.

1940

January 1940

ETA. Motor Trawler. 6th. Sunk after catching a mine in her trawl when 6 miles NW of Outer Gabbard Light Vessel, off the coast of Essex. None died.

LUCIDA. Steam Trawler. 11th. Sunk in position 55°00′N 00°53′W when bound for the fishing grounds. Ten died.

NEWHAVEN. Steam Trawler. 15th. Sunk about 18 miles SSE of Lowestoft. Eight died.

February 1940

BEN ATTOW. Steam Trawler. 27th. Sunk when fishing 7 miles E ½ mile south of the Isle of May, in the River Forth. All nine died.

March 1940

HALIFAX. Steam Trawler. 11th. Sunk SE of Aldeburgh, in position 52°06′30"N 1°59′40"E. All nine rescued by the *Ipswich*.

April/May 1940

Nothing found.

TEASER. Motor Fishing Smack. 22nd. Sunk in the River Blackwater, off Tollesbury Pier, Essex. Both crewmen rescued.

June 1940

RENOWN. Fishing Vessel. 1st. From Leigh-on-Sea, and helping in the Dunkirk Evacuation, when she developed engine trouble. Taken in tow by 2 tugs at about 1am, but sunk near Sandetti Light Vessel about 45 minutes later. All 4 died.

OCEAN LASSIE. Drifter. 3rd. Sunk 2¾ cables 55° from the Outer Ridge Buoy, Harwich. Six died and 3 rescued.

July 1940

REMEMBRANCE. Fishing Vessel. 4th. Sunk in the English Channel, position 51°53′N 01°22′E. Both crewmen rescued.

LEACH'S ROMANCE. Fishing Vessel. 29th. Sunk in the English Channel, about 10½ nautical miles south of Kemp Town, East Sussex. All 4 died.

August 1940

FLAVIA. Steam Trawler. 28th. Sunk in the North Sea. Cause unknown. All 10 died.

September 1940

SALACON. Steam Trawler. 7th. Sunk 5.3 miles 114° from Spurn Point Lighthouse. Eight died and 4 rescued.

October 1940

PRIDE. Motor Fishing Vessel.16th. Sunk off the East Pier, Scarborough. Four died.

ALBATROSS. Fishing Vessel. 17th. Sunk off Grimsby. Five died.

ENCOURAGE. Motor Fishing Vessel. 25th. Sunk 6½ cables 210° from Breakwater Fort, Plymouth. Four died.

WINDSOR. Steam Trawler. 25th. Sunk 2.1 miles 174° from Spurn Point. One died.

CARLTON. Steam Drifter. 25th. Sunk 3½ miles 131.5° from Spurn Point. Ten died.

November 1940

LORD HALDANE. Steam Trawler. 12th. In the neighbourhood of the Bristol Channel. Cause unknown. Nine died.

WIGMORE. 18th. One of 6 trawlers in an escorted convoy, heading for the Icelandic fishing grounds, when sunk at about 11.10pm in approximate position 57°59′N 2°11′W, about 25 miles NW off Rattray Head, by a mine laid by U.22 (Kptlt. Karl-Heinrich Jenisch). Sank within minutes and all 16 died.

December 1940

CARRY ON. Steam Drifter. 17th. Sunk east of the Nore Sand Light Vessel. Six died.

1941

January 1941

STRATHRYE. Steam Trawler. 12th. Sunk in position 50°35′N 03°59′W. All rescued. (Listed as *Strathrye*, but may have been *Strathyre*.

February 1941

THOMAS DEAS. Steam Trawler. 16th. Sunk 4 miles 273° from Spurn Point. All 13 died.

CHRISTABELLE. Trawler. 27th. Sunk in position 61°27′N 6°05′W, south of the Faroe Islands, by what may have been a British mine. Ten died.

March 1941

ALASKAN. Fishing Vessel. 25th. Sunk in position 54°49′N 1°07′W. All 5 rescued.

MILLIMUMUL. Steam Trawler. 26th. Sunk by a mine, laid by the German raider *Pinguin*, when in position 33°34′N 151°56′E, off the coast of NSW, Australia. Seven died and the other 5 picked up from a lifeboat by the collier *Mortlake Bank*, and landed at Sydney.

April 1941

ALPHA. Fishing Vessel. 21st. Damaged in the Whittaker Channel, Essex.

May 1941

Nothing found.

June 1941

AUDACIOUS. Fishing Vessel. 15th. Sunk in position 51°28′N 00°51′E. Skipper T.E. Meddle and Fisherman A. Noakes died.

DORIS II. Fishing Vessel. 18th. Sunk 3 cables SE of the Outer Bar Bell Buoy, off Sheerness. Both men died.

July 1941

STRATHGAIRN. Steam Trawler. 1st. Sunk approximately 20 miles SW of Barra Head. Five died.

August 1941

EXPRESS. Motor Fishing Smack. 12th. Sunk 1 mile SW of E Spaniard Buoy, off Whitstable.

September 1941

OPHIR II. Steam Trawler. Sunk about 15 miles from Spurn Point in Northern Approach Channel. Five died.

GLEN ALVA. Fishing Vessel. 19th. Sunk off Jenkin Buoy, Southend. Both men died.

MURIELLE. Steam Trawler. 28th. Nine miles SW by S from Morecambe Bay Light Vessel when a mine, caught in her net, exploded. Being towed to Fleetwood when she sank W by N of Blackpool Tower. None died.

October/November 1941

Nothing found.

December 1941

LORD SHREWSBURY. Steam Trawler. 8th. Sunk 1 mile east ½-mile south of the Chequer Shoal Buoy in the Humber Estuary. All ten died.

KINCORTH. Steam Drifter. 10th. Sunk 7 miles 82° from Lynas Point, Anglesey. All 11 died.

MOUETTE. Fishing Vessel. 19th. Sunk in Blue Anchor Bay, Minehead, Somerset. Two died.

1942

January 1942

BRACONBUSH. Steam Trawler. 29th. Sunk 2 miles SE of Duncansby Head, Caithness. All rescued.

February 1942

BELLEVUE. Steam Trawler. 22nd. Sunk 5 miles NW of Turnberry Lighthouse, in the estuary of the River Forth. Presumed mined and all 8 died.

March/April 1942

Nothing found.

May 1942

LITTLE EXPRESS. Fishing Vessel. 4th. Sunk ¾-mile SE of the West Pansand Buoy, Kentish Flats, Brixham. Three died.

BEN IVER. Steam Trawler. 11th. Damaged in position 59°39′N 09°25′W. Repaired and returned to service in 1946.

June 1942

MAGGIE. Fishing Vessel. 17th. Sunk 25 miles NNE of North Foreland.

July/August/ September/October/November 1942

Nothing found.

December 1942

BEN SCREEL. Steam Trawler. 25th. Sunk off St Abb's Head. Nine died.

1943

January/February 1943

Nothing found.

March 1943

EVG. Fishing Vessel. 17th. Sunk. All rescued, but no further details.

April 1943

BOY BILLY. Fishing Vessel. 10th. Sunk 6 miles 235° from Dungeness. All 3 died.

May 1943

Nothing found.

June 1943

CRYSTAL. Steam Trawler. 26th. Sunk 12 miles off Scarborough. No further details.

July 1943

Nothing found.

August 1943

STRATHLYON. Steam Trawler. 30th. Sunk off Iceland. All 15 died. (One source claims she was sunk off Cape Wrath.)

September/October/November/December 1943

Nothing found.

1944

January/February/March/April/May/June 1944

Nothing found.

July 1944

ROCHESTER. Steam Trawler. 27th. Returning to Hull when sunk in position 53°54′N 00°42′E. Eleven died.

August 1944

Nothing found.

September 1944

WOLSELEY. Steam Trawler. 23rd. Damaged 22 miles ENE of Great Yarmouth. Several died, but no details.

October/November/December 1944

Nothing found.

1945

January 1945

Nothing found.

February 1945

AQUARIUS. Steam Trawler. 25th. Sunk approximately 15 miles SE by E of Outer Dowsing Light Vessel. Ten died.

March 1945

Nothing found.

April 1945

ETHEL CRAWFORD. Steam Trawler. 20th. In the Firth of Clyde, and in position 55°13′N 5°14′W at 9.09pm, when sunk by a mine laid by U.218 (Kptlt. Rupprecht Stock) on the 18th. All ten died.

May 1945

Nothing found.

POSTSCRIPT

Mine clearing was a major and dangerous business after the War and, due to the huge number of mines laid, it was impossible to locate and dispose of them all. This has resulted in several ships being sunk or damaged after the War and, even today, it is possible for fishermen to catch a WWII mine in their nets.

Although the author's personal experience of mines was limited, it is worth recording here as it serves to illustrate what was happening in the post-war era.

His ship, the Liberty Ship *Samforth*, laden with wheat from the Argentine, was bound for Moss and Oslo. As they neared the British coast, he himself took a telegram from Landsend Radio Station saying that the charts to show them the way through the minefield across the North Sea to Norway would be awaiting their arrival at Kirkwall. This turned out not to be the case and the ship lay at anchor for almost a week, in August 1945, before the charts arrived and they could proceed.

During the passage across the North Sea, a floating mine was seen and the ship's gunners fired at it, with rifles, in an effort to explode it. As the mine could be exploded only by hitting one of its horns, this was not an easy thing to do and they failed. An XXX urgency signal was then transmitted to all ships warning them of the danger and giving the position of the mine, and a similar message was sent to the GPO Radio Station in Wick, Caithness. The latter would then inform the Admiralty and a Royal Navy ship would be sent to destroy the mine.

The only other occasion when the author saw a mine was shortly after leaving Venice on the *Samnesse* in March 1947. The mine, however, had already been reported by the *Sampan* so that the navigating officers were on the lookout for it.

Other seafaring books by Ian M. Malcolm

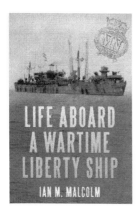

LIFE ON BOARD A WARTIME LIBERTY SHIP (print and ebook formats, published by Amberley)

Describes the author's wartime experiences as the 3rd Radio Officer of the Liberty Ships *Samite* and *Samforth*.

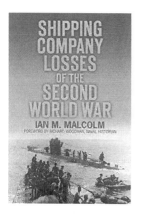

SHIPPING COMPANY LOSSES OF THE SECOND WORLD WAR (print and ebook formats, published by the History Press)

Describes the losses suffered by 53 companies in detail; giving masters' names, where bound, convoy numbers, positions when sunk, casualties and enemy involved.

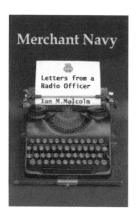

LETTERS FROM A RADIO OFFICER (print and ebook formats, published by Moira Brown)

Letters sent to the author from a former shipmate who, from 1951 till 1963, served with Brocklebank, Marconi, Redifon (ashore and afloat), the Crown Agents, Clan Line, the Royal Fleet Auxiliary (RFA), Ferranti (in Edinburgh), and Marconi again before settling for a shore job in London.

OUTWARD BOUND (ebook format, published by Moira Brown. Print format due out July 2017)

The author's first post-war voyage; on the Liberty Ship *Samnesse*, managed by Blue Funnel for the Ministry of Transport. The voyage begins with calls at Piraeus and Genoa, after which months are spent tramping to various ports in East Africa and the Red Sea. A very happy ship with a predominantly young crew basking in the post-war euphoria.

BACK TO SEA (ebook format, published by Moira Brown, print format due out July 2017)

A voyage to the Far East on the 1911-built *Atreus*, which carries pilgrims to Jeddah on her homeward passage. The author then attends the Lifeboat School in Liverpool and stands by the 1928-built *Eurybates* in Belfast before making his first two voyages on Glen Line's *Glengarry*.

VIA SUEZ (ebook format, published by Moira Brown, print format due out July 2017)

The author makes two more voyages on the *Glengarry* before requesting a voyage to Australia prior to swallowing the anchor. He then coasts the *Glengarry*, *Elpenor/Glenfinlas*, *Helenus*, *Patroclus*, *Medon* and *Clytoneus* after which he is told that his request has been granted. (Photographs/illustrations.)

LAST VOYAGE AND BEYOND (ebook format, published by Moira Brown, print format due out July 2017)

The Australian part of the voyage, on *Deucalion* (built in 1920 as the *Glenogle*) proves enjoyable, but is followed by a trip round Indonesian islands, loading copra, which, although a most interesting experience, is not. On returning home, the author spends two unhappy years in a Dundee office after which he works at GPO Coast Stations for three years, before resigning to train as a teacher in Edinburgh.

Printed in Great Britain
by Amazon

57090367R00133